BEYOND BETRAYAL

28 YEARS
LIES – DECEIT – INFIDELITY

NONI YATES

DAVID YATES

DISCLAIMER: In the interests of transparency and authenticity, please note that we are not professional counsellors. Any decisions made in our story should not replace advice from a professional therapist. The views expressed in this book are entirely from our perspective and personal experience. Although the story and events are factual, everyone other than the authors and relevant therapists are referred to by a pseudonym. Names and identifying details of affair partners have been changed to protect their anonymity.

CONTENT WARNING: Themes expressed in this book are consistent with covert abusive behaviours.

Editor - Cindy Draughon USA

Proofreading Editor - Laura Wilkinson UK

Formatting - Michael Davie, Grim House Publishing UK

Cover Design - Immaculate Studios, PK

www.behance.net/immaculatestudios

This book is dedicated to the courageous men and women who seek truth and authenticity.
Those who are honest with themselves and others.
Those who know how to love, be loved, and continue showing up 'unmasked'.

CONTENTS

ACKNOWLEDGMENTS

There are so many people to thank for bringing this story to life. I've always found writing easy and thought I wrote reasonably well. There is nothing like the brutal awakening of the editing process to keep an ego firmly in check. In fact, every process following the initial draft has been quite overwhelming, so here goes with attempting to cover all bases with my gratitude.

First and foremost, my amazing husband and co-author, Dave. Without you, the story simply couldn't be written *(in more ways than one)*. You are brave and bold. You stepped up to meet every challenge, overcome every obstacle, and face every discomfort regardless of how daunting the situation was. I love that you desire to be part of the healing journey for so many. I love that you see what is possible.

To our three long suffering children. Thank you for listening to my ideas with amusement even though you mock my enthusiasm and roll your eyes when you think

I'm not looking. Who am I kidding? You roll them regardless. You're all amazing humans and we are blessed to call you ours. May you learn from the mistakes we made while you're busy making your own. Life is interesting and unpredictable. Each one of you has your own books within, and even though I'm certain you won't admit it, I do hope that you're secretly proud of what we've achieved, and you'll understand that going public with our story may have a greater purpose for the benefit of others.

Charlie, our 'Uncle Buck'. You once said that good friends are hard to come by, so why cut people you like out of your life because the romantic relationship ends. Eternally thankful for the friendship and support you have shown me, Dave and the kids. We are all fortunate that you are part of our family. Thank you!

To the beautiful Samantha Gowing, our self-publishing mentor and friend, thank you; your expertise and dedication to ensure this project came to fruition has been overwhelming. To Nigel 'Noo', you kind and generous soul, helping me to be become somewhat tech savvy has been no easy task, thank you. To Luke and Ty, the best neighbours in the world, thank you for letting me pick your brains with my endless questions when I was clueless and scared that I might break the internet if I pushed too many wrong buttons. Massive gratitude and love to you all for the endless patience you extended to me while I floundered learning how to DIY. Thank you for supporting and encouraging me when I felt like throwing in the towel and for being there when I had meltdowns over website glitches, social platforms and other technical issues. This has been one steep learning curve, so thanks for encouraging me to persist.

Gratitude to Catriona, Shalini, and Mary for reading the roughest of drafts and giving honest feedback. To Dennis, Joy, and Jen, for reading a slightly more refined version whilst still rough and lending your honest feedback. Whilst not always easy to hear, we value and appreciate all comments. Cindy Draughon, our editor, thank you for your understanding and bringing our manuscript to life.

In addition, to friends who have given their support along the way, to those who have encouraged us, prayed for us, understood the motivation and determination behind our story, we are eternally grateful.

To those near and far, thank you!

"We either own our stories or they own us.

Only when we have the courage to own our history are we able to write a brave new ending to our story."

— BRENÉ BROWN

PREFACE

When I began writing in March 2019, I thought we had reached our last discovery/disclosure day, commonly referred to in the affair recovery world as D-Day. The day when I would finally learn the full extent of my husband's double life. However, like most of those who walk this harrowing road, another grenade detonated only weeks later. My heart was demolished. I was left reeling and wondering yet again, "Who the hell are you?"

When considering writing this memoir, Dave and I pondered whether we should wait until we had more recovery under our belt, or if we should just begin and tell our story from where we are now with what we know. We chose to go with it. Perhaps there are people in the same boat as us, and maybe if we can share our 'nothing watered down' madness, they may find the strength and courage to persevere in their own story whatever that may be. Twenty-eight years is an awfully long time to be swimming through debris from the ship-wreck of shame. Maybe our brutal honesty can offer hope to others floundering in the cesspool of secrecy and dysfunction.

When we went searching for affair recovery material in 2019, we found very little home-grown help. Australia seems to lack openness for couples finding themselves in our position. There is no shortage of counselling services but having access to others who have waded through the affair quagmire and overcome infidelity seems a rarity. Is it because the majority of us inhabiting this Great Southern Land are immune to adultery? Or are we not open enough to expose the reality of what goes on behind closed doors? Is our attitude one of 'She'll be right mate, S*#+ happens'? Do we brush the treachery of betrayal aside and get on with life without actually getting to the bottom of it? Do we even know what 'it' is? Do we keep our shame hidden? Is the topic simply out of bounds?

Online resources helped guide us to a path of recovery, and though invaluable in content, the material scarcely conveyed the intensity of emotions we were drowning in. Our experiences at times felt completely out of control. In the midst of our trauma, there was nothing remotely neat, orderly or sensible about us. It was messy, volatile, and unlike anything we were equipped to deal with. Perhaps we might be too damaged to come back from this. Maybe we'd damaged our children to the point of no return. We'd done so much so wrong, but then again, what is right about abuse and betrayal?

During rumination, I wondered if I was just a little bit crazy or a whole lot crazy. I mean, how does someone like me get sucked into something as insidious as this? How? Why would Dave, the person who swore to love, honour and cherish me, seem so hell-bent on destroying me? Am I stupid? Ignorant? Blind to the truth? OR...am I none of these things and stronger than I ever realised? Before this became my reality, I would have held a very different point of view. Until we find ourselves in a situation, we can never say for certain how we will handle it.

For those with no experience in addiction, infidelity or abusive relationships our story will be unrelatable and perhaps shocking.

For those who unfortunately have lived this nightmare, it may sound all too familiar. We wish it wasn't. We wish it wasn't a story we had to write either, but we want you to know that although it can feel like it, you're not alone.

Meanwhile, for others our story will pale in comparison.

We don't compare stories or pain, we share hope for healing and recovery and even though each situation is unique, we've learned there are more similarities than differences. We hope and pray that while you can relate to our story, you will also relate to our healing and experience healing in your own lives as well.

Dave and I both share our points of view throughout the story – my primary narrative is interspersed with

Dave's. We've included sections throughout the book and at the end which we've titled 'Lessons from Beyond'. They're an abbreviated list of aha's or learnings, some which we gleaned from our own experiences and some we've taken from the wisdom of others. We hope there may be one or two useful pieces you can implement in your own circumstances.

We would like readers to assume that at the time of writing this book, neither one of us have *arrived* anywhere. We are both on a journey, in the process of, and committed to our recovery and healing

We all bring baggage to relationships. When we met in 1990, we were no different. Dave brought his brokenness with him and I mine. I also came with an active two-year-old boy plus my new-found commitment, love and relationship with Jesus...

And yes, it has felt like a very, very long road to our *happily ever after*. We are works in progress, but we're not quitters.

This story cannot be written without being completely authentic regarding the source of our enduring love. If you are of faith, you will understand, and if not, our desire is that you will take some hope and encouragement from our journey and believe, no matter how bleak your circumstances may appear at any given time, *"all things truly are possible and will work together for good."* *Matt 19:26, Romans 8:28*

Sometimes the heart simply sees what the mind
cannot…

Noni x

"Permanent withholding will always be a permanent deficiency in the relationship, an obstacle to the love that could have been."

— JOHN POWELL

FOOTPRINTS

One night I dreamed a dream.
As I was walking along the beach with my
*   Lord,*
Across the dark sky flashed scenes from my life.
For each scene, I noticed two sets of footprints
*   in the sand,*
One belonging to me, and one to my Lord.
After the last scene of my life flashed before me,
I looked back at the footprints in the sand.
I noticed many times along the path of my life,
especially at the lowest and saddest times,
there was only one set of footprints.
This troubled me, so I asked the Lord about it.
"Lord, you said once I decided to follow you,
You'd walk with me all the way.
But I noticed, during the saddest and most
*   troublesome times of my life,*
there was only one set of footprints.
I don't understand why, when I needed You the
*   most, You would leave me."*
He whispered, "My precious child, I love you
*   and will never leave you*
Never, ever, during your trials and testings.
When you saw only one set of footprints,
It was then that I carried you."

— AUTHORSHIP CONTESTED

PROLOGUE
STANDING ON THE OUTSIDE LOOKING IN

NONI

Canberra winters are cold. Freezing, especially at night. None colder than the winter night when the man of my dreams told me he didn't love me and even though we were only six months into our relationship, my heart belonged to him. This same heart was now ripped from my chest, torn apart, crushed, and discarded. Those four words, "I don't love you" translated into *I'm unlovable*. I believed this lie and many others for the next nine years. Why was this the story I told myself, and why did I spend the next nine years with the man who didn't love me? He certainly wasn't getting my heart again, there was no way in the world I would ever let myself feel this pain again. This mandate influenced my adulting skills for years to come. What did I know about love?

At sixteen, not a whole lot...

I

∼

In the 80s, my world looked perfect. Outwardly confident, successful, living free and easy. My mantra: I am, I can, and I will. If it is to be, it's up to me! Although unseen, my self-sufficiency had roots.

Beneath the imagery and bravado lurked deep-seated doubts of self-worth accompanied by a bottomless pit of insecurity requiring constant topping up. I would fill the void with the trappings that society fools us into believing lead to happiness. Money, relationships, sex, beauty, power, success, drugs, and alcohol. Chasing the high but never addicted to one, I used the thinly veiled filter to disguise layers of emptiness. Each vice a weapon, to bypass pain from unhealed wounds of rejection and assumed responsibility for another person's actions. Pain I'd rather not confront. It was all fun and games until it wasn't.

"We manage to avoid being happy while struggling to become happy, fulfilling one desire after the next, banishing our fears, grasping at pleasure, recoiling from pain - and thinking, interminably, about how best to keep the whole works up and running. As a consequence, we spend our lives being far less content than we might be otherwise. We often fail to appreciate what we have until we have lost it. We crave experiences, objects, relationships, only to grow bored with them. And yet the craving persists." Sam Harris, American neuroscientist and philosopher, described this human condition in his 2014 publication entitled 'Waking Up'.

The Bible – a book more than two thousand years old – also addressed this concept.

~

C hildren of servicemen and women learn to fly solo, permanency is a foreign concept.

Frequent upheaval is what we're familiar with, and from an early age, we know to lean on self. We become independent. The majority of naval families relocate every two years.

Friendships are best accepted with open hands. We dare not grow too attached to anyone.

Learning with certainty that change is inevitable, we would do well to become comfortable with it. Being the new kid at school was always daunting, and this change is one I never grew accustomed to even after wearing the badge eleven times over. Though frequent uprooting is disruptive, our transient lifestyle helped establish a deep yearning for travel and adventure.

It wasn't all bad…

CHAPTER 1

PREGNANT PAUSE PURPOSE

NONI

I was all of sweet sixteen when I met Charlie at a Canberra club in the early eighties. Charlie was a handsome gentle giant, popular, a talented football player and twelve years my senior. Although appearing outwardly older than sixteen, at heart I was still the non-conformist teenager who concerned herself with pursuing this man vigorously. Initially, Mum and Dad believed Charlie was twenty-two. The first year we dated I fumbled my way into revealing the truth. Our age gap concerned Charlie far more than me. If my parents were bothered, they kept silent.

Quiet wild child was a description that suited me well. An oxymoron. My introverted self was kind-hearted and gentle while my alter ego, rebellious and feisty, took chances and usually secured the object of her desire. Charlie became my object of desire and something I clung to long after hearing him utter those four words which crushed my young impressionable heart.

After completing a hairdressing apprenticeship in Canberra at nineteen, my growing boredom with conservatism in our nation's capital led me to accept a job in Darwin. Disappearing to the Northern Territory in 1984 was a choice I made without considering how Charlie might feel, regardless of us being together for over two years. If polar opposites exist, these are it: Noni and Charlie, Darwin and Canberra. Twelve months passed and the excitement of Darwin's initial appeal wore off. Hitchhiking to Perth popped into my mind and sounded like a good idea, so after minimal planning I set off on a whim. Danger never entering my mind. Mum and Dad remained blissfully unaware of my antics until the adventure drew to a close and I arrived safely in Perth. A few wild months in the west with friends met along the way satisfied the itch momentarily before the time came to cross the Nullarbor Plain en-route back to Canberra. It was 1986 and I was heading home for my twenty-first birthday in March.

Although uncertain about my feelings toward Charlie, there was one absolute; I never wanted to live in Canberra again, ever. Returning from Western Australia for a few short months, convincing Charlie there were adventures to be had beyond the world he'd known since childhood, we packed up our lives and moved to Queensland, destination Sunshine Coast. There very little in the way of work opportunities on the coast in '86 and although our rent was paid by the football club Charlie played for, once the season finished, we hit the road and spent the next six months in the Northern Territory. Early 1988 we returned to Queensland and opened a hair salon in Noosa Heads. I was twenty-three years old with no business experience, possessed little more than a total lack of fear, and I was five and a half months pregnant. Seems I may have forgotten to marry somewhere along the way... According to my father, I always liked to do things the 'wrong' way around.

We welcomed Corey on August 8, 1988 weighing in at a healthy 8lb 8oz. I returned to work when Corey was only two weeks old, giving myself kudos for managing work full-time while continuing to breastfeed him until he was eighteen months old. Charlie cared for Corey while my work supported us financially. Corey's dad is a good man. I knew it then as I know it now. However, my relational immaturity and unsettled spirit would never satisfy nor be satisfied in that relationship. To be honest, I had no clue how to have a healthy intimate relationship, not even with myself!

Charlie and I were together for nine years. Should truth be known though, this rebel heart checked out emotionally on her return from Darwin in 1986. At the time, I was too lost and confused to understand why. I had it all – a career, good friends, material wealth and a great family. Despite my seemingly full world, a nagging emptiness persisted which I couldn't explain and eventually couldn't ignore. No matter how much external stuff I filled myself with, the satisfaction was fleeting. I wanted more...

Sometime during 1989/90, I took myself along to a church in Noosa. It was the first time I'd ever been in a church with comfortable seating. The only ones I'd gone to before were furnished with hard timber pews and even harder kneeling boards. It didn't look like other churches. This one was just a normal building with no statues of Mary or bowls of holy water for blessing yourself. The room didn't smell of incense and Jesus wasn't nailed to the cross. The priest was called Pastor instead of Father and he wore plain clothes instead of robes. People were friendly, they seemed like they were really happy to be there. My childhood memories were of going to mass with Mum and my big brother. The best part of going to mass was on the days Mum relented to our nagging and we left after communion before the end of the service. The fifteen-minute early mark was easily the happiest part of my religious experience! There were no organs or hymn books in this church either, just a projector.

Lyrics on the overhead projector displayed on the back wall are as vivid today as ever.

> *"You did not wait for me to be near to you*
> *Instead, you clothed yourself in frail humanity*
> *You did not wait for me to cry out to you*
> *Instead I heard your voice calling me*
> *I'm forever grateful to you*
> *I'm forever grateful for the cross*

I'm forever grateful to you
That you came to seek and save the lost"

THIS WAS ME! LOST, LOST, LOST!

This juncture was a defining moment when I finally admitted I wasn't so self-sufficient after all. This moment determined my future. An exchange took place at that moment and a magnificent transformation began.

I sensed an overwhelming need to love, be loved, and to belong.

My heart became putty, heavy, thumping in my chest.

Something or someone drew me closer and the flood-gates opened.

I surrendered my life to someone I couldn't see but whose presence I most definitely felt.

It had been three years since I remember crying over anything, such was the stony state of my heart.

This person/spirit/being – a stranger up until that moment – became someone I trusted would do a better job of directing my steps than I could myself. The miserable choices I'd been making were unfulfilling. My heart desired more; I was ready for change. In a humble brown-bricked Pentecostal church in Noosa, I became a Christian. With no idea of what this entailed or what was supposed to happen next, the only sure thing was that a transaction had taken place, an indelible one. Somehow, everything looked brighter. Colours were more vivid. Joy differed from happiness. I had a lightness in my spirit, and for the first time in many years, I felt free and unburdened. A tangible sensation, divine!

Arriving home after my encounter proved a different experience. I wanted so much to share the joy found, however, my epiphany sparked little interest in Charlie who was content with life as he knew it. We were very different people in almost every way.

I retreated to the garage and poked around, singing to myself and thinking about how this Christian life worked. Growing up in Catholicism we were not actively encouraged to read the Bible. I was only vaguely familiar with the Ten Commandments, so I figured this was as good a place as any to start and began with number one. What would it look like to love the Lord, my God, with all my heart, soul, and mind?

The deliberate choice I'd made to not attend church regularly stemmed from lack of desire to join a club. I had to explore this new relationship for myself, to learn about Jesus. I wanted God to show me if what I'd experienced was real. Is He who the Bible says He is? Could I trust Him completely? Could I rely on Him? My quest for truth began. Tired of running, I ran toward the goal. I needed Him, and from that day forward, I belonged to Him.

(Had I become part of a church family, I may or may not have saved myself a lot of pain looming on the horizon, but that's hindsight for you, did I mention I had a rebellious spirit?)

Not long after making Jesus my focus, I became brutally honest with myself.

Confronting some of the ugliest truths of my flawed character is when it dawned on me that I was living a lie by remaining in this relationship with Charlie. This enlightenment had nothing to do with religion or sex outside of marriage; instead, it had everything to do with being authentic. I believed something must be deeply wrong with me.

Charlie was a good man, yet my love for him was brotherly in nature rather than the type of love that should exist as the father of our child. What I felt was certainly not enough to sustain a long-term intimate partnership.

There were no discussions of my determination with friends or family. I had to be brave enough to make the clear unemotional decision of terminating our nine-year relationship.

A lot of grief and pain accompanied my choice; however, it was nothing compared to what Charlie was about to experience.

In addition to running our Noosa salon, a hair company occasionally engaged me to do presentations. One late afternoon in mid-September, Charlie collected me from the salon for an upcoming showcase on the Gold Coast. We took the three-and-a-half-hour road trip down the highway, my face hot, tears streaming down both cheeks for the duration of the drive. Charlie never once asked

why, and I offered nothing and saved my announcement for later.

Model preparation went late into the night. When we
returned to our accommodation, Charlie sensed imminent doom and faced me saying, "I really want this relationship to work."

"It's not going to for no other reason than because I
don't want it to," I replied. "When we return to Noosa, I
am going to move out."

It was as simple as that. It was torturously painful, yet
void of deep dialogue. As brutal as it appeared, discussion was pointless since I was clear about my decision.
I'd made the right choice. We arrived home after the
seminar and, true to my word, I packed a small bag and
walked out of the new home we had built six weeks
earlier. Noosa Heads was a very small town in 1990. I
had no idea where I would go but I knew it wouldn't be
far. I left Charlie and I left Corey with him.

An interesting side note from all of this is for the three
years before leaving, I suffered debilitating sinusitis and
was heavily reliant on medication and inhalers. I tried to
remedy my blocked nasal passages so I could breathe,
but nothing worked. The rebound effect from over-the-
counter nasal sprays was debilitating. I always felt like I
was suffocating. No lie, the exact same day I walked
away from my relationship of nine years, my sinus
problems disappeared, never to return. True story!

LESSONS FROM BEYOND

THE GOD I MET IN THE CHURCH IN NOOSA? HIS NAME IS JESUS.

I'LL BE REFERENCING HIM THROUGHOUT OUR STORY.

YOU MAY NOT KNOW HIM OR BELIEVE IN HIM OR ANY GOD, BUT THAT'S OK.

PLEASE KNOW THAT OUR INTENTION IS NOT TO PROSELYTISE IN ANY WAY, THIS IS PURELY OUR TRUTH.

WE FULLY APPRECIATE EVERYONE'S UNIQUE VIEWPOINT; THIS IS WHAT MAKES US ALL SUCH INTERESTING CREATURES!

WHATEVER YOUR SPIRITUAL ANCHOR, HIGHER POWER, OR GO-TO 'STRENGTH' IS, SIMPLY EXCHANGE THAT ANCHOR IN PLACE OF HIS NAME.

This chapter of my life was over. Now, let's meet Dave.

CHAPTER 2
MEET DAVE

DAVE

I've always considered myself a fairly laid back and uncomplicated guy. Late into my fifty-seventh year was an awakening to realise I was anything but...

Unfortunately, by then, I'd crushed and almost destroyed people I love deeply.

What does a person do with childhood wounds they don't even know they're carrying? How do they address their fears, insecurities, and emptiness? It's taken an awfully long time, but I've finally discovered how I did. Coping with hidden remnants of painful experiences, I found avenues to soothe my pain and ease my discomfort, hoping to feel good.

In short, I believed a whole bunch of lies about myself and took them right along with me on life's ride. In the coming pages, you'll read how a man professing to love, care for, and protect his family was actually the one they needed to be protected from.

∾

B orn the middle child of five and the eldest son, I was brought up in a loving, caring household in suburban Sydney. My mother, one of seven children, grew up on a farm four hours from the city. As children, we marvelled at her stories of riding a horse to school with two or three siblings on one horse. Mum met Dad when he was working as an announcer at the local radio station (he was also the station manager, cleaner, and gardener). My father was the middle son of three to an inner-city Sydney working-class couple. When they married, Mum moved to Sydney with Dad, 270km from her country home and family.

Christened Catholic, religion was a major component of our lives. Attendance at Sunday Mass and Catholic schools was mandatory and unquestioned. Dad was often involved in the local St. Vincent De Paul Society, the School Parent and Teacher Association's many fundraisers, and a regular reader at Sunday Mass. Dad adored Mum, placing her on a pedestal.

Mum kept busy with household chores and trans- porting and tending to the needs of five children. She undertook it all with enthusiasm and love, working hard to create a safe, supportive household. By any measure, our home life was stable and normal. Dad worked hard to provide for us, often with multiple jobs. Both parents openly showed us affection and took great interest in whatever we did. There was no shortage of positive affirmations. We were clever, smart, good, strong and handsome/pretty most of the time. Mum and Dad went to lengths shielding us from the *bad* or *unpleasant*. Arguments and conflict between them was never or rarely witnessed. Nor was resolution modelled. Conflict and anger were greeted with swift disapproval from my parents. "Don't talk like that to your mother, brother or sister!" Never was there any open discussion about bad things or conflict.

Late one afternoon, Mum called my two older sisters and me to the kitchen. She had something important we needed to know. She may as well have been speaking Greek with the phrases I barely recall like, "I need to leave," "I cannot live here anymore," "I am worth nothing to your father."

I couldn't understand what any of this meant, I was only seven years old.

A suitcase was packed, and my mother tearfully told us she loved us. I stood on the porch watching her. She strode out our back door, brown suitcase in hand, across the yard and towards the back fence she went. Opening the gate in the paling fence, she continued on to the footpath and didn't look back. Mum picked up her pace, walking away from home and disappearing to who knows where.

I chased her, calling and pleading, and she would stop and turn me around, telling me to go home. I would pause momentarily before resuming chase. She drew further away until we came to a busy intersection. Mum stopped to cross, I caught up. By now, my seven-year-old skinny, terrified self was wailing and begging her not to leave. I tugged at her hand trying to drag her back. I'm not sure if the prospect of crossing a busy road with a hysterical child swinging off her arm was the reason, but she stopped and turned around. Hugging me, we walked home hand in hand. I didn't release my grip until we reached the safety of our backyard.

Nothing was said about the incident in the days following, or ever. Assurance was given later one afternoon when Mum told us everything was alright and she was not going to leave. A fear of abandonment instilled early.

LIE NUMBER ONE

Even the woman who was biologically programmed to love me – my mother – could leave. Maybe I cannot trust love, maybe I am not able or worthy of holding love.

~

NONI

Hairdressing salons are wonderful meeting places; hair-dressers are a special kind of people. We are granted permission to be up close and personal in a way most professions are not. Clients divulge information to us that is normally reserved for trusted friends and confi-dantes. Hairdressers are privileged by the honour bestowed upon us by those sitting in our chair. We are vaults of secrecy.

Jenna was one such client. During one appointment, she asked whether I cut men's hair, explaining to me that her boyfriend, David, couldn't get a decent haircut anywhere. "Sure," I said, "send him in." And in he came, becoming a regular client who had his hair done every few months. His hair was fine and straight as a stick. Every scissor mark showing on his sun-bleached surfer's hair, plus he had a hairline funkier than a mosquito's tweeter!

(*Funkier than a mosquito's tweeter is a song by Nina Simone. What could be worse than the high-pitched buzzing of a mosquito? Amplified buzzing, Dave's hairline comes close.)

There was never a suggestion or hint of anything vaguely romantic about our connection. The strongest thought I had about Dave was, *he's a nice guy, but jeez, I know why he had trouble getting a good haircut.*

A year or so after Dave began coming into the salon, I noticed his partner hadn't been in for a little while.

Mentioning this to Dave, he told me they'd separated and she moved back to the central coast. I shared my condolences and his reply, whilst sorrowful, was, "The break-up is for the best." Without prying further, we switched topics, likely me asking for the umpteenth time what he did for work. He would have told me, and I would have nodded, pretending yet again that I knew what an orthoptist was.

~

DAVE

I had always wanted to live close to the ocean. When I entered the workforce, my aspiration expanded to having my own place near the beach. Now in my mid-twenties, living and working in suburban Sydney, those dreams were a long way out of my reach. I was in a relationship with Jenna, a divorced mother with a seven-year-old daughter who lived in her own home an hour north of Sydney. I spent almost every weekend with the two and together we celebrated holidays, birthdays, and family occasions. Our lives were entwined. Eighteen months into my relationship with Jenna, I was offered a position on the Sunshine Coast a thousand kilometres away. The decision to accept the job offer and move was difficult knowing it would practically put an end to our relationship. Though Jenna was willing to move, I did not want the responsibility of upending the established lives of two others. I loved belonging to this family unit on a part-time basis but I was not willing to take on the responsibility full-time. Complicating matters further, Jenna was in her early thirties. If we were to start a family together, a decision needed to be made sooner rather than later. The catch cry was, "I'm not going to be giving birth when I am forty." Making the choice to move interstate to follow my career and maybe fulfil the dream of a place by the sea also helped me avoid owner-ship of the decision to end the relationship rather than commit to it.

At the age of twenty-seven, I moved from suburban Sydney to the Sunshine Coast. I had no family or friends. My days were filled with work, so it was hard to make new friends. Evenings and weekends were spent alone. Jenna and I spoke on the phone regularly. Calls were often cut short as I ran out of change for the payphone. I missed Jenna and her daughter but was determined to try and make my independence work. At my suggestion, they came to visit during school holi-days. We did all sorts of family types of things, explored beaches, and had a great time. I was convinced it was a good idea for Jenna to come and live with me. Yes, I had decided we should be a family.

When I shared the great news with my father, I was filled with the excitement of taking what was a giant step.

He asked, "Do we have plans to marry?"

I said no. His next words cut right through me (as the truth tends to).

"In which case, I cannot support your choice at all. You are not doing the right thing by Jenna or her daughter."

I pressed on with all the wisdom of a twenty-seven-year-old who had lived at home for all but twelve months of his life. Jenna resigned from work, rented out her house and took her daughter out of school. Soon, we were all playing happy families and everything seemed pretty good to me.

The fact is, I had no idea how to be in a mature adult relationship. Conflicts arose between us occasionally, they were rarely resolved and instead buried or pushed aside. The reality was that Jenna wanted and deserved more than cohabitation with a boyfriend. I started with no real long-term commitment, and after a year, I was no closer to giving one. This created a volatile atmosphere, my evasiveness frustrating Jenna, I grew anxious with the mounting pressure and just wanted to preserve things as they were. Jenna issued an ultimatum.

"What are you going to do? Are we going to marry? Are we going to have children? We should have been married by now."

"I don't know," "I am not ready," and "I can't yet," were my lame responses.

This final ultimatum was a chance to shift responsibility for the relationship dysfunction and its disintegration. Taking the position that it was her decision to move back and it was probably for the best absolved my responsibility for the relationship failure and subsequent emotional fallout. Jenna arranged to move out while her daughter was visiting family so there was no farewell between her daughter and me. I had mixed feelings about that for a long time. We had a very strong bond. Saying that I had pangs of guilt is an understatement; deep down, I was engulfed in shame for the pain I inflicted. It remained for years.

~

NONI

During preparations for an upcoming event, Dave arrived at the salon for a haircut (this occurred during my decision-making time about leaving Charlie). As Dave left the salon, one of my models commented about him being cute. Jokingly, I responded, "Yep, he can park his shoes under my bed any day!" Evidently, this new Christian's halo needed some serious adjusting. As a mother in the process of leaving a long-term relationship, my sanctification was nowhere in sight! Still as flawed and carnal as ever, the redemption process was an ever-unfolding journey. Such is our need for amazing grace and mercy, every minute of every hour of every single day. As essential as oxygen.

Early in September 1990, I garnered enough courage to part ways with Charlie. My initial sadness morphed into relief once the hard part was taken care of. I kept myself busy with work, Corey, and friends.

Catching up with my staff for drinks one Sunday in September resulted in a chance meeting with Dave. The first outside of the salon. Dave was waiting for a friend at the beach bar and we struck up conversation easily. Natural and effortless, our hairdresser/client relationship ensured communication was neither forced nor awkward; squandered hours were spent talking, laughing, and enjoying each other's company. This conversation and stimulation had been missing from my relationship for some time. Invigorating interaction, the beginning of mutual attraction.

∽

DAVE

When Noni cut my hair, I avoided looking directly into her eyes. Instead, I'd gaze at huge posters on the salon walls featuring Noni working. This was a woman of intensity and focus.

She was and is still a uniquely attractive woman – she looked like a superstar! Although I didn't dwell on these thoughts outside my infrequent visits to the salon, the memory of viewing Noni's face from many angles reflected in the myriad of mirrors still makes me smile.

Our chance meeting at a bustling beachside bar was our first interaction outside of the salon. No mirrors, no distraction in this face-to-face encounter. I was immediately put at ease by how pleasant she was to talk to. Looking me directly in the eye, she exuded warmth and gentleness. I felt like Noni wanted to understand me as she saw into me. I wanted more of her presence – all that in the first fifteen minutes. We laughed at stories told, enjoying the warmth of a spring evening. Not wanting the brush with Noni to end, I eagerly tagged along with her and her entourage, moving from one bar to another. When we weren't talking, I found myself intently watching her interact with other people, observing the same softness and openness I experienced. She saw people.

~

NONI

Conflicted with thoughts about right and wrong, this random connection with Dave coincided with the week of my separation. Far from being interested in another relationship, it was surprising that there was something quite alluring about running into Dave.

BAD TIMING…or was it?

LESSONS FROM BEYOND

LIFE ISN'T ALWAYS AS GOOD AS IT LOOKS ON INSTAGRAM.

BEFORE WE CAN LOVE ANOTHER, WE MUST LEARN SELF-LOVE.

HONESTY IS THE BEST POLICY, AND OFTEN, THE PERSON WE FIND IT HARDEST TO BE HONEST WITH IS OURSELVES.

I COULD HAVE LIMPED ALONG MAKING EXCUSES ABOUT WHY I WANTED OUT OF MY RELATIONSHIP, ATTEMPTING TO SOFTEN THE BLOW, ACHIEVING NOTHING EXCEPT PROLONGING THE PAIN.

SEEK TRUTH AND COMMIT TO IT.

TOO STUBBORN TO ADMIT THAT THERE WAS A VOID IN MY LIFE, PRIDE KEPT ME FROM ACCEPTING MY WEAKNESS, BROKENNESS, AND VULNERABILITY.

GOD HAS PLACED ETERNITY (SENSE OF DIVINE PURPOSE) IN THE HEART OF EVERY MAN WHICH NOTHING UNDER THE SUN CAN SATISFY.

— ECCLESIASTES 3:11

NONI YATES & DAVID YATES

LESSONS FROM BEYOND continued

I WISH I HAD KNOWN EARLIER. THIS POWERFUL SCRIPTURE MADE SENSE OF MY LONGING, THE HUNGER FOR MORE, AN ENDLESS QUEST FOR FULFILMENT.

THE SPACE NEEDING CONSTANT TOPPING UP WAS RESERVED FOR GOD TO TAKE UP RESIDENCY, AND UNTIL HE DID, MY SOUL WOULD ALWAYS BE THIRSTY.

CHAPTER 3

BAD TIMING

DAVE

Noni was extraordinary, and I couldn't wait until we could be together again. Just hours after recounting my rendezvous with this extraordinary woman to work colleagues I was called to the phone.

"It's someone for you."

"It's her!" they giggled.

I'm sure I was blushing as I hid behind the reception desk relishing the sound of her voice.

My attraction and desire to be with Noni rapidly escalated. I was besotted. We seized every opportunity to be together. Noni fast became my best friend and I wanted more and more of her. Complicating this blissful new friendship was the combination of Noni juggling young Corey's needs and her enthusiasm as a new Christian. Corey's family unit had radically changed with Noni leaving his father the week we met, and the way her values shifted as she grew in her faith left me confused and frustrated, feeling as though I was competing with these other aspects of Noni's life. My underlying insecurity often took over and I retreated into the comfortable role of rejected victim or neglected partner.

~

NONI

Following our initial meeting, Dave and I caught up on a semi-regular basis. Having no fixed address after leaving Charlie, I house sat for different people around Noosa. Dave and I would meet for lunch, dinner, or drinks and share our love of live music, sun, surf, and sand.

We continued to enjoy an evolving connection and our friendship grew incrementally stronger with each date. Dave felt safe and kind. He was gentle with me, showing interest in my business and profession, and just like I pretended to know what an orthoptist was, he pretended to know what 'Bonfire' and 'Roxy Red' hair colours were. Dave was always generous with compliments and affection. We laughed at the same things, found beauty in nature, and communicated well. Even as the circumstances of our life shifted, this friendship has always been the foundation of our love and has never changed over time. Ours was a well-cemented bond from the outset.

Intentionally focusing on my personal relationship with Jesus rather than attending church with any consistency, I read all manner of material and often devoured up to five books at once. Reflecting, meditating, and absorbing as much as possible, I learned about authentic relationships with God and people. Integral to this period of personal growth and now for spiritual reasons, I had a new-found commitment to sexual abstinence until I married. Did my strong aversion to the concept of marriage mean I was looking down the barrel of a celibate future? There were certainly no plans to join a convent...

A whole new ball game emerged from brokenness and dysfunction. Prior to my nine-year relationship with Charlie, the resulting loss of virginity from sexual assault at thirteen drove my ability to use sex as control. Promiscuity masked my negative self-image for several years. (Assuming responsibility that this assault was somehow my fault, it wasn't until my mid-thirties that I saw I was not to blame for the perpetrator's actions.)

The time had come to confront the faulty sense of self I held onto so tightly. Determination spurring me on, like a swimmer on the starting blocks at a pool, I stood ready to take the plunge, conquering the illusion of self and discovering my true identity.

In a world full of Kardashians...be an Audrey! (A nice concept, easier to talk about than put into practice, right?)

In the modern secular world, promiscuity and sexual freedom are considered completely normal. Something to be celebrated rather than frowned upon, proudly flaunted through media, movies, magazines, and reality shows. Openly confessing to abstinence in an attempt to restore lost purity sounded quite ludicrous, yet it was true. I wanted to try to get it right.

I decided to share the news of this revelation with my new friend, Dave, and it left him a little confused, yet not deterred. Although the physical attraction and emotional connection between Dave and I had increased somewhat, he remained the perfect gentleman, understanding my announcement.

"The spirit is willing, but the flesh is weak."

— MATT 26:41

If only my willpower were enough to honour my intentions. Even though Dave was respectful of my wishes to not engage sexually, our desire proved too much on more than one occasion. The ongoing struggle and tension of passionate pursuits began. Sexual chemistry between us always has been and remains strong. If this felt so good, how could it be so wrong?

This is how...it wasn't sacred, and I was soon to find out that it also wasn't exclusive...

Conversation between us flowed easily, we spoke about anything and everything. Long lingering exchanges often went into the wee hours; keeping company with each other warmed our souls and satisfied our intellect. Before our relationship progressed to physical Dave told me about seeing five girls all at once. He made a point, however, to only sleep with one. He seemed pretty pleased with his juggling capacity. Not one girl was aware of the others; he thought this was something to boast about. Less than impressed, I recall alarm bells ringing. However, my ears foolishly remained deaf to them.

∼

DAVE

Despite being shy and a little self-conscious like most teenage boys, I found it relatively easy to strike up friendships with girls. When it came to dating, I was a late and slow starter and really only dabbled with the whole boyfriend-girlfriend thing. In my late teens, I lost my virginity to a girl I had been dating for a short while. She lived 100 metres from the local squash courts where I worked part-time, so besides going out on weekends, I would regularly drop by and see her after work. We had been an item for several months when one weekday evening, I called by her place and there was no answer. Strange. I thought I was expected? Hearing faint music coming from inside, I knocked again but got no response. I went to the window. There was no mistaking the sound of voices inside. Returning to the front door, I knocked again. She opened the door in a bathrobe, and from behind her, emerging from her bedroom, was a man I recognised. He had been an occasional visitor and had been introduced as just a friend. The fact that he was married with a young child dampened my initial suspicions. I was given no real explanation or apology. She merely shuffled her feet and shrugged. Plain sickened and hurt, I walked away in silence. It unfolded later that my girlfriend always had multiple partners. Feeling foolish and unable to hold the affection of someone I cared for, I promised myself that I would not let it happen again. There was no strategy in place to prevent it from recurring, just an innate desire to save myself from the pain of rejection in all future relationships.

The story I told myself became LIE NUMBER TWO:

The only thing I know for sure about relationships is that they end.

~

NONI

Not long after commencing our physical relationship, Dave travelled to the USA for work. I was still without permanent accommodation and stayed in his house during his absence. He told me he intended to stop in and visit his ex-girlfriend on his way to Sydney and that they had been discussing a possible reconciliation. My recent separation and not wanting to rush into a new relationship left me encouraging him to do what was right for him. I was in no position to promise or offer anyone anything.

The uncertainty around my future meant I could barely make decisions for Corey and me, let alone be capable of considering another. I had peace around this little snippet of wisdom, but if truth be known, I secretly hoped they wouldn't reconcile and that we might explore where our relationship could go.

The morning after Dave visited Jenna, he called me, noticeably upset. Their meeting didn't end well. Dave decided it would be a mistake if they got back together and she didn't take his decision kindly. I shared my sympathy, though was quietly pleased for what this may mean for us.

When Dave returned from the states, our romance escalated to a greater frequency and he got to meet Corey. (What I know now but didn't know then was that Dave not only stopped in to see Jenna, but he also spent the night with her and they had sex. No wonder she came unhinged after he told her he couldn't *do* the relationship; a cruel, selfish, and insensitive act on his part. She, of course, knew nothing of me and likely anticipated a different outcome. My heart broke for her when this truth finally came out. None of this was fair!)

By now, I had found stable accommodation. The unit we once shared when our little family was intact becoming vacant. Charlie and I took turns caring for Corey equally. One week with Mum and one with Dad. Corey would have his little black duffle bag full of clothes and

treasures and bounce between us. His nanna, disheart-
ened by our arrangement, grieved that her grandson's
life would amount to the sum of all his bag contained.

Corey, my active two-year-old, was adorable, spirited,
and definitely the most important and loveable little one
I knew. He was my greatest blessing. My joy. He taught
me about love. I could and would be a good mother, I
loved being his mum. Corey was my priority, and his
security, safety, and well-being were at the top of my list
along with my God connection. Continuing to seek
divine guidance daily, my own wisdom had a ceiling. I
needed more.

Before long, tension began to appear in the new relationship with Dave. The onset of the *terrible twos* created a
measure of discord, giving Dave reason to become
agitated and disenchanted with the reality of being in a
relationship with a single mum and her toddler. Harsh
words and attitudes occasionally spewed from Dave
which I didn't appreciate. If forced to make a choice
between my relationship with Dave or Corey, Dave
would never come out on top. A mother's love is like no
other. Corey needed stability, not more turmoil.

Wanting to share gratitude and appreciation for Dave,
yet at the same time explain my thoughts and feelings
in-depth, penning a letter to Dave seemed most appropriate. I needed to be clear about my intentions and how
I felt without any diversions. Words written expressed
that no matter how strong my feelings may be towards
him, it made me very sad to witness how the boy I cher-

ished and loved dearly made the man I saw myself growing to love so angry. My suggestion was that it might be better to wind back our relationship and return to a platonic friendship. Dave agreed, so we parted with respect and love.

Evident early with Dave was how easily impressed he appeared to be by status and power. Apparent that he wanted to please people, the outworking was a rapidly changeable personality. Depending on whether he desired to impress or not, he could be genuinely charming and engaging, yet down the other end of the spectrum, he could be condescending, rude, and disinterested. The early warning signs were present, and although observed, they did not deter me from continuing to see him.

A week after reassessing our relationship status, Dave and I caught up for a casual breakfast. We were both pleased, sitting opposite one another chatting about a myriad of interests. Both fully engaged and eager to connect. I must have been sitting a little to one side of Dave because it wasn't until we changed angles, that I noticed the purple mark looking suspiciously like a hickey on the side of his neck. A wave of nausea swept over me as I questioned him. Defensively, he replied that it was none of my business. I had broken up with him and in his mind, he was free to do what he wanted.

OUCH! That hurt!

As sickened as I was, I had pity for him. How could someone be so needy? Why would someone who I thought had strong feelings for me quickly move on with another? I was really confused and so was he.

~

DAVE

Around this period, I had been flattered by the attention of a female friend of a workmate.

A series of selfish outbursts on my part left Noni questioning the wisdom of us continuing as we were. Interpreting this as harsh judgement and rejection, I retreated into a well-ridden victim cycle, simplifying the situation to one where I wanted the relationship, but couldn't make it work well enough for Noni. Rather than approaching the situation maturely, working through the challenges and being accountable for my feelings, I readily took consolation in the easy attention of Linda. Telling myself that if Noni didn't want me and someone else did - then Noni must be wrong. I convinced myself there was nothing wrong with feeling or acting the way I did.

The friendship with Linda escalated into a physical relationship. My fragile ego, propped up by the attention received from another woman, proved that I was worth something to somebody else. I had gained a sense of power and control over the situation now that I had another option – one that was far less challenging. This was an appealing alternative to the risk and potential discomfort of having to face myself and be vulnerable instead of angry, and then commit to growing my relationship with Noni. The easy reassurance and attention from Linda did nothing to curb my deep longing to be near Noni.

~

NONI

During this initial discovery my mind drifted to the story of Jesus' crucifixion.

Nailed to the cross, He said, *"Forgive them Father, for they know not what they do." Luke 23:34.* Under no illusion of the past and present sin I was relishing in, there was forgiveness in my heart for Dave even though he was not asking for it.

This was the beginning of many lessons and growth opportunities for me.

Dave and I parted amicably later in the day, not sure of any plans to meet up again even just as friends. That night, at my dysfunctional best, I went out to see a band and blotted out my emotional disappointment with a cocktail of tequila and wine. WTH was happening?

The magnetism between Dave and I was strong, and without discussion or clear direction, it wasn't long before we reignited our friendship/romance. Falling back into a familiar pattern there was no unravelling of his hook-up with this other girl, Linda. In all honesty, my impression was I had no place asking questions, especially after Dave's initial reaction and response. He led me to believe, or perhaps it was the story I told myself, that she was merely a rebound, a one-night fling, and because I had broken it off with Dave, it was my fault. More than likely, this belief was an unhealthy combination of my own insecurity and it suited Dave perfectly. Hindsight is a wonderful thing, there was a lot more going on than leaving marks on his neck. Naivety and denial at its best.

~

DAVE

I bounced between the two relationships for a couple of months, never willing to give up one for the other, keeping information to a minimum, preserving the facade. My need to maintain control over circumstances and wrestling with my desire for Noni required energy. Despite my time spent with Linda, attempting to soothe my lost self-certainty, the desire to be near Noni never diminished. Relinquishing the affair to pursue my connection with Noni was a natural choice. We settled into a relationship that grew in depth over time, becoming best friends as well as lovers. Often on a Monday, Noni would meet me for lunch in a park opposite work. These lunch breaks were eagerly anticipated and always a highlight of my week. Being her day off, Corey accompanied her. Sitting under the Eucalypts, we would eat, chat, and play the hour away, laughing hysterically while we all dodged swooping magpies in spring as they protected their nests. The journey wasn't without hiccups as I stumbled along.

$\sim$

NONI

Central to this mess, I was still wrestling with where and how God fitted into my current circumstances. Dave wrote a letter and it was clear from his writing that he was frustrated with me, describing how unfair I was because I had melted the icy walls he'd built to protect himself from pain. He was angry that he'd permitted me access to his hardened heart when he unintentionally dropped his guard and lowered his defences. At the core, he wasn't stoked that he'd allowed himself to develop feelings for me. I was throwing him more challenges than were welcome.

As my feelings grew stronger for Dave, my spirit ached for an honest and truthful bond with him. Dave struggled with his own demons, determined to retain a firm grip on them, keeping me at a safe distance. Inner conflict manifested in his behaviour and words. This was difficult to watch, let alone understand. The very first time I was moved to pray for another person out loud was then. I'd seen it done in church, I'd read about it, I knew of people laying hands on each other for healing, and now I was going to give it a go. What did I have to lose? Tentatively, I asked Dave if I could pray for him. Thankfully, he welcomed the comfort of prayer. It was an exercise in trust, trusting God, Dave, and myself. Once more, we moved toward each other with hope.

LESSONS FROM BEYOND

STEPPING OUT ON A LIMB IS SCARY BUSINESS.

IF YOU WANT TO WALK ON WATER, YOU MUST GET OUT OF THE BOAT.

TRUST AND VULNERABILITY INVOLVE RISK.

TWO BROKEN PEOPLE DON'T MAKE ONE WHOLE.

CHAPTER 4

IT'S GETTING REAL

NONI

Valuing my career and financial independence, Corey and I enjoyed a comfortable, secure lifestyle with an occasional luxurious splurge. Empowered by having control over our freedom gave me a sense of safety. I was a strong, capable, and independent woman.

Dave and I continued growing more committed to each other, spending increasing amounts of time together, having fun, laughing, and generally enjoying life. His improving relationship with Corey was interspersed with moments of angst and tension needing resolution. Both boys competed for my attention, sometimes neither were great in sharing me and likewise I didn't always achieve balance.

Dave and I had a lot in common. Apart from our love of good food, wine, and travel, we were both raised

NONI YATES & DAVID YATES

Catholic and had a Catholic education. Remnants of guilt accompanied by a 'works' mentality carried considerable sanctimonious weight. We thought we understood what constituted a 'good' person. Much of the religion rooted in us from an early age took some shaking off. Developing greater comprehension of being in a relationship with Christ versus religious indoctrination took time.

Our strength together was anchored by a depth of communication I'd not enjoyed with any other man. Coincidental or God-ordained, a quest for truth and transparency persisted front and foremost. Desiring an authentic and meaningful relationship with God, myself, and others became my primary pursuit.

Somewhere around the eighteen-month mark of Dave and I being 'an item', the thought struck me; this is the man I want to spend the rest of my life with. My best friend, I didn't want to live without him. I could envisage myself committing a life to him in marriage. This change of heart was a significant shift from my former self and a revelation that terrified me for a plethora of reasons. Fear of rejection played its part, but the greatest doubt by far, was my proven track record. During one of my many 'honesty hours', I uncovered an ugly little truth about myself; the thrill of the chase excited me more than the acquisition. Pursuing and then claiming my heart's desire only to discover once mine, expectations failed to live up to reality. Not as fascinating as initially thought. My remedy was to simply discard and move on to the next challenge. Everything disposable, even relationships...

Cautious and fearful there was every possibility this might be the case now, I reluctantly approached Dave and shared my fear. If I loved him like I believed I did, he deserved the truth. To his credit, he did not back away or recoil, neither did he reciprocate the same desire.

We had simple conversations around the prospect of a future together, and although the M-word was temporarily shelved, we continued to be and act like a perfectly infatuated couple. Little did I realise that Dave had his own set of deep-seated fears about love and marriage. I didn't think it was possible that another human existed as confused or frightened by the commitment of lifelong relationship as myself. Trust me, I found him; Dave was the one. Even more so!

This to-ing and fro-ing went on for another six months or thereabouts. As the frustration increased, it became painfully clear to me that Dave was extremely commitment phobic. Even though we were so good together, it appeared we might exist in this state of inertia indefinitely. Continuing to *try* and do my best at being a good Christian wasn't cutting it. Frequently succumbing to temptation only compounded confusion. Never in doubt though, the bar slowly rose on what I would and wouldn't accept as the standard of commitment I sought.

During the year, I bought a house in Noosa. The quaint four-bedroom Old Queenslander was a dream come true. Managing the purchase independently as a twenty-six-year-old single mum, this was absolutely winning. I had a home to call my own!

Although I was getting to the end of my tether with Dave's indecision around our future together, my prayer was never that he would marry me. Even though our relationship felt so legitimate, I remained hesitant to trust my own ability to *get it right*. Rather than pray, *please let Dave appreciate what an incredible catch I am. Have him drop to his knee and confess his undying love and make me his wife*, even though undeniably this was my fleshly desire, I did believe our eternal reward is in Heaven. So, my heart's honest prayer was always for Dave to receive the gift of pure love from Christ. To be free from the bondage confining him. Yearning for him to relate to and love Jesus as I did. To understand how incredibly precious, we are in God's eyes, and most of all, for him to know how much he is loved. I wanted Dave to experience what it was like to be free from the constraints and lies of this world. To identify the truth of where his identity lay, not tied up in performance, possession, approval, success, or ego. I wanted him to have the deep unshakeable joy that comes from being in a relationship with the divine. I truly wanted the best for him. I have always wanted the best for Dave and still do today.

A corporate opportunity came Dave's way. The position in Sydney meant relocating, an exciting change for Dave, new start, and direction. We had mixed feelings about the impact of the move on our relationship, but I actively encouraged Dave to accept the job. I'm not averse to change, change equals growth. They are called growing pains for a reason. On the flip side, we were going nowhere fast in our comfortable little arrangement. My choice was to view this through spiritual eyes and believe the opportunity was divine intervention and would break the inertia one way or another.

~

DAVE

The career opportunity appeared too good to pass up. Noni and I discussed it and agreed the job offered significant long-term employment benefits. Anxious about making a decision, I arranged to talk the offer over with my current boss, hoping that when I told him the details, he would simply ask how much it would take to keep me (I had a number in mind already). This would spare me separation from Noni and life might continue comfortably.

"I reckon you should take the role as I can't give you the same prospects. All I could do is offer more money, but that won't help you," he said.

Disappointed an offer of more money wasn't on the table, I reasoned that my career might have been limited but at least it could have helped me avoid making a difficult choice. His answer confirmed what Noni and I were resigned to. The move would be smart career-wise and an easier one to make than the far more important decision of whether I could commit to this wonderful woman. Moving back to Sydney was difficult and painful. I sat in my car waving goodbye to Noni and Corey as they stood in front of me on the timber wrap-around deck. Both of their images blurred by the tears my eyeballs were swimming in. Turning on the ignition, our favourite Absent Friends song filtered through the car stereo: "I don't wanna be with nobody but you..." Wendy Mathews' voice hauntingly beautiful. I sobbed aloud and began the eleven-hour drive ahead of me. Even though I had family and friends in Sydney, I was going to be lost without my best friend.

~

NONI

The month before Dave joined the firm in Sydney, he moved in with Corey and me. This did nothing but solidify and intensify our love and desire for one another. Dave could still not establish whether he wanted to make this a permanent commitment. I believed it better for us to end our relationship rather than try our luck at a long-distance 'thing'. We discussed this and agreed no contact was best for all of us. The day Dave drove out of our driveway in Noosa for the last time is one of the most painful moments etched in my memory. Before he left, we stood on the timber wrap-around veranda holding each other tight, hearts heavy and shirts drenched with tears of sorrow, not wanting to leave the embrace or comfort of this love. Climbing into his red Honda civic, Dave started the engine, labouring for an agonizingly long moment before shifting gears to reverse. Time stood still. Then movement as his car disappeared down the street. Gutted, gone was the love of my life.

Australia's largest hairdressing convention was held in Sydney some weeks after Dave's departure. He knew I would be in the city for a few days. Accommodation sorted for all but one of the days conveniently left a night free before returning home to Noosa. Shall I contact Dave or not? Who am I kidding? Of course, I would, and I did. Five weeks had passed with no contact, so our re-connection was intense. We were cautious, however, the attraction toward one another had not dissipated in the slightest. All it took was one night together and we transitioned into an arrangement neither of us wanted, embarking on the passionate roller coaster of a long-distance relationship. Dave's work involved a lot of travel and he advantageously arranged work in South East Queensland. Many opportunities for weekends and nights in Noosa coincided with his schedule. We saw each other frequently and spoke on the phone most days. One weekend, I literally drove from Noosa to Port Macquarie (an eight-hour drive one way!) just to spend two nights with him. What I would consider madness now was effortless at the time. A little like opening a hairdressing salon when five and a half months pregnant!

～

DAVE

Given any opportunity to travel near Noni, I jumped at the chance, extending trips to squeeze in more time together. Over the months, our reunions became regular and intense, like mini honeymoons without marriage. Indecision and lack of direction led to Noni's growing frustration. Work was exciting and challenging, a significant learning curve with plentiful positive support and recognition. My job, co-workers and customers made me feel like I was someone special, precisely the culture nurtured in most sales organizations. The business unit I worked in was a close-knit group. Celebrating each other's successes and supporting one another, my co-workers were good company. Travel, the celebration of wins, team building, socialising regularly, all common-place in this new corporate environment. Another common occurrence in this corporate world was office affairs. These affairs appeared to be openly accepted and tolerated. This may have been a reflection on the character of senior leaders or underlying organizational culture. Evidently, this same attitude of 'tolerance' was exhibited across the industry. I can recall at least a dozen individuals stepping well outside the boundaries of their marriages with seemingly little consequence. At times, people were cheating all around us, no one saying a word to them. We gossiped and surmised, yet these dalliances remained unchallenged. A few months after starting work in Sydney, I began a relationship with Karen. We first met at a work lunch, hit it off immediately, experienced a level of attraction, and agreed to continue our conversation over dinner that evening. Our friendship transitioned to a physical one in the space of weeks, despite her being in a long-term relationship and myself continuing my fly-in fly-out romance with Noni. Karen ended her existing relationship soon after we increased the frequency of our catching up. Though never considering us an 'item', emotional attachment and intimacy developed. There was no way I would let go of my relationship with Noni, though. She knew nothing of the other woman, yet Karen knew of my relationship with Noni. Noni has never been someone I've wanted to keep hidden. Karen was working in a different area of business when we first met, but soon after we commenced seeing each other, she accepted a position in the business unit I was in.

Sharing customer meetings and events provided ample opportunity for us to be alone, allowing the relationship to develop further within work hours. Though the friendship and emotional and physical attraction to Karen was enjoyable, it felt nothing like the overwhelming intensity or level of connection I experienced with Noni. I recall trembling when standing near Noni the first time after a period of separation. However, Karen made no demands. I continued unchallenged, maintaining both relationships to the extent I needed to. Extracting the best from each of them as opportunities presented while avoiding commitment as best I could.

~

NONI

We carried on like this for about six months when I realised abruptly that I had compromised the standard I'd set out to maintain, once again lowering the bar of expectation and giving in to my flesh. Damn! Sorry, God…

I recall Dave and I had dinner at a Hastings Street restaurant one night, discussing how I was feeling about our relationship, which was now nearing the two-year mark. Matter-of-factly informing him he enjoyed all the benefits of a married man with zero responsibility, i.e., someone who had a child he could 'play' family with, someone who cooked meals, paid her own way, owned her own house, etc. Although I'm not a big gift-giving or receiving kind of person, I think words along the lines of, "It would be nice to get some flowers every now and then" may have emerged from my mouth.

Turning to me he said, "You're a hard taskmaster, Noni."

Needing to lift my jaw from the table, I said, "I don't expect anything I don't think I deserve Dave!"

I totally meant it! I do believe flowers arrived the following week and have made regular appearances since.

Speaking up and voicing opinions I believed fair and reasonable has never been a problem for me. The more I matured, the stronger my belief that I am worthy of respect and honour. Yet even with this conviction, I still found myself tolerating less than acceptable behaviour more than I ever should have. I'm not sure if I over-looked the grievances because the good outweighed the bad, or if it was a case of not being able to see the wood for the trees.

~

During one of Dave's visits to Noosa, he told me two of his good friends whom I knew were marrying in Switzerland later in the year. Excitedly chatting about this great European experience without one mention whatsoever of me joining him, I quite boldly asked if he'd even considered I might go with him? Apparently not! This must have given him something to think about though. A couple of weeks later, I received an invitation to the wedding in

Switzerland and we began planning a wonderful five weeks of travel through Italy, Switzerland, and France.

Although making a decent go of the long-distance relationship, it was never going to be sustainable. The novelty began to wane. Being married to this man was the only option for me. Discussions throughout the year about marriage – more specifically, our marriage – looked promising. Dave seemed to be coming around to the idea of us making our commitment official. Before leaving for our overseas adventure, I broached the idea of our nuptials again with him by asking if we could shop for engagement rings while we were away, his answer was, "Maybe."

My reply, "Whenever my dad said that, it meant no," and just like conversations with my dad, this was the end of any further discussion on the matter.

~

DAVE

A European Wedding.

The invitation to my best friend's wedding in Switzerland presented me with an opportunity to travel and see Europe as well as present a defining moment of consideration. Do I go alone? If so, then I am saying I am a single man free to enjoy the accompanying freedom of that status. Is this what I really desire? *No*, was my honest answer. Do I take Noni – my best friend and lover for years? After all, I relish every moment spent with her. Any experience shared with Noni is always a better one. If I do, am I making a bold statement about who Noni is in my life? Will the next logical step be that we make plans to marry? This decision was not one I could make lightly. Committing to a lifetime is a lot bigger than five weeks travelling overseas. However, if I was going to be celebrating the biggest day in my best mate's life, then I wanted my best friend right by my side to share it with me. Ultimately, there is no one on earth I would rather share new experiences with. We started planning.

LESSONS FROM BEYOND

THAT WHICH YOU TOLERATE WILL NEVER CHANGE.

CHAPTER 5

THE WORDS THAT CHANGED
EVERYTHING

NONI

Dave and I flew from Sydney to Rome on Boxing Day 1992; Corey stayed with Charlie. This trip would significantly impact our lives in a way neither of us could imagine. I went with the expectation of a proposal but received so much more. We journeyed around three countries by boat, train, and car. We mistook blocks of butter for cheese, sinking our teeth into tasty wedges of fat, ate bread and drank wine on the side of the road, and made love often. (Yes, still guilty of fornicating! Yes, still fumbling my way through my Christian walk, and yes, still a sinner. Did God condone what I was doing? No, He didn't! Did God still love me despite this? Yes, He did!) We laughed and made precious lifetime memories, joyfully witnessing the celebration of two beautiful friends, their stunning wedding one of epic proportion. We visited many cathedrals and churches, not to take part in any services, merely to admire the grand buildings of historic significance. The definition of church is the body of people, the believers, not the structures used for gatherings. We explored many such buildings, coining the phrase ABC; translated to Another Bloody Cathedral.

~

DAVE

Travelling through Italy, France and Switzerland with Noni was filled with memorable adventures. Dining, shopping and visiting museums often resulted in hilarious situations as we absolutely massacred the foreign dialects. Noni and I came close to arguing once during our five-week European vacation. Hiring a car in Paris, I drove and Noni navigated. She turned the map in circles and upside down trying to work out which direction we needed to go.

Without realising that 'Rue' is the word for road, our first wrong turn was the one leaving the Avis terminal.

I'm not certain how many times we circled Notre-Dame that day, but each time it came into sight, according to Noni and her map, it was supposed to be on the other side of the river.

Eventually making our way out of the city, both of us chose silence while our heads cooled.

I didn't regret the decision to have Noni with me on this trip for one second. Apart from the hours of fun and laughter, it was like the honeymoon without the wedding.

~

NONI

Our last stop was Paris, the city of love. I was convinced this was where the proposal would happen, just like in the movies. True to tourist status, we visited the Eiffel Tower, Arc de Triomphe, and the Louvre, but unfortunately, it was closed for a private function. We went to Sacre-Coeur which I can tell you is no ABC. Dave and I were inseparable on this trip and never left each other's side, yet as we entered this cathedral, we inexplicably went in different directions. I don't recall where Dave was. Other people were inside the building, but they were merely slow-moving objects to me. There was no controlling what happened next. Not focusing on anything in particular, I began to weep. This scenario was not necessarily new. Memories flooded back to when I first walked into the little church in Noosa, sensing God calling. I needed to find a seat and rest. Without a doubt, this was inexplicably the audible voice of God. Hand on my heart, I kid you not.

Initially, I didn't know where the sound came from. I turned around to see if others had heard. Were they listening to what the man's gentle, yet firm voice was saying to me? No one was paying the slightest bit of attention to this fathers' loving chastisement. His exact words were, "Why should he marry you? He has his cake and he's eating it too. Surrender it ALL to me." Tremendous calm and peace accompanied His words. My loving Heavenly Father, promising I would be OK no matter the outcome. The Lord, ultimately in control could be trusted with every part of my life. Our finite human brain limits God to what we are conditioned into believing He is like. What I've learned is He meets us right where we're at, communicating in ways we individually can understand. God's words to me were astonishingly simple. They were not harsh. Every word was spoken and delivered with pure love. A gentle scolding from someone who cares for and loves me more than I love myself.

After what must have been an eternity, I stood up and walked to the exit. This is where Dave and I reconvened. The voice inside the church never mentioned. No longer crying, the warmth from this encounter created a complete, all-encompassing serenity. The remainder of the day was a blur. The next thing I recall is being at Charles De Gaulle airport waiting to board our flight back to Australia. With no proposal likely, I turned to Dave and spoke resolutely.

"The ball's in your court."

Confusion was written all over his face as I continued, "When we get back to Australia, you make this relationship what you want it to be."

This time, I was confident. I meant it.

~

DAVE

The spectacular Basilica of the Sacred Heart is better known as Sacre-Coeur. Although Noni and I visited on a clear crisp day, a cloud in the shape of the *what now* question mark loomed heavily over me. It was a day of both confrontation and clarity for me.

We moved in different directions not long after entering the Basilica. I was drawn one way and Noni another. After strolling around absorbing spectacular architecture and artwork, I sat in the stillness of enforced silence. Inner turmoil raging, there was no avoiding the question, What next, Dave? Perhaps I was hoping for divine inspiration, guidance, or deliverance from the moment. A voice cut through the stillness, "What you are doing to her is not right."

Sitting a while longer, I let the words sink in. These were not my own thoughts, but a clear revelation, a moment of truth. Meeting Noni outside on the steps of the basilica, a panoramic view of Paris spread out in front of us, just like our future. Convicted by these words, there was no surprise for me when Noni told me she was at the end of the line as far as continuing our relationship in its current state. Other than lamenting why throw what we have away, I didn't try to persuade her otherwise. I knew it wasn't right of me to continue taking up her life without the commitment she and Corey deserved, particularly as my secret involvement with Karen persisted. The ball was well and truly in my court, where it rightly belonged.

I was frustrated because it was up to me whether I kept Noni in my life, but I couldn't dodge responsibility for the relationship's future any longer. Noni's commitment and desire for our partnership was as clear and unwavering as ever. We returned to Australia in this state. Noni, clear, concise, and committed. Myself, full of doubt, insecurity, and fear. The memory of failure in my relationship with Jenna was never far from my mind. The pain I caused was the weight of shame I carried. A child was involved again. It wasn't just the lives of two adults at stake. What if I messed this up as well? What if I am not enough? Noni and I parted.

~

NONI

The white flag raised, jammed firmly in the ground. I went back to Noosa, Dave remained in Sydney. From this moment forward, I ceased initiating any contact with him. Our friends who married in Switzerland had three weddings, the next one a few weeks after we arrived home. Previously confirming our attendance, Corey and I accompanied Dave, enjoying a stunning weekend. Corey and I returned to Noosa with no future plans of heading south, keeping firm my resolution not to contact Dave.

~

DAVE

Soon after returning to Sydney, I continued the casual but regular relationship with Karen. This relationship offered comfort and companionship with no demands – a poor substitute for the deeper connection, unconditional love, and acceptance I had with Noni. My longing grew, I missed Noni more and more. A month or two passed and then I approached a friend who had been married for about twenty years and asked, "How do I know if this is the person to marry?"

"Dave, ask yourself one question; can I live without this person in my life?"

That question I answered in a heartbeat. In a matter of days, I devised my plan. There was still the matter though of telling Karen of my decision. She was tearful but fairly gracious, conceding, "I expected as much."

~

NONI

Thankful for good business and great staff, there was always plenty of distraction keeping me busy and occupied. A few weeks passed. Dave called once or twice each week, chatting about nothing in particular, regular stuff. Although nice to hear his voice, I had no desire for small talk.

One day at work, a guy walked in for a haircut. He was a confident, good-looking American guy. I had zero attraction towards him, flat out no interest. As he left the salon, I sensed he would ask me out on a date. Nothing surer, he called the salon that afternoon with an invitation. I wasn't the slightest bit attracted to Paul (my heart was firmly attached to Dave), however, I decided to go out with him. His confidence was off the Richter scale, ensuring there was no chance of breaking a heart or bruising an ego the size of Texas. We went for dinner, saw a movie and chit-chatted about light stuff. I was dead honest about my heartache and love for Dave. Cocky, confident, and emphatically sure, the remedy for my sorrow would simply be to go on a few dates with him. Little did he realise how much I truly loved Dave. I hung out with Paul a couple of times, it was harmless and pleasant enough. Always making sure of driving myself and paying my own way, avoiding any false expectations or mixed messages. Dave continued weekly calls, I told him about Paul and other activities filling my time.

One night, Dave called, asking what I'd been up to. I told him about catching up with Paul. He had a dummy spit, reacting angrily and saying, "Oh, your boyfriend."

Our conversation became heated and I retorted, "Dave, he's not my boyfriend, I don't have a boyfriend. Actually I don't want a boyfriend, what I want is a husband. NO, NOT just any husband! I want you to be my husband!!!"

With that, I hung up. The first time I'd hung up on someone since high school. This felt good. A few minutes later, the phone rang again. I had nothing more to say to Dave. I listened, without uttering a word.

"Noni, please don't do anything, please give me some more time."

Quietly thinking to myself; it's been two and a half years, how much more time does this man need? Keeping those thoughts to myself I instead blurted out, "Time, how much time?"

"Give me a month, please."

In stunned silence, my heart softened.

"OK."

Dave gave himself a time frame. No ultimatum needed, his request one easily accommodated. I didn't exactly have any immediate plans.

Three weeks after that phone call, I was arranging a dinner for my twenty-eighth birthday. Dave called asking who would be going to the dinner. I told him who I thought would be celebrating with me. (I had a sneaky suspicion he was checking to see if my American friend might have been coming. I could be wrong). At work the day before the dinner, I popped out of the salon for an errand. One of my staff found me, saying I was needed at the back of the salon. I walked out from my staff room to see Dave climbing out of a taxi with his surfboard. Bursting into tears, he uttered the words I'd been waiting to hear:

"Noni, will you marry me?"

My eyes still grow misty at the most exquisitely memorable moment of my life. I visualise and am touched by emotion, as powerfully now twenty-six years later, as back in March of 1993.

~

DAVE

My intention was to surprise Noni with a visit, and a marriage proposal. I anticipated sweeping her off her feet with dozens of roses in front of cheering onlookers. In my eagerness to get to Noni's salon from the Noosa airport, I completely forgot to ask the taxi driver to stop and find a florist. Thankfully, when I surprised Noni at the back of her salon with my heartfelt invitation to a life together, her answer was yes, even in the absence of something a little more grandiose.

~

NONI

Dave gathered himself, overcoming arguably the biggest decision he'd made to date. He was ready to put a ring on my finger immediately. Now it was my turn to press the pause button.

I had a wedding to plan, a business to sell, a house to organise, and a son to consider. The date was set for October 2, 1993, seven months after Dave's proposal. Our wedding fondly regarded as magnificently simple. It couldn't be any better than marrying my best friend, living the rest of my life sleeping and waking next to this wonderful man whom I adored.

Happy days!

After Dave's surprise proposal on my birthday weekend early in 1993, he went back to Sydney. We spoke frequently on the phone and saw each other as often as possible during the seven months leading up to our wedding day. I hadn't met Dave's work colleagues, but several names, both male and female, were familiar. One name popped up regularly, a woman Dave worked with – Karen. I recall questioning Dave about what kind of *friendship* he had with this woman. "Just a friend," he said.

Something didn't feel quite right. He occasionally went to a movie with her, took her flowers because she was off work sick with shingles... stuff like that. My hackles rose. One night, Dave called whilst driving home from indoor soccer, interestingly taking a completely different route to the most direct way. Although a little uneasy about several aspects of his interaction with this woman, he always gave seemingly plausible explanations to questions I asked and would become abrupt if I pushed too much. Concerned with appearing insecure by continuing to question, I buried my fears. Earlier, during courtship years when querying a relationship, he had with another casual female acquaintance, Dave told me in no uncertain terms I had a 'nasty suspicious mind!' I suppose from then on, my thoughts were guarded, and I was wary of asking too many questions, particularly surrounding Dave's female friendships.

LESSONS FROM BEYOND

NO MATTER HOW MUCH WE MIGHT WANT THE BEST FOR OTHERS, UNLESS THEY HAVE THE DESIRE FOR THEMSELVES, OUR BEST EFFORTS ARE LIKE CHASING THE WIND.

WE TEACH OTHERS HOW WE WOULD LIKE TO BE TREATED.

TRUST YOUR GUT INSTINCTS, THEY MIGHT NOT BE EXACT, BUT THEY'RE RARELY COMPLETELY OFF THE MARK.

CHAPTER 6

THE HONEYMOON'S OVER!

NONI

Our wedding took place in a stunning sandstone Church in Noosa, the reception at The Beach Chalet. Seventy guests joined our celebration. Corey played a pivotal part as our ring bearer, suiting up to match Dave. Exchanging our vows was undeniably the most precious part of our day, loving and cherishing all this meant for us. Before God and mesmerised in the moment, we wholeheartedly pledged vows to each other.

My salon sold ten days before the wedding. We married on Saturday, October 2, had a family gathering at my home in Noosa on Sunday, October 3, and left for our Bali honeymoon on Monday, October 4. My precious home was now a rental property and my roots were no longer in Noosa.

Returning after a glorious two weeks in Bali, I gathered Corey and drove straight to Sydney. Married life for our little family would begin on Sydney's Northern Beaches. A whirlwind couple of weeks had me failing to anticipate the enormity of changes set in motion.

Bali is one of our shared travel destinations, both holidaying on the Island of the Gods before meeting. Having visited since 1980 and familiar and comfortable with the Balinese people and culture, Bali was a natural choice for our honeymoon. Conjuring up a fantasy Cinderella story of how our honeymoon would unfold left me underwhelmed. The only person I had to blame was myself. Too many Disney movies set me up for disappointment. The stark reality was that Dave's checked baggage was surfboards. A surf trip with his new bride would be amazing, he had his own story going on. Newlywed Mrs. Yates would surely share this adventure, his pillion passenger holding tight to her man. There was endless motoring in search of secret surf spots that, in 1993, still existed.

Alas for Dave, his bride detested motorbikes, all the more when ridden without a helmet and carrying a surfboard under one arm while holding onto him for dear life with the other. None of our preconceived ideas had been discussed beforehand, but eager to please Dave, I played along for a few days. After skidding into gravel and unceremoniously dismounting the bike and ending up ridiculously sunburnt, I fessed up to be a scaredycat. Telling him I would be ecstatic, over the moon in fact, for him to buzz off and surf by himself. In the interests of saving my sanity, we agreed that relaxing at the resort, soaking up quiet time and chilling by the pool would suit me better than anxiety-inducing bike rides. We still spent plenty of time relishing one another, consummating our love and desire as husband and wife.

During dinner one evening, we chatted about wedding gifts. The Sydney relocation prompted us to request gift vouchers rather than physical items. A purely practical option. Dave mentioned his work colleagues gave a couple of nice bedside lamps which suited the bedroom perfectly. A little perplexed, I thought this was an unusual gift from workmates. I said nothing of my surprise, instead, asking who bought the lamps. His response; Karen. My gut churned and my mouth went dry. Sharing troubled thoughts about them being an unusual gift and how uncanny it was that they fit in with the bedroom décor so well, I think I said something along the lines of, "Maybe she knows the bedroom a little better than she should."

Dave became defensive, angry with me for having such stupid thoughts. Once again, I was forced to deny and bury unfounded suspicion. His stern response silenced me yet left questions circling in my mind.

The weeks leading up to our wedding and honeymoon were as exciting as they were rushed, so now that there was time to be still, I reflected on the past and with some trepidation, pondered the future.

I lived in Noosa for seven years, longer than I'd lived in any one location. Now Corey and I were moving to a city we'd never lived in. The anticipation of relocating to Sydney was no problem; I'd nailed this kind of change many times over. The fear causing my anxiety was a trust issue. Not only did I need to trust another person not only with my life, but also the well-being of my five-year-old son, I also needed to trust his integrity. But I had niggling doubts about that. I had no business, no work, and no income of my own. On top of this, I had a brand- new surname. No longer Noni Kopp, I was now Mrs. Noni Yates. Who the heck was she?

It was time to find out.

This identity crisis in the midst of our holiday surely wasn't part of anyone's honeymoon script. I needed to pull myself together real fast. Gaining composure, gently persuading myself back from this ledge, guaranteed the majority of our two-week holiday was incredible.

Our arrival in Sydney was an exciting and busy time. Settling Corey into school, I turned the house into a home and found myself a part-time hairdressing position. Things were motoring along well, apart from an underlying agitation and annoyance in Dave which was difficult to put a finger on. Acrimony was not far beneath the surface of Dave's personality and I was never aware of what might set him off. He rose to anger quickly over minor irritations. In addition, red flag moments arose regarding Dave and this woman he worked with.

By now, I'd met others Dave worked with, including Karen. She gave him a small but concerning gift, a cassette she recorded. It was just a playlist of music which I didn't think too much about at the time. More alarming was the carefully cut letters from magazines and newspapers decorating the cassette case. This minor detail made me think she went to an awful lot of effort listing music on the tape. If this was a friend of mine, they'd receive the tape with scribbled song titles on the cardboard insert and be thankful. Expressing my apprehension to Dave, he casually shrugged it off, dismissing my unease as not being something he thought mattered or was important. Try as I might, I couldn't let it go. This thought gnawed away internally until I realised, I didn't trust Dave. I hated to admit this to myself. My gut conceded that if I didn't have a marriage based on trust, I had nothing.

Waking one morning with heaviness of heart, I had to confess this burden.

While preparing breakfast for Dave before he left for work, I dissolved into tears. Glancing at me in dismay, he said, "Darling, what's up?"

I replied solemnly, "Dave, I have a real problem, I don't trust you."

Astonishment was written all over his face. He held both of my hands as I continued,

"Do I have any reason not to trust you?"

Me at my most vulnerable. Frightened yet confident of what I must do, I had to be honest. He kept a hold of my hands looking straight into my tear-filled eyes.

"No, Noni, I love you and place you above all others."

Holding me, he gently kissed and hugged me tightly. His answer, even though I was unsure about what the 'above all others' meant, gave me comfort, alleviated my unfounded fears, and he went off to work. I had been silly, nothing to worry about. Taws naught but my own rotten insecurity. I set about clearing my mind of such negativity. Openly, honestly, and humbly, I asked a direct question and in return received all the assurance needed. Never once did it occur to me this might not be the truth. It was inconceivable to me that a person could look another straight in the eye and blatantly lie, especially someone who had pledged to love, honour, and cherish me. Laying my fears aside, I continued to go about my business of nurturing our happy home life. Early months into marriage, adjustments are to be expected. For the most part, we were progressing nicely in our post-nuptial bubble, giving our best shot to navigating minor disagreements and learning how to communicate as a family. Sharing plenty of laughs and family gatherings, we explored a couple of local churches, enjoyed weekends at the beach, and were busy making new friends as a couple. We enjoyed a healthy, active sex life, savouring frequent lovemaking. The epitome of wedded bliss... what could go wrong?

Dave's work has always required significant travel. Corey and I often joined Dave when he worked in regional New South Wales. We all loved a road trip, the drive through the Blue Mountains on the way to Orange is divine, especially in Autumn. Twilight skies, falling leaves and pre-winter crispness. We appreciated the changing landscape.

About a month after my meltdown over the fancy cassette cover, Dave scheduled another Orange visit and would be away for only one night. Corey and I stayed home. It was winter 1994, cold in Sydney and even colder in Orange.

I was lying with Corey reading him a bed-time story when Dave arrived home. He paused at the door to Corey's room before walking in and giving us both a greeting kiss and an extra goodnight one to Corey. The light was dim. As Dave approached the bed, my eyes couldn't avoid the hideous purple mark on the side of his neck. My mind started swimming. Were my eyes playing tricks on me? The breath was knocked out of me by the assault and my heart thumped. I could hear the reverberation pounding in my ears. Try as I might, I needed to suspend my fear and maintain control for Corey's sake. Once I knew he was off in the land of nod, I climbed off his bed and willed my shaking legs to inch toward our bedroom. I had to investigate what I thought I saw and see if it was, indeed, there. Dave was getting ready for bed. When I entered our room, he began chatting away mindlessly, making polite small talk. For him, nothing was amiss, he was clueless to how sickened I felt, unaware of my complete and utter disbelief and the absolute traumatic shock that stunned me. Although the internal screams were deafening, words failed me. With only five steps separating the front door from the back in our two-bedroom fisherman's cottage, our home was no place for a screaming match. Once I caught my breath and found my voice, I managed to control the volume as I said, "WHAT'S THAT?"

He echoed a quizzical, "What?"

I pointed again to the grotesque bruise on his neck which triggered my nausea. Turning from me, he walked into the bathroom massaging his throat. A feeble attempt, trying to erase that which my eyes could not. Staggering to my feet I followed, watching him rub furiously at the mark.

"Come back here and explain to me what has happened!"

"I had dinner with Karen last night."

I retaliated. "It looks like you had more than dinner!"

I was furious, devastated, and shattered. It was unthinkable that he would do something like this. My world disintegrated, fell apart. How the hell was I going to recover from this? I had trusted him wholeheartedly and gave up my independence to make a life with this man. I had walked away from being in control of my future and dared to become someone's dependent. My greatest fears were realised in that moment. Surely this was the coldest, darkest night of my life. If you've not personally experienced this trauma, I hope you never do. It's not easy describing the level of pain and despair I was drowning in at that moment.

This night was one of the longest in living memory. We both cried, terrified for what this might mean. I remember lamenting that our marriage was a complete sham. Dave insisted it wasn't. How could it not be? If he really loved me, he wouldn't have done this, would he? No decisions were made in the cold the of night, but as soon as first light peeked through the blinds, I was on the phone to Air New Zealand. I had a good amount of money left from the sale of my business. I just wanted to pack Corey up and run as fast and as far away as possible. I knew how to run from pain.

Before daylight broke, I drove to the salon and left a resignation letter and the salon key. Back home, Corey was still in bed. While I was making calls to book flights, Dave came out begging me not to go. Facing me, he spoke dejectedly, "I need help, can we please go to counselling? Christian counselling."

This caught my attention. I hung up the phone and cautiously explored what he was suggesting. But before entertaining the thought of any counselling, I insisted Dave call Karen and explain that their night together in Orange had been one huge mistake and that I knew about their coquetry and it would never happen again. Standing beside him as he made the call, she seemed confused by Dave's words. Call me naïve, but Dave had led me to think this indiscretion was a one-off, a one-night dalliance and that they didn't have sex. Foolishly, I believed him. My initial thought about their working relationship was that one of them would have to look for work elsewhere. This didn't eventuate.

After composing ourselves enough to function in some capacity as parents, we drove Corey to school. Pretending things were normal with great difficulty, we wished Corey a wonderful day before driving to meet with a pastor. I let Dave do all the talking. He opened with, "I've done something terrible to damage my marriage."

I'm certain this dignified man had heard the same words on more occasions than he'd like. He was gracious, gentle, and wise. He ascertained I was a believer and had a relationship with Jesus, surmising Dave did not. After some discussion, Pastor Barry asked Dave if he would like to surrender his life to Jesus. To my surprise, Dave wept and accepted this invitation. The worst and best of days combined. How did darkness become light in this instant? Although we had been through the most excruciating night, I now had to acknowledge that God, who I'd wanted so desperately to show me He was real, once again answered my prayer. I'd prayed regularly for Dave to meet Jesus the past three and a half years. GOD, why did it have to happen this way though? Why? Nevertheless, true joy emanated from what transpired. We began a new chapter of our marriage as an equally yoked couple. I also had a deep conviction. This betrayal was more about Dave and the battle raging within him, rather than me, the affair partner, or deficits in our marriage. I wish I could say this conviction lessened the intensity of pain. It didn't.

～

DAVE

My decisions and actions over the years are my responsibility alone, not that there was any admission to this at the time. Our marriage was good. I wasn't lacking sexual fulfilment, never thought of marriage being anything but monogamous, nor did I ever wish to leave my wife. I do, however, want to share insight into how a man who truly loves his partner can betray promises and cross lines he never thought he would.

My ability to live in duality was well established before Noni and I ever married. Entering into our vows with the knowledge of my secret affair was already lying by omission. I reasoned if Noni didn't know, then it wouldn't hurt her, and I certainly didn't intend to maintain the relationship with Karen once I was a married man.

Soon after Noni and I married, my affair with Karen started again. Seeing her most days as part of the same sales team gave us many reasons and occasions to interact. I was unaccustomed to placing healthy boundaries around myself and was unaware of my underlying vulnerability. My finely crafted compartmentalization skills were about to get a real test. Deflecting and diverting suspicion became a way of life for me. Stealing time to get together around work functions or on trips with Karen became almost routine. This self-deception took a ton of energy to keep in place, though it was met with little internal resistance. Rationalization of my actions and deceit took form in the following lies. I can keep this part of my life separate – if not found out, no one is harmed. I still want and love Noni and my family, I am not nearly as bad as those unfaithful husbands who want to leave their wives and children. Karen seems happy with the situation, there's no obvious pressure from her, it's harmless whilst ever the two worlds are kept separate. I must be worthy of this extra attention, otherwise, it wouldn't be happening, there must be something special about me.

Living in this deception is far from easy and constant fear of being found out stalked my thoughts. What if the image I portrayed as a wonderful husband and father was exposed as a fraud? I lay awake at night dreading that Noni might ask one more question, uncover a detail exposing the truth. On the nights at home immediately following any trip where I had been unfaithful, I laid in bed next to Noni hoping she was asleep while I tried to stop my thoughts from spinning. I'd replay every word I'd spoken to her and examine her reactions to my deception. Had it worked? I wondered whether she believed my edited account of events and timelines. What if she realises, I'm awake and asks one question that uncovers my lies? What if she senses my anxiety and trusts her instincts? Sleep does not come easy when you're trying to duck and dive to avoid being found out. I couldn't stand this feeling, and in those moments, I vowed to stop. I vowed to, but I didn't, so I needed to become more practiced in my charade.

When Noni asked me the simplest things, my mind would race ahead and wonder if she was suspicious or just genuinely interested in my day. As I gave my false accounts, I was sure my pulsating temples could be noticed across the room. Through a dry mouth, words were carefully handpicked as I selectively left out details of where I had been and who I'd been with.

Moving on to hastily change the topic with as much casual ease as I could muster became a necessary diversion. Other times, I blatantly lied to direct questions, lies accompanied by a measure of conviction that almost had me convinced of their truth. The moment I looked into the eyes of my beautiful bride, held her hands, felt her fear and vulnerability, and promised her she had nothing to be concerned about, this cowardly act took me to a new level of self-loathing. Leaving for work that morning and driving down the hill from our humble cottage, a wave of disgust rose from the pit of my stomach. The company car I sat in was taking me away from my greatest love and straight towards my workplace and playground.

It wasn't the affair I was hell-bent on protecting, I was protecting myself from the consequences of my infidelity.

Each time, the twinge of pain and shame was accompanied by fear. The crushing fear of exposure, exposing me for what I was – a cheat, a liar, a fraud, and a coward – would certainly result in the loss of Noni and Corey. A most certain I would crumble under the weight of my deception, when the two compartments of my life appeared to collapse, I would say anything to avoid discovery.

And that's exactly what I did on the cold winter night Noni pointed to the mark on my neck.

Walking to the bathroom off our bedroom, desperately wanting to consult the mirror before making comment, scrambling to collect my thoughts, I frantically wanted to believe there may be another explanation. My head began to throb, the face staring back at me from the mirror flushed violently. Like a menacing stranger peering through a bedroom window, there was no denying that this person I had tried my hardest to avoid was now looking at me head on. There was no escaping this time.

Reluctant to confront the full extent of my deception, I did everything possible to control the disaster, somehow hoping to minimise my complicity. Walking back in to face Noni, I stood at the foot of our bed unable to utter the words my neck screamed. Stammering pathetically as if this would explain anything, "I had dinner with Karen last night..."

The hollow words were the best I could come up with, not technically a lie, yet a galaxy away from the truth. Minimising my actions by understating the frequency of betrayal and length of time I had been unfaithful made everything more tenable.

A sleepless night ensued, the shrapnel from colliding worlds bombarding my mind, body, and soul. Images of my infidelity, carefully scripted lies, and reflex impromptu lies all swirled around. Smack bang in the middle of it all was my precious wife, Noni, absolutely drowning in her pain. Desperately wanting the impossible, how I wished I could undo this mess, somehow take it back and erase the whole ugly sordid affair. At the end of myself, I needed to surrender, but to whom, and how?

The world outside Pastor Barry's office looked clearer and cleaner the day I knelt down, repented, and prayed for forgiveness, inviting Jesus into my life. There was an airiness in my step as I walked the path through the trees to the carpark. Clasping renewed hope for our future, my mind and spirit was noticeably weightless after sharing my shame. Despite the new buoyancy and hope, I was light years away from being completely honest with anyone, including myself.

Determined not to wound Noni more than I already had, I chose to maintain the fallacy of a single act of recklessness and indiscretion, reasoning that any more might destroy Noni and any chance of saving our marriage. It was also easier to admit being the man who disgraced his marriage in a moment of weakness rather than one who connived and calculated ongoing deception from his wedding day. In this decision, I was still aiming to protect myself.

Baring genuine remorse for my actions, I wholeheartedly welcomed the acceptance and understanding shown to me by Pastor Barry and Noni. Although wanting to end the double life I led I was still unprepared and unable to face myself entirely.

~

NONI

We both began individual counselling and couples counselling. Nothing specific to infidelity, more a generalised talk therapy, addressing little if anything about the nature of the affair.

My impression was that it was a one-night casual encounter, and they didn't have sex. Never encouraged to explore deeper, therapy sessions focused on marital deficiency and moving on. A great deal of social shame still exists today for unfaithful and betrayed partners of affairs. In 1993, infidelity was a perceived moral failure, subject closed. We began recovery from this setback. Though the infidelity was not fully addressed, counselling sessions helped open a new pattern of behaviour.

Regular church attendance as a family allowed us to meet great friends.

Though Dave and I grew closer to one another, fear and doubt about the betrayal ruminated within. Consciously applying my best effort was not enough to quell involuntary thoughts and previous suspicion. My mind drifted to how she chose bedside lamps which fit so well in our bedroom. In bed one night, I came straight out and asked Dave again how she could possibly have known what would suit our bedroom.

"She's been here, hasn't she!"

In hushed tones, through clenched teeth I continued, "You've slept with her, here, in our bed!"

"You've F*^#%* her haven't you!"

Heightened hysteria flooded me as the realisation hit hard. Dave's silence answered my questions. Positioning himself close, he faced me, sitting on the side of the bed. In fits of rage I began thumping his chest, I wanted him out of my sight. I hated him, not only for what he did but for not telling me the truth. For lying to me and deceiving me into thinking this indiscretion was a lapse in judgement, an unfortunate mistake we would overcome.

He looked at me forlorn, trying to calm me and hold me. Then he said he would go. I asked where and he replied to his parents.

I barked "What? And lie to them too?"

"No, I'll tell them the truth. The hardest thing was being honest with myself and then you. Now it doesn't matter."

Picking up my Bible, I hurled it at him as hard as I could. Walking out of our bedroom Dave handed me the Bible on the page it landed, Matthew 18:22 "seventy times seven" is how many times we should forgive each other...

NO WAY! NO GOD DAMN WAY!

The next day, Dave's mum phoned offering her support. Making little sense through my sobbing, her words clearly conveyed her thoughts, "Well, he didn't need to go and have an affair, did he!"

Dave was very much the wonder boy of the family. The comfort and support I received from Ma was graciously appreciated.

In the days following, Dave showed remorse. He said and did everything to show me he was committed to healing and to saving our marriage. We spoke in greater detail about the betrayal. He was tested for STI's and I believed him to be deeply grieved for the pain he caused. The efforts Dave made and the steps he took, all allowed me to cautiously soften my heart toward him once again. It was 1994. We had no internet and sweet little resources existed for a newly married couple left shattered by this bombshell. We continued marriage and individual counselling. Dave moved back home; our pastor's wife voiced concern that I had allowed him back prematurely. I was comfortable working through this under the same roof.

Ultimately, the choice was ours.

Couples counselling offered nothing to adequately address the 'why' of infidelity. Instead, it was primarily focused on what was lacking in our marriage that caused Dave to stray... As a newlywed couple passionately in love, sexually active and robust, we believed our marriage deficits minimal.

There must be reasons though, and we innocently bought into common misconceptions and looked externally for the *why*. Some reasons Dave offered; I wore flannelette PJ's in winter, he was curious whether it was possible to feel what he felt for me with anyone else. Does this sound like a good enough reason to stray? NO! Although none of this is a true or legitimate reason to commit adultery, as a young woman and new bride, I accepted these lame excuses as being true for him at the time. Nevertheless, we continued with counselling, hoping to learn all we could about us and marriage. We were both ready and willing to do whatever was needed to get past this hurdle. Our depth of communication increased as we began the process of rebuilding.

Through the discovery/disclosure process, it came to light that Dave had been having an affair with Karen for eighteen months by the time he was caught out. Interestingly enough, forgiveness came easily for me. Perhaps a little too easy for my own good. Understanding the power of grace extended, I was fully aware that harbouring unforgiveness would lead to separation from God. This was the one thing I wanted to avoid at all costs.

Intimacy with the Lord is a warm safe place for me. I feel his presence. He is my closest and most trusted friend. Even during challenging times, conversations with Him are characterised by peace and comfort. My girl friendships are tight. They're valued, but nothing compares to the strength I feel in God's presence. When there is distance growing in our communion, I know something is amiss. During this recovery period, I began experiencing difficulty connecting with God.

In one particularly barren session, I picked up my Bible and began reading. With no plan of where to start I opened at Matthew 5:22;24. "But I tell you that anyone who is angry with a brother or a sister will be subject to judgement. Again, anyone who says to a brother or sister 'Raca,' is answerable to the court. And anyone who says, 'You Fool!' will be in danger of the fire of hell. Therefore, if you are offering your gift at the altar and remember that your brother or sister has something against you, leave your gift at the altar. First go and be reconciled to them; then come offer your gift." The passage smacked me like a bit of two by four right between the eyes.

Raca was a word used by the Jews as an expression of contempt, the meaning is *worthless* or *good for nothing*, its root meaning is to *spit*, yikes! Admitting to myself I used words far harsher than *You Fool* when thinking about the other woman, and grasping the concept that obedience is better than a curse, I chose to obey this word from God. My flesh burned in complete opposition to God's Word and my ego felt justified holding onto the contempt I felt for Dave's affair partner. It was my constitutional right. She knew about me before Dave and I were married, had met me after I became Dave's wife, and still had the audacity to step into our marriage and continue an affair with full knowledge. She and Dave had a choice, when I had none. This wasn't fair! But none of my justification could appease the stirring in my spirit of what I must do.

I may have forgiven Dave. The next step was to forgive her.

The same afternoon I received this revelation, I sat with pen and paper and constructed a letter to Karen. It is a letter I wish I had the foresight to copy. To this day, I believe it is one of the best letters I've written to anyone. My words didn't trivialise the excruciating pain caused by the affair or the hurt experienced by everyone, including her. I acknowledged her feelings in this mess and separated the sin from the sinner. I told her that although I hated what they had done, I had no hatred towards her. I explained my marriage to Dave was made in the eyes of God. No man (or woman) could change that. Our marriage was a sacred and holy commitment to each other. A commitment God would guard jealously. I wished her well, apologising for her pain, encouraging her that she had a lot to offer the right person. That person was not Dave. The words written were genuine. Moistening the back of a stamp with my tongue, I attached it to the envelope, sealed it, and posted the letter. Immediate peace followed this act of obedience, a testament of God's faithfulness. I had forgiven. Freedom was my reward. My day grew brighter. Why would I choose to hold onto anger when I was able to receive incredible lightness emanating from a burden released?

Dave arrived home from work and I told him I'd written a letter to Karen. He almost stopped breathing for a moment until I told him what was in the letter. His face lightened up in true joy for me. We were going to get through this, we were going to be alright!

A few days later, dressed in my daggiest tracksuit bottoms and hoodie, blissfully ironing away and singing at the top of my lungs, a knock on the door interrupted my mood. Yanking the entry curtains open, I saw Karen standing in front of me on our doorstep. My heart momentarily skipped a beat. Thankfully though, peace and calm materialised, no feeling of dread or discomfort, not an inkling.

Welcoming her, she began to cry. "I'm so sorry."

Embracing her, I said, "I know you are."

After holding her in my arms while she wept, I invited her inside for tea. We sat and spoke for two hours. Able to counsel and comfort her with an outpouring of love was nothing short of the Lord's love and grace. I thought it brave of her to face me and respected her courage. It felt instinctively right to demonstrate love to her. There is no explanation of how comfortable I felt. Peace and confidence are two of the many blessings of obedience. We spoke of many things. I distinctly recall her saying she felt that if it hadn't had been her then it would have been someone else, my response simply, "Yes, I agree, I believe it would have."

Asking if I could pray for her, she accepted willingly and was tearful as I began. Thanking the Lord for her and our time together, I prayed for healing for us all. As she was ready to leave, another knock at the door announced the arrival of our pastor's wife. Time for my counselling session. The bewildered look on Pastor Pat's face said it all when I introduced Karen to her in passing.

~

DAVE

No one knew the overall magnitude of my deception and weakness. I controlled every detail surrounding the betrayal and lies, and measured out truth, never admitting the full extent of involvement with Karen. I rationalised that God knew it all and was forgiving me so that was enough!

The following months were punctuated by questions from Noni as they occurred to her. Partial truth trickled out in my answers, and with every reluctant disclosure, a fresh wound was created for Noni to handle. A new rush of sickening shame enveloped me on each occasion as I witnessed Noni reliving acute incapacitating pain, adding to existing betrayal and humiliation. Every reluctant disclosure prolonged the road to recovery.

Lost for words on the night Noni point-blank questioned me with the accusatory truth of joined dots, I was relieved as her fists found my chest. In that moment, I would rather be beaten like a dog than hear my own words describe my duplicity.

Later that evening at the front door of my childhood home, I witnessed grief and disappointment eclipse Mum and Dad as I recounted to them what I had done. The force of my infidelity stretched further afield than myself and Noni. Noni and I lament not having access to the people and resources we do today. There were no serious attempts or inroads made to unravel the reason for my betrayal. We had little if any guide for affair recovery and rebuilding. Ambiguity and inexperience shrouded our efforts to delve further into why I did what I did. Even with the right support, the reluctance I had to owning my actions and confronting myself would likely have sabotaged and hindered progress.

When Noni told me of her letter to Karen, my first instinct was one of dread. She had every right to send the mistress a poisonous pen letter. After telling me what was in the letter, my heart rejoiced. Noni stands with love and dignity, demonstrating strength, Christ-like compassion, and forgiveness beyond betrayal. In my opinion, she's shown true superhero qualities. At times, Noni has been the only Bible I've read.

I determined my heartfelt remorse and best intentions were enough to make good; they would get me through. Over time, surely, I could craft myself into the person I wanted to be, and the husband Noni deserved. Believing my new relationship with God, genuine remorse, and the blessing of a second chance would catapult me along the right path. I did embrace my faith and found true comfort, encouragement, and inspiration in His word. Eagerly accepting God's forgiveness and Noni's, I was still a long way from inviting illumination into the dark caverns of my soul. That area was out of bounds, too broken. My thoughts and deeds were unforgivable. I wasn't worth unconditional love. I needed to earn it. Shame became a poor substitute for humility, continuing to secretly undermine my attempts to grow.

Embracing the second chance I didn't deserve, I applied myself to being present as husband and father and loved it. Rather than leave the company Karen and I worked at, I thought I could keep interaction with her restricted to an as-needed basis, strictly professional. I felt confident I could make this work.

～

NONI

A great deal of healing took place over a short period. The affair no longer occupied my mind and I felt we were moving in a good direction. We were hit with debris periodically, especially seeing as how Dave was still working with this woman. Extensive work travel made way for a lot of crossing of boundaries that upset me to no end. Dave failed or refused to acknowledge how harmful this was. Ignorance and lack of clear counsel specific to infidelity had us on a collision course for trouble ahead.

LESSONS FROM BEYOND

NONI

It is easy for us betrayed to believe affair partners are wicked, immoral people.

Even though they make choices which inflict incapacitating pain, they have their own stories going on.

I had no voice or choice when Dave and this woman decided to deceive me.

Forgiving the affair partner catapulted me into my own healing. This is where I could exercise my own power. This is a choice I was free to make. My choice enabled me to continue experiencing joy in daily life without being trapped by the offence.

～

LESSONS FROM BEYOND continued

DAVE

I've come to understand my destructive beliefs were formed to protect myself. Unexamined and unchallenged, these beliefs limited my emotional and spiritual recovery. Not only did they rob my family of me as a complete person, but they also kept me fractured and fragmented for decades. A highly developed instinct preserved this coping mechanism, holding it firmly in place to keep me safe and help me avoid discomfort and pain.

CHAPTER 7

CRUISE CONTROL,
DEPRESSION & POTHOLES

NONI

Our first baby, Ruby, was conceived in September 1994 and joined us in June the following year. Ezekiel, our youngest, arrived in September 1997. Everything about these years was joyous. Conception, pregnancy, birth, and our growing family were all celebrated with pleasure and delight. Dave still experienced bouts of agitation and shortness of temper, but I considered these more annoyances rather than anything too troubling.

I stopped working a month before Ruby's birth, starkly different to Corey's arrival seven years earlier when I had a total of four weeks away from the salon. Ruby was six weeks old when we set up a modest home-based studio allowing me to work around the needs of our growing family. This gave me tremendous flexibility to remain active in the kid's lives as well as maintaining my professional identity. Dave has always been supportive of the balance I need to feel connected with people outside of our immediate family. There has never been pressure placed upon me to go out and earn money. I've been blessed that I'm able to contribute financially without sacrificing precious time with him and our children.

These were great days, weeks, and months.

Renovating our home, being active in church life and community involvement, and welcoming our first boxer puppy, we were a run of the mill normal family. The Yates clan enjoyed plenty of social gatherings and wonderful holidays. Life was good. We were cruising along nicely.

Dave was a 'fun' dad. He played all the games I was too tired to play. He is incredible at keeping active young children occupied, his energy and humour matching theirs to the point of exhaustion. Apart from work gatherings where the family was included, he often appeared most comfortable playing with kids at social events rather than mixing with adults. Most of the time, Corey, Ruby, and Zeke all benefitted from the fun antics of their playful dad.

As years went by, Dave's demeanour gradually began taking a slide for the worst. Travelling a lot for work, he became increasingly angry when home. Aggressive, spiteful, agitated and hot-headed adequately describe his temperament. Asking if there was a problem was no use, nothing was ever wrong. The kids and I tiptoed around his prickly moods. I yearned for adult conversation to get to the bottom of the horrible behaviour, to change what we needed to clear the atmosphere.

In complete exasperation one night as we lay in bed, I said to him, "This is going to sound harsh, but things are easier here when you're away."

He sat silent. I asked him what he was feeling. His response angered me as he sullenly replied, "I wonder how I became this person no one needs or wants around."

I recanted, "That's NOT what I said. You can choose to sit and wallow in your self-pity or you can do something about it."

Dave stayed silent. Quietly, I turned to him and asked if he might be suffering depression? There must be a reason, right?

In the days following he spoke to our pastor who also suggested this could be the case.

Dave made an appointment with his GP, was officially diagnosed with depression and began a two-and-a-half-decade medication journey.

~

DAVE

The following months and years I diligently applied myself to be a better father and husband, believing I had myself under control and home life was good. A blanket melancholy began to creep over me, minor inconveniences caused irritation, and at times, the frustration festering inside erupted in an angry outburst. Each episode had me retreat further into a state of withdrawal. I sought counsel from our pastor (also a pharmacist), and he suggested it sounded a lot like depression. He encouraged me to see a doctor. The diagnosis of depression and treatment gave us all minor reprieve from excessive moody behaviour. Medication took the edge off the uneasy anxiety that grumbled below my skin.

A diagnosis though, in my mind, allowed me to avoid responsibility and accountability for my outbursts. Now I had a disease state to explain periods of melancholy, irritability, and anger. Not only that, but I also had something else to blame my infidelity on or apportion responsibility to it. Comforting myself with thoughts and stories alleviating me from full ownership.

I was weakened by my illness. My actions were probably due to my untreated condition. I was vulnerable due to an illness. I probably wouldn't have carried on this way had my depression been under control.

Frustration and insecurity with my life was a daily companion. Rather than share and discuss these, I avoided conflict and confrontations. Internalizing anger was my resolution. Medication has limitations, though, especially when the patient is not playing their part.

For me, the prescription ceiling resulted in episodes of erratic outbursts, periods of sulking, withdrawal, or all of these in rapid succession. Self-medicating with alcohol led to the appearance of my nastiest self. Arrogant, rude, abrasive and loud. This wasn't a person I enjoyed sitting with. What right did I have to expect Noni and the kids should? In a convoluted way, this was my expectation. A cycle of conflict, withdrawal, and remorse followed by people-pleasing, performance and shame continued. Depending on where I was in the cycle, my inconsistency was unsettling for everyone, especially Noni. Noni's description of *going around the mountain over and over* is apt. I continued lapping the mountain several times a year for many years to come. I would often neglect filling my prescription for antidepressants, procrastinating rather than prioritising the fifteen-minute diversion to the chemist on the way home from work. My irritable persona resurfaced – a source of repeated frustration for Noni and the children. This simple measure to protect my family, I considered an inconvenient burden even though it was my responsibility. Perhaps I resented being 'that' guy needing his medications. Either way, it was me first and everyone else second.

~

NONI

Anti-depressants lifted Dave's mood for a while yet did nothing to change ingrained behaviours. It also didn't help that for the first few years following the diagnosis, Dave lacked vigilance with taking his happy pills. Often running out of scripts or not filling them, his moods swung up and down like a yoyo. The kids and I all shouted a ticket on this emotional roller coaster ride.

Dave and I have worked well together on projects, particularly real estate ones. We found a block of land at Palm Beach with sweeping views of the Pittwater. We would build our dream home, relishing in a prestigious Palm Beach address. In 1999, Dave's mum was diagnosed with cancer and then suffered a stroke. Dave went to Amsterdam around September, leaving me with his car and mobile phone. (These phones were the size of a brick, so they remained in the car charger.)

On the day Dave left, I bundled all three kids in the car and drove Corey to soccer training. Corey was twelve, Ruby five, and Ezekiel three. Pulling the car into the soccer field parking lot Dave's phone lit up with a text message. It read:

"Hope you have a great trip. Enjoy Amsterdam. Behave, Beth xxx."

I almost choked on my spit. WHO THE HELL WAS BETH AND WHAT THE HECK IS SHE DOING TELLING MY HUSBAND TO BEHAVE HIMSELF!

Corey read the message first. He grabbed the phone from its holder and punched out a message with more expletives than is acceptable of any twelve-year-old. After regaining my composure, I explained to Corey we wouldn't press send on this message, but I was glad he expressed his feelings. Calmly pressing the buttons for my reply, I typed, "BIG MISTAKE BETH. Dave left me his phone while he's away, Noni 'WIFE' Yates." I hit send. Furious!

Arriving home after soccer training, I contacted one of Dave's work colleagues to find out where he'd be staying in Amsterdam. Even through past betrayal, I chose to trust Dave. Our pastor's wife told me it must be a conscious choice I make to repeat over to myself and Jesus my intention to trust. Young, naïve, and following unsophisticated advice led me, perhaps stupidly, to never become hyper-vigilant or need every detail to his whereabouts.

I found it hard to believe he would do this to me again. Knowing he would still be in transit; I called the hotel he would soon be arriving at and asked the reception staff to urge him to call me as soon as he checked in. The kids were having dinner when the phone rang. Phones were still attached to the wall then so I couldn't take the call in another room. Stretching the coiled line until it could go no further, I crept outside and hoped the children would be spared my anguish.

"Hey, darlin', what's up?"

"WHO'S BETH?" was all I could manage.

Dave stumbled through some weak dialogue. I repeated, "WHO'S BETH?"

Beth was someone he worked with. They would catch up for lunch, etc. They didn't have sex, they kissed, cuddled, and talked. According to Dave, this was not classified as an affair. They were 'just friends.' This is about when I wanted to smack him in the face. He sure as hell better be kidding. He has GOT to be kidding me! How the heck could this not be an affair?

I hung up as he begged me not to leave. What right did he have to request anything of me?

Once again, my instinct to run the hell away from this living nightmare was overshadowed by his pleas.

The next day, a girlfriend from church came over with a long email Dave sent them. Giving them a sanitised, watered-down version of events, asking them to speak to me. Reading the letter with a complete lack of emotion I looked at her and said, "This isn't the first time."

She left, speechless.

The grief experienced during Dave's absence left me numb. When he returned from his trip, I had simmered down and listened to his excuses. He needed to talk to someone, and she was it. Yes, I thought the excuse lame. I told him he should be speaking to me instead of with-drawing and seeking solace in the arms of another woman...

~

DAVE

In the years following the discovery of my initial infidelity, I started to let my boundaries loosen. Believing significant penance done, behaving myself, what harm could come in relaxing a little? Convincing myself I was much better and entitled to some latitude. This decision was made gradually and unilaterally. Little by little, my contact and conversation with Karen increased with frequency and warmth. I had missed our connection, sharing lunch and conversations around work became a regular occurrence. Our emotional relationship re-established easily and quickly, developing sexually soon after. Falling back into the same was inevitable. Hooking up at sales conferences, out of town customer meetings or trade meetings. If staying overnight in the same place, the likelihood of spending the night with her was strong. The nature of our work provided plenty of opportunities, just as it had in the past. Why on earth would I do this again? Didn't I remember the pain and hurt I caused? Had I forgotten what I had risked? Of course, I remembered the carnage. How could I forget obliterating the woman I loved and desired more than anyone? Fuelled by my own desire to be wanted and ease my self-loathing, I hadn't recognised the underlying beliefs and insecurities that made me vulnerable. The allure of having a member of the opposite sex validate me with zero accountability was a powerful prospect. An escape from the responsibilities of a family and the excitement of an illicit affair proved too seductive, and off I went down the familiar path; this time I would not be discovered.

Over the next few years, my unfaithful behaviour and sexual relationship with Karen swung back and forth. There were periods one or both of us instigated ending our affair. Whether it was out of guilt or fear of being caught is still lost on me. The restraint, however, didn't last. Time would pass and the pattern would be revived. Sometimes soothing a disappointment, other times a lapse in self-control. An excuse, justification, reason, and opportunity were never far away.

During an ebb in the activity of my affair with Karen, I sought the attention of Beth, another woman working in a related part of the organisation. What began as sitting together at a work function progressed to the occasional lunch in a park, a casual smile across a room, flirting in person or via phone. All suggestive to what might be and all serving to bolster my self-esteem. Now I had the attention of yet another woman, another married woman to stroke my ego. This routine carried on for about six months. My first morning in Amsterdam, I received a call from Noni. Initial anxiety, fearing that my mother had passed, gave way to horror as Noni unleashed, fuming at me. The text message from Beth made it obvious to Noni that we were not 'just friends'. Anger resounded through Noni's voice as I desperately tried assuring her it wasn't as bad as it appeared, and I pleaded with her not to do anything rash.

What if Noni left me? Suddenly the compartments of my life looked like they were crashing together with painful and ugly consequences. Aside from desperation and trying to contain the damage taking place 16,000 kilometres away, in that very moment and over the coming days, I also had to face the reminder of how damned conniving and dishonest I'd become. I had arranged to meet with Karen on this trip! Caught in the middle of leading my double life, I was sickened to the core by the reality of my duality and the plain depravity of who I'd become. The next few days were a blur of attending meetings and events. I was detached from my surroundings, preoccupied with the consequences of my lies and deceit. Yet I still proceeded to share the few days and nights with Karen as planned and offered her no explanation for my often sullen mood. On the twenty-two-hour trip home, I replayed every word that might be spoken, all the possible reactions and every outcome I could imagine. All of it was exhausting; none reassuring. Do I come clean and reveal the full extent of my relapse and ongoing affair with Karen? Should I purge myself of this weight? But what would happen then? Noni and I would surely be finished. What about our gorgeous children? I resolved to tell Noni all about Beth and I did. I was filled with remorse for my relapse as well as a fair helping of embarrassment for paper-thin explanations. There were moments when facing Noni that I pictured myself uttering the words, "That's not all. I need to tell you about..." It was too big a leap to take. Instead of disclosing the truth, I figured it was best to navigate this act of stupidity and weakness. Hide the rest… yes, that would be better for both of us I told myself.

~

NONI

Dave is smart, he's convincing, and I loved him. Once again, I accepted, we could move on from this. No desire on their part to continue the affair, her only concern being for me not to tell her husband. In my mind, I was thinking *I have my own crap to deal with chick, the last thing I want is to be involved with anyone else's.* It never entered my mind to unleash my pain upon her poor unsuspecting husband. I'd never met this woman and knew zip about her.

In hindsight, Dave's anger, defensiveness, and sharp tongue left me feeling frightened and unentitled to ask details. Reluctant to push for more information, I became satisfied with the fact that this affair had run its course and he would not continue seeing her. I believed this to be the case and had the same intuitive hunch as previously. This affair was more about his *neediness* rather than a reflection upon me or the state of our marriage. Each time light exposed an affair relationship, and once the pain of discovery subsided, we grew closer to one another. There was never any doubt in my mind that Dave loved me, and I loved him. I trusted he wanted to be with me, confident he never desired a permanent outcome with the affair partners.

This absolutely confounded me though because his actions demonstrated enormous incongruity to his heart.

After this affair discovery, even though enjoying plenty of great times together, Dave's irritability didn't subside and become dormant like before. Something was going on, but I couldn't quite put my finger on it.

Sadly, not long after this, his mother passed away. Like many of our friends and family, she had no knowledge of this other wounding. I'm not sure whether this was a conscious choice. Infidelity is not discussed openly now, let alone back in the 90s, and even less when it happens more than once. This other *seemingly* less serious affair flying under the radar was brushed off as another mighty blunder.

We continued with house plans and waited patiently for council approval. Close to finalising building details after two years in the making, we finally received long-awaited news. The plans were approved. The reason for the delay was that a neighbour opposed the plans from the start. Wanting and needing our land to expand on a development he had in mind, he fought us tooth and nail. In the end, we won.

Beginning to source quotes for our house, it became evident the project would put us into significant mortgage stress. The driveway alone tendered at $150,000. In 2000, this was astronomical. Even by today's standard, it is a heck of a lot of money to spend before getting out of the ground. Dave determined we could do it. I wasn't so sure and grew increasingly nervous at the thought of having so much debt.

Taking my stress to the altar one Sunday morning, my prayer request concerned finances. The leader prayed:

"God wants you to know all will be ok. He is in control. You don't need to worry about anything."

Sweet, I'll take that, concluding we would be in for a windfall. A few weeks later, on receipt of the contract, I called Dave and shared the exciting news. That same afternoon, Dave called back, "Don't sign anything, I've lost my job."

Arriving home early, we sat together in stunned silence. A few personality clashes within the company resulted in a couple of employees losing their jobs. A day later, we received a letter from HR reporting allegations of 'harassment and intimidation' made against Dave.

My head was spinning. Had his irascible disposition gotten him into strife? Did this have anything to do with his affairs? OMG, what was going on? He assured me the decision was in no way affair related and had every-thing to do with company politics. Thankfully, this turned out to be true. He had been with this company for eleven years, giving them blood, sweat and tears. Dave excelled at his job and believed he would stay and grow with the company for all of his working days. And now he was terminated, just like that. Shockwaves enveloped us as we anticipated what lay ahead. It was our first wake up to the fanciful concept of job security.

We sat one night drinking a glass of cask red wine with dinner (straight to the mentality of penny-pinching, figuring we could save by giving up a nice bottle for a nasty cask LOL). During our ten years in Sydney, we spent many hours dreaming about and considering living on the northern New South Wales coast. This night, we revisited the dream. Without the commitment of a career in Sydney, we had the flexibility to pack up and make a new start up north. Suggesting we contact our neighbour who wanted the land, we'd let him know we'd consider selling if he was interested. Much to his delight, this was another win for us. He accepted our asking price which was twice as much as we paid two years earlier. Once again God had provided. This was our windfall albeit not as my mind had imagined. Jehovah Jireh is one of the twelve names of God, meaning 'My Provider'.

The land contract settled, and with the money from the sale of our house, we were cashed up. A breach of Dave's employment contract was next in line to deal with. What ensued was another lengthy crazy roller coaster ride. The company's legal team agreed to an out of court settlement in our favour. Our mood lifted, rising from the ashes. After tidying up loose ends, we hosted a party bidding farewell to ten years of Sydney life.

Dave's workmates came and yes, Karen joined us. Our farewell was the only time I had seen her outside work events since facing me nine years earlier. Plenty of friends and acquaintances occupied our attention throughout the evening. Though harbouring no ill will towards her, I sensed a measure of awkwardness in our interaction. Paying minuscule attention to this unease, the emotion fleeting, our goodbyes were said. Loading the Volvo with our belongings, kids, and dog, I headed north. I can't quite remember why now, but Dave came a little later.

CHAPTER 8

A NEW BEGINNING; THE QUIET YEARS; OR SO I THOUGHT

NONI

The next couple of chapters are best described as in-between years. A period when apart from the obvious stresses of day-to-day life and Dave's Jekyll and Hyde personality, there was no reason to suspect anything was terribly amiss in our relationship. We didn't understand Dave's unpredictability or short temperedness, but we were so used to living with him, it became the norm. We neither enjoyed, nor tolerated it. Admittedly, though, I'm guilty of excusing the behaviour as part of his depression and anxiety diagnosis.

In all honesty, it became increasingly unpleasant discussing Dave's temperamental issues.

I grew tired of dealing with the angry juvenile. Even though we had ongoing conversations, his understanding of the behaviour rarely progressed further than skin deep. It was only ever a matter of time before we revisited the same scenario. To fill in the gaps, I've written a simple chronological timeline of events as they occurred.

Before leaving Sydney, we put a holding deposit on a block of land on the far north New South Wales coast. A contract of sale was slow in eventuating and our solicitor left us in the dark as to why. Dave arrived from Sydney and we approached the sales agent hoping to find out the reason behind the delay. Apparently, the developer and his wife recently separated, and all assets were frozen, including this parcel of land. Dave and I were both in shock. We had packed up our entire lives and family thinking we were going to begin our dream coastal lifestyle.

Awesome! WTH do we do now? The agent offered us a couple of other options and we settled on one similar to the ideal block we thought was ours. A quick dusting off of initial expectations and we adapted to the new dream. Working with a local architect, we designed and built our first gorgeous beach house.

We treated the initial relocation period as somewhat of a holiday. Settling the kids into their new school, I developed friendships easily through the gym, church, and community. This was the first time I chose to work voluntarily rather than pursue a career. We had substantial savings in the bank allowing this hiatus to happen. I believed this period was a season of growth and leaned on the Lord without relying on a career to prop myself up. Involvement in school, community, and ministry fulfilled every personal desire although did nothing to add to our financial situation. In these early days, spending time with Dave was as tenuous as our fiscal future. Undoubtedly, Dave felt enormous pressure and uncertainty which only increased his temperamental turns. Foolishly, I began neglecting my own health which caused increased levels of anxiety. Making poor food choices and drinking more than I should, I knew I was on a downward spiral. Dissolving into tears during a routine doctor's appointment subsequently resulted in me leaving with my own prescription for anti-depressants. Awesome! Now our children had two parents relying on tablets to keep them stable!

Not a place I ever anticipated we'd be, but completely necessary under the circumstances.

Three months passed with me doing everything possible to regain my health through exercise, diet, counselling, and friendships. Taking the small white pills helped. They lifted my mood to the point I could reinstate my once resilient character. The chemical assistance was a welcome reprieve, yet I knew I'd had all I needed. My conversation with Dave let him know I was finishing my three-month trial on meds.

"Dave, I'm not going to be medicated for your condition."

We agreed this was the right thing to do.

Dave was mostly without work, but consulting contracts occupied hours when they came his way. He did his best to remain connected in the industry. Funds from our Sydney gains supported us for a while, however, they'd eventually run dry. In 2004, after twelve months of life in northern New South Wales, Dave secured full-time employment back in Sydney, this time choosing a weekly commute over relocation.

∿

DAVE

I wasn't too sad about leaving Sydney, even though we had a great circle of friends and loved the area we lived in. I knew this was an opportunity for us to build a new life together, a life away from my hidden betrayal and lies. This was a chance for a fresh start, leaving my personal defects behind.

Initially, we were financially comfortable. However, if we were to finish building our dream home, I needed regular employment. While revelling in the free time this recess allowed, I also experienced bouts of worthlessness and lack of direction. Without a job or title, I was also without the career identity I'd previously appreciated. Along with the loss of identity and self-worth a career provides, I also lost the avenue for my secret self-indulgence. The opportunity to bolster my self-esteem and soothe my insecurities with ready access to other women was gone. That favourable vanity mirror of my affair partners was lost, now it was just me.

Alcohol served to fill this emptiness, guaranteeing the same results it always had. Ugly outbursts, inflated arrogance, overcompensating, smart arse behaviour. These episodes caused embarrassment, awkward stand-offs, and emotional distance.

Long periods spent in front of the computer researching ways to make a living led me to casually view pornography. The justification? I would reward myself with a break from reality and escape boredom with a brief excursion into fantasy and pleasure. This pastime became a habit that remained completely hidden and unknown to anyone. Believing this was all OK, I was in control, it didn't take over my life. I rationalised my occasional indulgence in pornography the same way someone who is health-conscious might justify an occasional binge on junk food.

About twelve months after moving North I was offered a management position back in Sydney. I jumped at the chance to be back in an industry where I was known and my experience valued.

~

NONI

For eighteen months, Dave worked fly-in fly-out. The Gold Coast airport was only a short distance from home and made for easy transfers. Home on Friday, work on Monday, life was visibly good. Except when the weather turned foul and his Friday flight home got cancelled, delayed, or diverted. This sucked, for all of us.

Dave lived in a granny flat beneath a house on Sydney's Northern Beaches during the week, a wonderful location in familiar surrounds. We appreciated his dedication and provision.

Assuming my role as project manager for our new house kept me busy and supported Dave by coordinating everything to do with the running of family. Chief Organisational Officer and Domestic Goddess.

At home during the week, I could complete most of the mundane household chores freeing up weekends for beach and family fun. We had become actively involved in a local church since our spiritual family was an important connection.

Our beach house completion took six months. Moving in and embracing our coastal lifestyle was wonderful, not imagining a few short months later we'd be on the move again.

On a dark and stormy Sunday, Corey and I drove to town to buy fish and chips for a family movie afternoon. The most expensive fast-food mission to date! A block of land slightly north of us caught our eye. Dave didn't need too much convincing, and before we knew it, our next family project was underway.

Living in our first home a total of only six months, Dave continued commuting back and forth to Sydney. Filled with contentment, I relished in caring for family and home. Increasing involvement with church and community activities, I wore many different hats; frequently resembling a human doing rather than a human being!

A satisfying sense of purpose was more than adequate payment. I had the time and capability, the mission virtuous, so why not? The husband of a close friend told me,

"Just because you can do it, doesn't mean you should."

Wise words I hold firm today.

Dave appeared happy commuting. Home on weekends, which were R&R time, meant we sidestepped the mundane day to day routine of family life. Weekends were always chill time. Through the week, I ran a fairly tight ship, chores, homework, fun, order in the house, safety and consistency for the kids. We had a reprieve from Dave's anger and irritability on a full-time scale, and any flare-ups extinguished knowing the flight to Sydney was at the most two days away. We did miss him during the week. The sacrifices we all made worked, they helped us do the necessary to stay afloat.

After keeping this arrangement for more than twelve months, I did the commute and flew to Sydney for a weekend with Dave. I was looking forward to going back to our old stomping ground and having time for the two of us. Dave picked me up from the airport and we planned a quiet romantic weekend at his pad. Walking into his place my heart sank.

An awesome location, comfortable accommodations, and while he didn't actually spend too much time in the unit, I felt terrible. Working his butt off to accommodate us, providing for his family, living our dream yet this deprived him of actually living the dream with us. As someone who loved him desperately, I couldn't bear the thought of him coming home four days a week to an empty room, no meal ready, and no company. With my heart heavily burdened, I told him so. I didn't think this arrangement was fair. He didn't mind so much and if not for seeing where he was living, I probably wouldn't have raised the subject. However, I had seen it, so I couldn't unsee or erase the weight on my heart.

Dave began looking for work opportunities around South East Queensland and secured work with a finance company that enabled him to relocate and live back at home with us. This was another great opportunity not only for us as a family, but it was also the financial vehicle for our building our new home.

Dave finalised work in Sydney while I found a rental property, packed up our home, and moved. Dave literally went to work one day and came back to spend the next twelve months in a place he'd never laid eyes on. We trusted each other with these decisions, knowing we were both more than capable of making them.

Excited to have my husband home for another new start, the idea of renewing our marriage vows was birthed. My rationale: our original vows were taken under a shroud of lies. But now, the past was behind us and our future ahead. Certain Dave would be on board to welcome a new beginning, I planned to surprise him on his birthday and exchange new rings and vows to signify our never-ending commitment to love one another. The plan carried out seamlessly.

Dave's return brought many challenges. He was now working from home, no office building to go to, working autonomously in a completely new work environment and industry.

The new field of Medical Finance stretched him with much to learn. We all had to adjust to him being around full-time. I had set routines and a good network of girlfriends. Most days, Dave would ask, "What are you doing today?" I'd reply, "Nothing."

My nothing usually meant gym, school duty for three kids, postal/bill paying, groceries, connect groups and the likes. It was certainly nothing exciting, so I figured the details weren't important. What I didn't understand was he wanted to spend time having a cuppa or simply liked having me around. This is something I cherish these days and have learned to put busyness aside to be still.

The transit year in the rental didn't bring too many challenges. Major flooding damaged all our stored boxes in the garage, and we lost treasured memories, but in the scheme of things, this was more unpleasant and inconvenient than any great hurdle.

Caving into the age of technology, we invested in our first family computer. A short while after installing the space station sized PC, Corey and his friends discovered internet porn.

In those pre-Net Nanny days, Noni and David made up the only parental control system under our roof. The browser history was checked often. Corey, now in his teens, began testing how far boundaries could bend before breaking. He was ready to party as soon as we had our backs turned. His father, Charlie, remained connected to our growing family and became a regular addition to shared meals and family gatherings. Although Corey lived full time with Dave, me, Ruby, and Zeke, Charlie would step in to care for Corey if we travelled away during school terms. Charlie had to contend with several baptisms of fire and teen parenting intensives through our absence. They both survived, not sure who came out in front though.

The kids were settled and relatively happy at school.

Our building project commenced, we had plenty to look forward to. Dave didn't travel too far for work, mainly day trips to Brisbane and around the Gold Coast. Although he didn't mind the nature of the work, frustrations were creeping in with his job satisfaction at a personal level.

After four years in the role of providing finance options to the broad healthcare industry, Dave became increasingly restless, so sought out opportunities in his area of expertise. A representative role presented itself.

Although this position offered a lesser salary than previous management positions, it required little travel and thankfully no need to relocate.

I call these the quiet years. The usual dance of daily routine, nothing terribly significant to worry about. Kids involved in extra-curricular activities, dance, soccer, rugby, drama etc. They were all connected at church, had sweet friendships, and a fairly regular kid's life.

~

DAVE

Making an effort to turn my back on the past, in 2004, I made an agreement of sorts with myself that there was a line I would not cross again. The line of having a sexual relationship with another woman outside of my marriage. I believed I was a better man for finally acknowledging the significance of this boundary. I was stronger, had learned from the past, and was lucky not to have been exposed again. My internal agreement included that the past should remain safely where it was. Locked away and out of sight. These secrets I pledged to take to my grave. Thinking my days of extramarital affairs behind me didn't stop me from venturing close to the boundary as opportunities arose. Cultivating interactions and relationships, 'friendships' with women satisfied my needs. The feeling of importance, the boost gained through the attention of the opposite sex was as enticing as ever. There was also a level of adrenaline, like leaning over the edge of a cliff with one hand on the safety rail. I reassured myself that this is okay. Another lie readily accepted. *'I wasn't physically involved outside of the marriage and I wasn't going to be.'* I wasn't going to step off the cliff and I convinced myself that I was maintaining a degree of integrity by not crossing that line.

~

NONI

Dave was still taking anti-depressants as well as releasing the pressure valve of his ever-apparent agitation. Unleashing occasional caustic remarks was his style. Uncomfortable as this was, we patiently trudged through episodes and buried our angst. In between the peppered sprays of bitterness, the kids and I still enjoyed the wonderful side of Dave we were showered with. We just couldn't understand how he could be so angry and irrational one minute and then just as quickly return to being nice and pleasant the next, as though nothing had happened. I often questioned whether I had missed something. Did I not read the situation correctly? Seeing these words written plainly on paper in their entirety now makes it difficult to understand how anyone could not name the behaviour as abusive sooner. Being so enmeshed, the constantly shifting goalposts, and regularly being undermined was the beginning of doubting myself. Maybe I was the one who wasn't being fair?

~

Moving into our new home in 2005, only steps from a pristine beach and in the same community we'd enjoyed for the past couple of years, was a definite high moment. Setting ourselves up nicely, we could start over with modern interior décor and furniture. Simple yet stylish, clean and minimalistic. Those wretched bedside lamps were cast aside and no longer occupied a place next to our gorgeous king-size master suite. A large beautiful home, soon becoming a greater burden than asset. Overextending ourselves with a larger mortgage than we'd ever held, as well as failing to adjust spending habits in line with our current financial position, soon placed us in a tenuous situation. There was certainly no luxury of a cleaner and two full days each week were dedicated to cleaning the place.

I was still heavily involved in women's ministry and Dave was actively involved in men's groups and also part of the church's financial advisory team.

Our pastor's wife asked me to speak at a women's event sharing part of my testimony, encouraging others in God's love and faithfulness.

Hearts were touched as I recounted the 1994 affair discovery. Sharing how overcoming horrendous betrayal through God's grace, mercy, and love was possible. Dave was in the room. Two girlfriends knew what was about to be disclosed and both stood by Dave holding his hands, offering support. The finale to my story was introducing Dave. Acknowledging his courage and commitment, I was so proud of him. Women in the room were visibly moved, some in shock. Several women approached me who'd been betrayed, only one still married, none of them had been able to speak to others who had experienced the same pain. Our vulnerability and transparency unlocked necessary dialogue in the room that evening. Unfortunately, the conversations amongst the wider community went little further than the duration of the meeting.

∼

DAVE

When Noni shared the story of my early infidelity, the power of forgiveness and experiencing God's grace, I was so proud of her and incredibly thankful of where we were in our lives.

That's the extent of compartmentalisation I developed. I had built reinforced concrete bunkers, housing secrets and fears I determined would never see the light of day. Knowing the absolute truth, I continued deceiving my wife for years. Noni made a public account of betrayal and forgiveness while I allowed myself to be misrepresented as a brave, supporting, and rehabilitated husband!

The prospect of identifying as the chronically unfaithful man was not nearly as appealing as being the forgiven, reformed, and loving husband. Choosing the image of the latter, I tried to live up to it as best I could. Although forgiven, I was a long way from being repaired. Restoration evaded me while I controlled and concealed the complete truth. Functioning at this level of deception day in and day out highlighted my ability to compartmentalise, the misdemeanours occurring in another place and another time, therefore, should be left there, in the past where they belonged.

∼

NONI

The extended period of reduced income in his sales representative role led Dave to become curious about alternate income streams. He befriended a parent on the sideline of one of Ezekiel's soccer matches. This man with entrepreneurial spirit sought investors for a commercial development. Cash flow was tight for us, however, our home held significant equity valued at over 1.2M. The timing of the potential business opportunity coincided with Australia being caught in the grips of the Global Financial Crisis.

Although present and involved in day-to-day family life, Dave regularly retreated to a place of distant withdrawal with the aggravated, irritated personality his constant companion. I detected increasing disconnection between us. Shutting me out, he swung between his need for physical intimacy to being angry with me, or angry at me. Our bedroom sessions became more a desire to have sex for Dave than making love to me. A conversation in our lounge room, standing apart yet face to face went like this:

"I know you want to have sex with me. I don't feel you love me."

Although he strenuously denied this, I had been left feeling almost violated after several sexual encounters. Preferring rugged intercourse opposed to gentle tender lovemaking, I began feeling like an object and not his precious bride.

~

DAVE

Taking personal inventory of my history with pornography during recovery, I initially underestimated the frequency and impact. Estimating my indulgence was on average a monthly occurrence, longer and deeper reflection revealed when active it was closer to weekly. Periods of several months existed with no activity. At times of stress or boredom though, I retreated into a fantasy world where there was an image of women always eager and ready for sexual gratification and misadventure.

Rather than investing emotionally in my marriage, which would take energy, I was satisfied with the quick shallow fix to a physical need, requiring zero emotional connection. I was essentially commoditizing sex through dissociating sexual fulfilment from emotional intimacy.

Each time sexual sensation was sought from online pornography, my emotional bond with Noni was inadvertently undermined and weakened. Yet I fully believed my foray into fantasy was a simple, harmless diversion. The result, a growing feeling of distance between us. Noni communicated how she felt less connected and respected during the act of making love. I failed to see any correlation between my secret pasttime and our sex life. A continual decline in the regularity of our physical intimacy ensued, corresponding with growing frustration on my part. My familiar cycle of emotional withdrawal and irritability would ultimately kick off another lap around the mountain... I couldn't remain consistent in attempts to bridge the gap, let alone identify the source. This would be a pattern for a long time.

∼

NONI

The investment deal Dave involved himself with held little interest for me, not that I had a voice in the matter. As primary breadwinner and head of our home, his ego kicked into overdrive. Dave brought me documents asking for my signature. I looked at him and said, "What are they? Divorce papers?"

Denied of any partnership discussion about why and how this agreement would work, Dave was determined to go ahead believing it infallible. My only question, "Is there any chance we could lose the house?"

His answer, an adamant "No."

The commercial development we financed as unsecured creditors hit a massive pothole soon after we signed documents. In the absence of discussion with me, Dave went ahead and agreed with the developer to finance another project. Dave can fill in the details.

∿

DAVE

Blake was a handsome man with an interesting background as private chef and now aspiring property developer. His energy for exploring new projects and opportunities was infectious, and we would occasionally discuss the pros and cons of different ideas. I found the process of recognising and unlocking the potential value of property developments exciting. From time-to-time Noni and I would have those what-if discussions. Exploring different scenarios often gravitated to living somewhere in Indonesia and being active in a humanitarian project. During one of these chats, Noni quipped, "Dave, you'd like to be doing what Blake does, wouldn't you?"

Admittedly, I was a little envious of his ability to create income and wealth through various deals while we were just getting by month to month on my salary. Buoyed by recent momentum of local development I was quickly swept up in the glamour and scale of a new plan he shared with me. Although I discussed it briefly with Noni, my mind was set that we should find a way to buy into this opportunity. Whether driven by ego or a genuine desire to provide a comfortable future for my family, neither fully explains the impulsivity and poor judgement which followed. In the absence of any written agreement/contract from the developer and without asking Noni, I handed over a cheque for $275k of borrowed money. I just did it. Although uneasy when handing the cheque to Blake, this feeling intensified when Noni found out.

I was also afraid of being swallowed in embarrassment if I backed out.

PRIDE COMES BEFORE A FALL, THE BIGGER THE EGO THE GREATER THE FALL.

In the coming months, anything that could go wrong did go wrong. The main tenant died suddenly and half the ground floor was back on the market. The GFC hit and the cost of the debt on the building skyrocketed. Prospective owners backed out of contracts and cash to complete the building was scarce. Our return on investment evaporated quickly.

Tragically, succumbing to the mounting pressures of an investment gone wrong, Blake ended his life, leaving behind his devastated wife and young family.

~

NONI

By now, I had resumed working for a wage to increase our household income. No matter how many hours of work I could manage, though, I would never be able to make enough money to see our way clear of this mess. We were now staring down the barrel of complete financial ruin. Suggesting to Dave many times that we should sell the house, he continued insisting we could manage, we could make it work. He wrote out a budget of how this would work.

Honestly, when a budget allows no room for the slightest bit of fun, no money for a movie, a coffee out or kids' activities, this is not the way I wanted to live. Merely existing and even then, barely. Living so close to the edge with a constant threat of going under is plain ridiculous!

This house had become an idol and while we held on too tightly, I couldn't see how we were open to God's blessing. We became so accustomed to receiving monthly statements from the bank informing us we were another $3500 behind that we stopped opening them. A pile of unopened envelopes as thick as a Besser block rapidly stacked up on our kitchen bench.

Dave continued juggling with financial institutions attempting to hold onto our property, more house now than home. With the tension building, the cracks appearing were not only in the building structure, but also in the foundation of our family. Dave's arrogance and prickliness escalated and went from being horrible to working hard to try and smooth things over between myself or the kids. Overcompensating rather than addressing poor behaviour.

My struggle increased with the ideal of us keeping the house. I couldn't for the life of me envision how this could be possible. New Year's Eve 2008, three years after we moved into our new home. Heavily laden, I walked the beach for two hours alone. Crying out to God, "Show me whether it was I who had little faith or was Dave completely out of his mind." Walking and talking with God, I prayed, I cried… nothing. Absolutely zip. I went home, drained, and hopped in the pool to freshen up. Dave jumped in. Exhausted, I stayed silent. He swam over to me.

"You're right, we will sell the house."

I was relieved and elated. Dave and I were in agreement and could move forward. Being in agreement was a good start. But listing a house for sale is one thing, selling it is an entirely different matter.

I've become used to the fact that God rarely answers prayers exactly how we think He should. We come to Him with our agenda, but His ways are infinitely greater. He will make a way, and it's always in His timing.

In 2009, Dave was rewarded with a work trip to the U.S.A to attend an industry-specific international meeting. The meeting was in San Francisco, a city I love. Dave bought a ticket for me to travel with him. We spent a few days together exploring the city and sights, ate great food, made great love, and just hung out when he wasn't attending the conference. A wonderful networking opportunity for Dave, he arranged a meeting with a company director to discuss future employment opportunities.

There is a limit to how long one can expect other family members to care for three children, so I left to come back to Australia before Dave. A great trip. One we considered ourselves blessed to take together considering our dire financial distress.

CHAPTER 9

NIGHTMARE ON ELLISTON STREET

NONI

In January 2010, Dave began working for **** due to the successful meeting in San Francisco. The new job required a lot more travel and the head office was in Sydney. Dave negotiated to take the position if he could work remotely, primarily from home. Apart from greater remuneration, this position suited Dave perfectly. He was well qualified with incredible knowledge and is well respected by peers and clients. He had a new spring in his step and things were looking up. We were reasonably comfortable for a while financially but were emotionally constrained. Even with all the benefits his new job provided we had financial difficulty meeting monthly commitments. Our mortgage was astronomical because of the commercial deal. With the GFC fallout lapping at our doorstep, this investment opportunity quickly lost its shine. Financial pain loomed on the horizon. We needed options to ease our financial stress before total GFC annihilation.

One option was to remove Ezekiel from private schooling and enrol him in the local public school. It made sense doing so at the beginning of entry into grade five, middle school. Ezekiel seemed to us the most adaptable, definitely more resilient than Ruby. Since Corey had begun year twelve, disrupting his final year would be unwise. To this day, our biggest regret is making this decision. What followed for Ezekiel and us has been nothing short of a nightmare.

Ezekiel had friends at a local primary school, and he appeared excited to be joining them.

When he came home from his first day of school noticeably quiet, I asked him as all mums do, "How was your day?"

"Good," he replied unconvincingly.

Probing gently, hoping he might elaborate, he innocently and sadly said,

"Mum, they all swear."

This young boy possessed the gentlest of hearts and was kind and funny. I needed to help him with this new experience.

"Mummy has plenty of friends who swear, that doesn't mean I can't like them or need to swear to fit in with them."

My advice was to ignore them and spend more time with one boy in particular.

His response, this boy swore as much as the other boys and was friends with them all.

OH, aahhh, well, maybe just ignore them.

Arriving home from school on day two, Ezekiel was more withdrawn than the previous day.

He wouldn't tell me why, so over the next half hour, I continued extricating details of his day. Swearing obviously affected him badly as he was unaccustomed to the onslaught of vulgarity. He innocently asked one of the boys why he swore so much and the kid beat him up. Ezekiel spent his lunchtime locked in the toilets hiding away from this bully. Ezekiel's reason for being reluctant to say anything to me was because I would want to do something about it. Damn straight I will! It's one thing to ignore foul language but absolutely NOT ok to ignore abuse and intimidation. I charged up to that school at lightning speed. A couple of teachers listened while I explained what transpired. They gave me the culprit's name, nodding yes, both teachers echoing they thought as much. Disciplinary action was taken with the boy concerned. Ezekiel settled in slowly, linking up with a couple of boys although remaining relatively tentative after the initial teething problems. He continued here for two years, completing primary education before transitioning into high school.

We continued doing our best to make ends meet, coming to grips with a worsening financial situation. Our beautiful big home needed building rectification. The builder was tardy in tending to repair a significant waterproofing problem. A lengthy battle ensued between fair trading, the builder, and us. Our case ended up in a tribunal hearing whereby the builder didn't bother showing up. We didn't need this extra battle on our hands.

In early 2009, Corey moved to Sydney to pursue work opportunities. He returned briefly for his twenty-first birthday in August. Our gift to him was an around the world trip funded with Dave's frequent flyer points. Corey embarked on his trip in July 2010 and I planned to meet him in New York in August. My fare also bought with points. Somehow, I managed to scrounge a little spending money to cover accommodations, etc. (not such an easy task when you're living and surviving on credit).

In early 2010, Ruby, almost fifteen, became unwell with frequent headaches. She was often nauseous and always tired. She deteriorated over the ensuing months even though we had regular doctor's appointments trying to find out what was wrong with her, including numerous blood tests and a CAT scan. Her GP could determine nothing that would cause these symptoms. The only anomaly was that her blood revealed exposure to the Epstein Barr virus. It took six months before we received the diagnosis of Chronic Fatigue Syndrome. CFS is one of the most debilitating illnesses and can remain with a person for a lifetime. To witness our girl's dramatic decline in health was utterly heartbreaking. Ruby missed all of year nine schooling and went partially for year ten. Physically a very sick girl, emotionally she found it hard to go on. Her despair, chronic illness, and pain led her to act in ways completely contrary to her character. Desperate for help, we needed police assistance to locate her when she was at risk of harming herself. We had to remove locks on doors, keep a watchful eye and we were on constant alert and living in hyper-vigilance. This period alone could be its own book! Its relevance to this story becomes evident in chapter 12. These dark months were my first foray into dealing with the mental health crisis system.

I'm happy to report that Ruby's schooling finished well. Still contending with lingering traits of CFS, she self manages, self regulates, and self-moderates. Her life is full, she has completed three years of photojournalism, and at the time of writing, is completing a double degree in Nursing/Midwifery. She's a strong, deter-mined, kind-hearted soul who isn't afraid to stand up and speak for truth!

CHAPTER 10

OUT OF THE FRYING PAN
INTO THE FIRE

NONI

My trip with Corey went ahead, despite mixed emotions of guilt and fear. After a whirlwind few days in New York, we flew across to the west coast. I booked the cheapest possible accommodation in West Hollywood much to Corey's dismay. It was clean, in a good location, and safe. We checked in, by the time we caught the elevator to our room the front desk was calling. Our taxi driver returned to reception. My credit card declined our fare payment from LAX to Hollywood. Not a great start to four nights in the City of Angels.

Despite financial limitations, we created memories of a great trip.

At the time we listed our home for sale in 2009, the market value was $1.395M. With the delay in the rectification process due to the impact of the GFC and the subsequent declines in property values, our home sold and settled in January of 2011. Our debt on the house was $950k and it sold for $900k, so we walked away $50k in the red. We also walked away with palpable relief. This nightmare finally appeared almost over, but in reality, it was just beginning.

The pressure of these last few years had been enormous, not only on Dave and me, but also on the kids. Even though we tried to shield them from a lot of the turmoil, they didn't completely escape the trauma. We did our best, but at times it wasn't enough.

The first priority once the house sold was to return Ezekiel to the private school he left four years earlier. Two years at the public high school coexisted with plenty of unrest.

Ezekiel started year nine back at his old school with a few friendships from earlier years remaining intact. But he was still the new kid and needed to integrate into his new environment. The move appeared to be a positive one, however, Ezekiel refused to leave the car at the shopping centre if he was dressed in school uniform. He has never told us why.

Renting a house locally, we began to breathe a little easier. We were all adapting to the recent changes. Ruby improved in health and returned to school full-time for year eleven. Her friendships were tested throughout her illness so it became necessary for her to also find out where she fitted in once she returned.

Unfortunately, and sadly, as we were climbing out of our pit, Dave's dad passed away.

He had begun showing signs of dementia a couple of years earlier and he gradually worsened until he needed full-time nursing care. Through disciplined stewardship of his finances, he left a generous inheritance to Dave and his four siblings. We were able to clear our remaining debt and make a fresh start.

Dave and I both agreed we would never buy or build a house again unless mortgage repayments were equivalent to or less than rent payments. Chiming in agreement, we were done with taking financial risks. We were determined to live life in the present and to the fullest.

Now it was 2012. Surely this would be our year. Still prone to regular mood swings, Dave became noticeably worse and nasty when he drank alcohol. So much so that I didn't like being around him. Arrogant and obnoxious, he asserted too much cockiness for my liking.

When I spoke to him about this, I was often left wishing I'd kept my mouth shut. He turned and twisted things on to me. Sometimes I spoke up, other times I kept my mouth closed. A dance I greatly disliked.

He continued taking medication for depression/anxiety and had irregular counselling sessions, usually after trying my darnedest to help him recognise his own destructive behaviour. Marriage and relationship counselling throughout the years, both secular and faith-based, failed to help us get to the root of the problem. The kids and I resolved that his rage, aggression, and abusiveness were part of his medical diagnosis. Hard to excuse, but I guess we became accustomed to ignoring the behaviour and also him to an extent. Sometime during the year, Dave asked me to touch a lump on his neck. I did and felt a small bump and thought nothing of it. I actually didn't know what I was feeling for anyway.

Throughout 2012, Ezekiel began having difficulty sleeping at night and then finding it hard to wake up in the morning. For no obvious reason, his body clock switched to nocturnal, there was something bothering him.

Our efforts to help Ezekiel overcome insomnia included enrolling him with a personal trainer. Conducting group activity and mentoring for adolescent boys and girls, these sessions provided much more than physical work-outs. The guys often sat around talking about life issues and current events pertinent to them. They offered each other moral support and had a lot of fun giving as good as they got with frequent light-hearted ribbing. Ezekiel enjoyed the sessions, although they fell short of being the panacea to his sleeping problems. He wouldn't open up about anything that might be troubling him. A doctor wrote him a care plan for ten sessions with a counsellor. Ezekiel began therapy in conjunction with his group training.

Nothing made a difference to his sleep pattern. He wanted tablets to help him sleep which would never happen as the first port of call. We explored every other possible alternative.

We tried to get him to open up to us. We tried diet, counselling and training. You name it, we offered and provided every available option. I worked closely with the school to see if they could offer any insight. They, too, were at a loss. We kept plugging tirelessly away, praying for a solution. All the while, Ezekiel became progressively more withdrawn.

Mid-December 2012, we moved to a house next door which had become vacant. This place had a pool and a floor plan which suited us better since we expected to be renting for the long haul. We must have looked like hillbillies painstakingly carrying all our belongings bit by bit across the path.

During this move, Dave asked me again, "Non, feel this lump on my neck."

I didn't need to touch anything. I could see a bulge the size of a lemon sticking out of his neck.

Touching it, I exclaimed, "How long has that been there?"

In true Dave style, he retorted, "I asked you to look at it six months ago, you said it was nothing."

Now I'm no nurse, but this was definitely something. I told him he had to hightail it to the doctor pronto.

His regular GP was away so he made an appointment with the first doctor available who insisted he have a CT scan as soon as possible. Dave had one the next day, and the day after that we returned for results. Both of us conceded that this scan would merely confirm what we already suspected. How bad it was, though, neither of us could tell. The results, a stage IV Squamous Cell Carcinoma of the neck. This cancer began in Dave's tonsil and was now present in his pharynx and lymph nodes. Holy heck, what next?

We left the surgery in shock. Moving to a new house on December 16, we received this news on December 22. There was only one certainty; we didn't want to ruin everyone's Christmas with the big C bombshell. The news would be kept between us until after Christmas. Corey and his father, Charlie, were joining us on Christmas Day. Aware Dave needed the CT, they arrived and in unison asked about the results. They were visibly shocked as we told them and swore them both to absolute secrecy. Ho, Ho, bloody Ho, the four of us put on our best jolly faces and kept the facade for the day. It may have been a thinly veiled mask of festive joy, but we pulled it off.

A couple of days before Christmas, one of Ezekiel's close friends from rugby went missing. No one had heard from him for a few days. Christmas 2012 may have been lugubrious for us, but nothing could possibly come close though to the Christmas his family experienced.

These boys, at fifteen, were not only teammates, but class buddies at school. From that same year group, three young men with their whole lives ahead of them, independently of one another, and at different times throughout 2012, tragically took their own lives. It fills me with such grief how anyone might be consumed with such overwhelming desperation and loneliness that they would contemplate suicide as an option to end the pain.

"Suicide, a permanent solution to a temporary problem." Phil Donahue.

No truer statement.

Christmas Day came and went, Boxing Day rolled around and Dave and I hatched a plan of how we should tell the kids. A turn of events ensured this wouldn't be the day to face our two youngest with their dad's diagnosis. The body of a young man had been found. As I pulled into our driveway, Ezekiel was walking back from the beach. His posture and gait told me something bad had happened. Retreating straight into his bedroom, I followed him.

One glance at his face said it all.

"They've found Tom, haven't they?"

Collapsing in tears, my baby of nearly six-foot sat on my knee as I cradled him and wept with him, trying to comfort him in his grief. We were all shattered and agreed that our news would have to wait a little longer. This was the last time I saw Ezekiel cry.

The funeral for Ezekiel's beautiful young friend was held on January 2, and by then, we couldn't stall telling the kids any longer. We were out of time. Dave's treatment was imminent.

As we shared the news of Dave's cancer Ezekiel asked, "Are you going to die?"

Ruby asked if she could have the car...

Although said in jest, Ruby had grown tired of her father's passive-aggressive behaviour. She'd been thinking of moving out if he didn't stop drinking. She was only seventeen and sick of her dad's caustic remarks, angry demeanour and duality. All of the kids were impacted by the inconsistencies in our parenting styles.

A few weeks after this, we began the process of what would be our reality for the next year. Dave's mate is an Ear Nose and Throat specialist who admitted Dave into the hospital system under his care. An enormous blessing. John took control and explained exactly what we should expect and how everything would happen.

After our first visit John told Dave to take the next twelve months off work. Not only because of how sick he would be, but because, and in his exact words, "You're going to irritate and piss off everyone around you."

These words sent chills down my spine and filled me with dread. Digesting the mind-boggling information given about this mountain we were about to climb, I turned to Dave.

"Don't let this illness be an excuse for your behaviour to escalate. I can do 'sick', but I can't do angrier and more irritable."

It was true. Ruby wasn't the only person close to the end of her tether! I kept a blog giving regular updates for family and friends over the year of treatment. Revisiting the blog now feels like I'm reading about someone else's life though I acknowledge it as fully ours.

It is uplifting, yet simultaneously heart-wrenching.

2013 became a surreal bubble in which we literally lived on the razor's edge of life and death. In months following Ezekiel's friend's death, Ezekiel became further estranged, going to school less and less and barely attending training sessions before giving up altogether. It was evident that he had succumbed to deep depression. His doctor thought it timely to trial medication, hoping this may help lift his mood.

During this period, I was notified that Ezekiel was on the receiving end of severe cyberbullying. Transcripts from an anonymous chat site ASKfm were alarming enough for me to contact the police. Viewing the threats as serious, they came and spoke with Ezekiel.

He wouldn't tell them anything. They believed he knew who made the threats but was most likely too afraid to tell. This site was popular at the time with teenagers. A place where people could ask questions while their own identity remained completely untraceable. The police officer told me that ASKfm was one of their biggest problems and a dangerous forum. Here is a small sample of the nature of threats to convey their seriousness:

"You better watch over your shoulder next time you're out you queer C***, I'm going to F****** glass you."

"Why don't you go and neck yourself you faggot."

The keyboard warriors hiding in anonymity also unleashed a barrage of assaults on Ezekiel directed at his older brother's sexuality, and the list went on. To his credit, when replying to any of these horrible messages Ezekiel answered in a mature and measured way. Corey and Ruby encouraged him to delete his account on the site and to stay away.

Although moving past this hurdle, there was no significant shift in Ezekiel's turmoil.

Night-time sleep continued to evade him and we continued watching, waiting and hoping the fog would lift. There was no shift in the atmospheric pressure, a dark cloud became darker.

Juggling full-time shift work, a sick son, sick husband, and a daughter recovering from illness left very little in my tank. I really needed my family to each do their bit. If that bit was simply taming their tongue or getting themselves out of bed, I didn't think this was too much to ask.

So much for forewarning Dave about how close we were to the edge. It's fair to say his behaviour peaked at an all-time high about six months into his treatment. Blame may be attributed to cancer-killing chemicals pumping through his body. I don't accept that to be reason enough for inflicting the vilest verbal assault and profoundly wounding your children.

Ruby and I were in the lounge room one afternoon when Ezekiel walked in visibly upset.

Dave had driven him and his mates to several beach breaks looking for a surf.

Although I offered to take them, Dave insisted, placing unnecessary pressure on himself.

He had a scheduled appointment to keep. Nevertheless, he was adamant he wanted to, and they went. When I asked Ezekiel what was wrong, he said,

"Dad told Ben he was talking sh*#."

Ezekiel felt humiliated by his father speaking to one of his friends in this manner. Thinking it was inappropriate that an adult would speak to a teenage boy this way, I called Dave into the lounge room and asked what happened. He admitted saying this, all the while justifying his language.

Ezekiel called him an ars*****. Glaring at me angrily, Dave said,

"And you're going to let him get away with speaking to me like that?"

Ruby interjected, rebuking her father, "Is it any wonder he speaks like that when you're his role model?"

Dave stormed off, mumbling the most horrific unleashing on her. No way would I let him off the hook this time. Calling him back into the room, my insistence overruled his reluctance.

Once facing us I asked him to repeat what he had said. Defiantly, he obliged. Ruby stormed off to her bedroom in tears, devastated by what her father had said, and Ezekiel retreated to his room. Dave sat deflated and sorry, realising too little too late. The words had left his lips and exposed what lay in his heart. His poisonous tongue injured his princess like never before. Barely able to contain my rage, I said, "What kind of a loving father would say that to his daughter? It's one thing for you to lash out at me, but how dare you do this to our children? GET OUT, JUST LEAVE!"

ARGGGHHH! I realised that he couldn't go, he was sick, I couldn't kick him out. I approached Ruby and Ezekiel in their rooms.

"Get dressed, we'll go to Max Brenner's for chocolate."

Nothing else sprang to mind which might console their hurt. Ruby dried her tears and readied herself for the small comfort. Ezekiel stayed in his room, silent.

He didn't want to go anywhere. We'd bring goodies back for him. Lingering in the lounge room when we left the house, Dave was absent on our return. Pulling into the driveway, Ruby piped up, "I bet he's written a letter", inferring that Dave would leave us a note apologising for his outburst. Ruby saw through her dad. On her bed was a piece of paper. I can't recall if one was on our bed, but it was highly likely. Screwing up the letter, she threw it in the bin.

The problem with Dave's well-intentioned notes was they were as predictable as the bank statements rolling in each month. Although the words said 'sorry', the behaviour only changed momentarily. Words wound far deeper than a slap. Once abuse leaves lips, the words spoken are impossible to retract and they leave bruises and scars invisible to the eye, but the injury is felt deeply within heart and soul.

This was the first time since committing my life to the Lord that I actively questioned my faith. I not so much questioned God as I asked myself about whether my faith in Christianity had kept me in a place far longer than I should have stayed. This place was having a detrimental impact on our children. I hated myself for not protecting them from his moods and angry smile.

I hated myself for not being able to make it stop.

I recall meeting our pastor's wife in the days following and telling her what had occurred. Ps Jen openly asked why I had never left. I genuinely responded with my tearful reply that I never considered God had directed me to do so. Even though it was the truth, in all sincerity I added, "Jen, this is such an awful thing to say. It would be easier if God just took Dave rather than us living with his horrible hurtful behaviour."

It was true. I couldn't stand this torment.

Life with Dave resembled a snow fight. Throwing snowballs at each other, seemingly innocent fun except the snowballs he threw had rocks inside. They sure hurt when they hit.

The cruelty is covert abuse at its finest. No one outside of our immediate family could ever imagine how changeable Dave was and no one except me raised the topic and challenged any of his behaviours.

LESSONS FROM BEYOND

"One of the obstacles to recognizing chronic mistreatment in relationships is that most abusive men simply don't seem like abusers. They have many good qualities, including times of kindness, warmth, and humour, especially in the early period of a relationship. An abuser's friends may think the world of him. He may have a successful work life and have no problems with drugs or alcohol. He may simply not fit anyone's image of a cruel or intimidating person. So, when a woman feels her relationship spinning out of control, it is unlikely to occur to her that her partner is an abuser."

— LUNDY BANCROFT: WHY DOES HE DO THAT? INSIDE THE MINDS OF ANGRY AND CONTROLLING MEN

Ezekiel remained in his bedroom. Checking in on him, he was still quiet. I sent a message to Dave asking him where he was, but rather than giving me a direct answer he played the game of "You told me to go," etc...

Not the question I asked.

I needed to repeat myself several more times before he finally told me he was at a mate's place. Thanking him for finally answering me, I ended the confrontation for the time being.

He was sick, in treatment, and although I had enormous distaste toward him, I did care that he was safe. The next few weeks were uncomfortable. Caught in a dilemma, I needed to protect our children but I was also committed to their father. Dave came home. The air was thick.

At Ezekiel's final counselling session, his therapist asked to speak with me.

Ezekiel didn't want to stay so I went in by myself. The professional said he had never met a boy of Ezekiel's age so unable to express what he was feeling. All Ezekiel knew was that *feelings* were bad.

The counsellor advised that he knew Ezekiel had problems with his father and he asked me to tell him what kind of a man Dave was. I shared an abridged version of our reality, but he stopped me and looked directly into my eyes. With absolute seriousness he asked, "If this man was hitting you, would you stay?"

"Of course not," I replied.

He continued telling me that how Dave treated us was abusive and while Dave remained under the same roof, Ezekiel would feel unsafe. Shell shocked, again, I had to admit to myself I was tolerating a relationship that I never thought I would. Yes, we blamed depression and anxiety. I also felt sorry for Dave. It must be terrible struggling with these demons. Then I had a revelation of enormous magnitude. My sympathy and compassion for Dave was ENABLING him. Tragically, our children were the collateral damage!

After this session, I told Dave of the discussion with Ezekiel's therapist. Quiet and sad he said, "I will move out."

I was sad too, thankful though that he had taken initiative.

He moved up to a farm with some dear friends for a week then into a spare room in a house close by. We enjoyed peace in the household. Dave lived away from home for a few months, visiting regularly, and eventually worked his way back to living with us full-time.

Although the house was calm during Dave's absence, Ezekiel's sleeping remained the same.

He went to school intermittently and became obsessed with finding a job. He wanted to earn money. No one opposed this. If it gave him another interest then I thought it a good thing.

He found a part-time job at a local restaurant earning a few dollars for himself. I suspect but can't be sure it was around this time that he was introduced to marijuana to help him sleep.

The slippery slope to a living hell began. Ezekiel's detachment from familiar relationships and pastimes he'd previously enjoyed increased. He no longer surfed or trained. He developed friendships with people he didn't want us to meet. We were still trying to offer solutions. By now he was under the care of a psychiatrist.

As mothers at a loss do, I began searching Ezekiel's room looking for clues to his darkness. Regularly finding bags of weed which I disposed of, I also found disturbing notes. These notes talked of taking his life, ending the pain. Drawings graphically depicted the darkness in his soul. Sketches painted an extremely bleak picture of what was going on for him. His doctor and psychiatrist acknowledged that Ezekiel had contemplated suicide but had not gone as far as making a plan. This thought terrified me. Was I supposed to console myself with the fact that he hadn't gone as far as making a plan? This is small comfort when your beloved son is the one they're talking about! The anguish we went through is indescribable.

Where could we turn? Who could help us? Would Ezekiel be the next statistic, devoid of all hope? Would he go down the same path as the other boys he went to school with who had perceived no other way out of their darkness? Oh, God, how I cried out in anguish and fear during those days and nights. Dave and I tried to work together on this, but the crevasse of our differences was a major obstacle. Our communication was strained. He was fighting to stay alive and I was fighting for my son and to hold the family together. We weren't fighting fair and were far from fighting together. Dave barely made it through intensive rounds of chemo-therapy. He did and continued with thirty-five rounds of radiation. Surviving 2013, – just.

Dave and I planned a trip to Bali for early in 2014. Ezekiel was still not interacting with Dave; I flagged the idea that we ask if he would consider joining us on the holiday. Ruby was in her final year of school and stayed home with Charlie and the animals. Much to Dave's surprise, Ezekiel agreed. Dave and I flew first and Ezekiel came a couple of days later. The day Ezekiel flew over, I received a call from a teacher concerned that Ezekiel wasn't at school. Even though I informed the principal of our leave, the message hadn't been passed to teaching staff.

Apparently, Ezekiel posted a Facebook status the previous evening and two students, concerned by the nature of the post, confided in a teacher. They chose not to divulge what alarmed them about the post and the girls asked to remain anonymous. I am grateful they showed courage by sharing their concern with an adult. The teacher calling was visibly relieved to hear that Ezekiel was on his way to be with us.

(An interesting side note to this phone call; in all my years of international travel, I have never received a call on my mobile phone. My phone is kept on aeroplane mode without global roaming. I am still clueless about how his teacher's call came through. There is absolutely no way I had reception or coverage. In the street, I had no Wi-Fi, the call a regular number failing to show on my call register. I have no explanation. It remains a mystery to me.)

Bali has always been a healing place for our family, this holiday was no exception. Ezekiel spent four days surfing by himself at a beachfront surf resort while Dave and I went further up the east coast. Ezekiel sent an iMessage thanking us for the trip. Although I was unsure of his reference, he added, "It couldn't have come at a better time."

Our Bali holiday coming to an end, Ezekiel looked to be in good spirits reconnecting with us.

Sadly, this connection was short-lived once we returned home. The following is an extract from notes I kept. We had no control over the comings and goings of our six-foot sixteen-year-old son, a young man, driven and determined...

Wed 19/3 O/night flight from Bali

Thurs 20/3 slept and went to friends, home after dinner/bed

Fri 21/3 school/funeral/ went to friends stayed out overnight

Sat 22/3 home at 12 red swollen sore eyes. Slept all afternoon, up very late at home

Sun slept until lunch/surf for a while/bed and sleep

Mon 24/3 school

Tues 25/3 school/went to friends at 6 pm home at 9 pm

Wed 26/3 up for school doesn't go/ sleep all day. Scored somewhere between Tues/Wed

Thurs 27/3 school after school friends, home at 7.30 straight to room, took food

No talking/eating rubbish/ stays in bedroom

This pattern continued for weeks until he sent me another message in April saying that he wanted to make changes. He wanted to "stop smoking everything, have normal relationships, normal friendships." Asking us to let him be, told us he would be in a "Sh*# P***# mood" we were to leave him alone so he could make the right decisions for himself. Pleased to hear his heartfelt desire, although apart from the weed I'd found in his room, we really had no clue what else he might be smoking. Respecting what he asked, every motherly inch of me wanting to help him through withdrawal.

This was April 2014. He tried, I know he tried and did so with the best intentions. Intentions alone are never enough though, no matter how honourable. This 'addiction', this giant, was bigger than he or we anticipated.

The one day of the year I can gush about my mum without ruining my street cred! Thank you for your unconditional love, your grace, your wisdom and your support in everything I do. Thank you for still feeding me and braiding my hair because I don't know how to adult. You're my rock, my best friend, and the best mother I could ever wish for. Love always, your favourite xx

TOP LEFT, March 27, 1993, Dave surprising me in the Noosa Heads salon with his proposal. TOP RIGHT, "I do". The day we became Mr. & Mrs. October 2, 1993. BOTTOM LEFT, Adoring Corey with his much-loved little sister Ruby, June 1995. BOTTOM CENTRE, a social media Mother's Day shout out from our Princess of the Pretties. BOTTOM RIGHT, big sister Ruby and our darling Ezekiel just a few days old.

TOP LEFT, Dave, Ruby and Zeke, relishing in the laughter and fun at home on Sydney's northern beaches. Neighbour's wondered who on earth would buy such a shack TOP RIGHT. This was our first house renovation, the tiny two-bedroom fibro fisherman's shack, lovingly transformed into our substantial family home. BOTTOM PHOTOS, our beautiful baby boy, Zeke and us at Warriewood Beach.

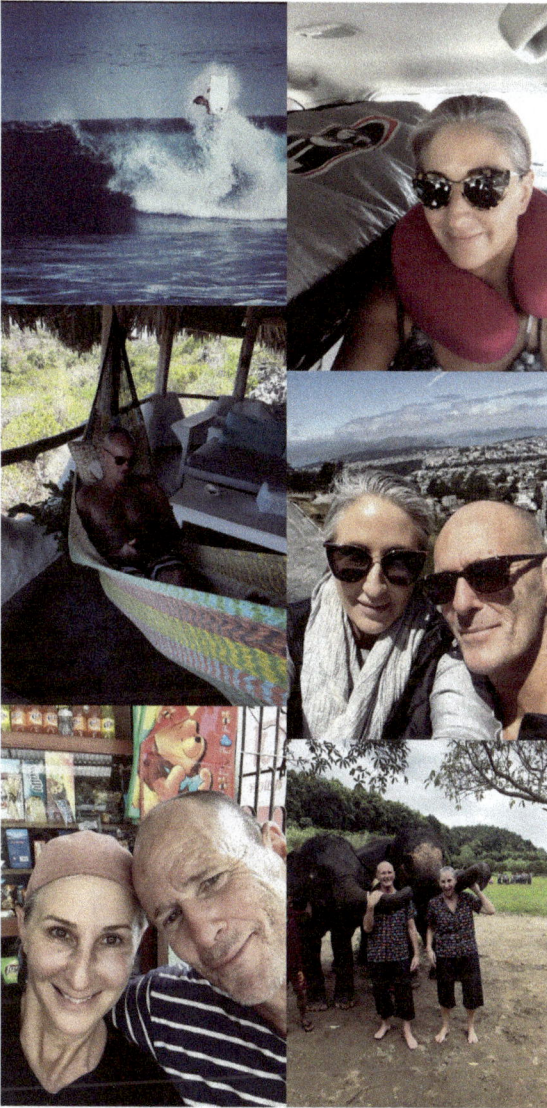

A GLIMPSE OF TRAVEL TOP LEFT, *Zeke catching a wave at Keramas Indonesia. TOP RIGHT, This, is how we roll, squished amongst surfboards on the way to Rote Indonesia. MIDDLE LEFT, Rote life, in a hammock trying to escape the heat. MIDDLE RIGHT, Dave and I with San Francisco in the background. BOTTOM RIGHT, At the completion of a 5-day Poon Hill trek in Nepal. BOTTOM LEFT, bathing elephants near Chiang Mai, Thailand.*

The straw that broke the camel's back. *Bali Villa, August 2018.*

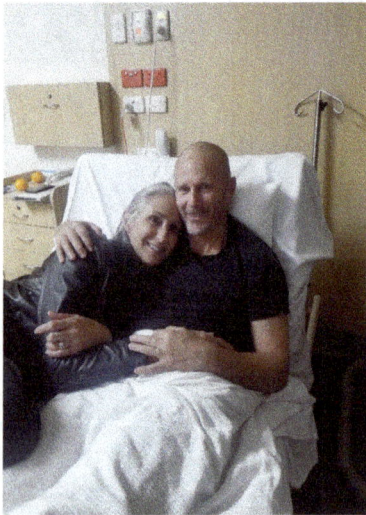

June 5, 2019, the night before Dave had his left lung removed.

CHAPTER 11

IN THE WILDERNESS

NONI

Ezekiel's battle was enormous. School was no longer a place he wanted to be and it was pointless us persisting that he go.

He appeared to gain a tiny spark once we leaned toward unenrolling him. Zeke was just shy of seventeen and legally required to remain in school, however, his pastoral care team agreed it was pointless to demand that he stay and allowed him to leave.

Over the space of two years, from ages fourteen to sixteen, we watched the life joy of our youngest son dwindle into desperation. He became a stranger in our home, aggressive, detached, dark, and secretive. Four short months after Ezekiel's message desiring change, I received information he was selling drugs. Approaching him with this news, his stance aggressively blocking the doorway to his bedroom. His only concern was who told me. I emphasised to him how I found out wasn't important, but that he should understand if a shred of evidence proved the information correct, he would need to find somewhere else to live.

LESSONS FROM BEYOND

ALTHOUGH DAVE AND I WOULD DISCUSS DIFFERENT COURSES OF ACTION AROUND SUPPORTING AND REPRIMANDING THE CHILDREN, IT WAS MORE OFTEN THAN NOT LEFT UP TO ME TO BE THE MESSENGER AND UPHOLDER OF ANY DISCIPLINE. DAVE'S CONFLICT AVOIDANCE, WORKING AWAY FROM HOME, HIS EMOTIONAL ABSENCE EVEN WHEN PHYSICALLY PRESENT, AND THEN ILLNESS ULTIMATELY LEFT ME SOLO AT THE PARENTING HELM FOR MANY YEARS. THE UNDERLYING DISHARMONY WHEN KEEPING A STRING OF HIDDEN UNHEALTHY SECRETS HAS A WAY OF SPILLING OUT INTO ALL AREAS OF LIFE. EVEN THOUGH I HAD NO INKLING OF THE EXTENT OF DAVE'S SECRETS AND DUALITY, THERE IS NO DOUBT IN MY MIND THAT THEY WERE A CONTRIBUTING FACTOR TO THE UNSETTLING OF OUR TRIBE.

Discovering evidence a couple of weeks later left us with no alternative but to carry through with the consequence. Before giving Ezekiel his final chance, we tried speaking to him again.

We asked how he would be able to live with himself should one of his friends have an adverse reaction to something he gave them. Ezekiel, unperturbed and disinterested, didn't care.

Holding the drugs in my hand, I pleaded.

"Ezekiel, someone is going to want their money for these. You're earning eleven dollars an hour, how many hours will you need to work to pay them?"

His curt response, "They didn't cost me anything."

Our hearts sank. We suspected he was in far deeper than we ever imagined. We had lost track of him. This was Thursday. He was rostered to work that night and he could come home to sleep, but the next day, Ezekiel would need to find alternative accommodation.

We believed we had the endless patience and perseverance needed to be supportive and caring while Ezekiel was in active addiction. That's one thing. It's something else entirely to ignore illegal dealings and enable them to continue unchallenged under our roof.

Ezekiel showed no remorse for his actions and there was no sign he was going to give up his illegal hobby.

When he was ready, I drove him to work then took his drugs to the police. Yes, I turned our son into the police, telling them I believed he was selling drugs. Initially, they didn't take me seriously. Not until I produced a pouch of pills and trips did the officer pull out his notepad and began scribbling. The amount was borderline possession/supply. Bikies infiltrated our precinct, looking for vulnerable kids to be their hands, feet, and faces of criminal activity.

The narcotics were handed over to the drug squad who would speak with Ezekiel. The officer asked if I wanted to remain anonymous. "Of course not," I said. I had no reason to be fearful of truth, firmly believing this would be Ezekiel's turning point. Perhaps I felt a mother's attachment, certain Ezekiel and I still had a connection. From my perspective, this rang true. Once more I was about to find out just how wrong I was. The ensuing agony over the next five years was undoubtedly our most excruciating parenting experience.

Ezekiel spent Thursday night at home. The police called Friday morning. I took the phone into Ezekiel. After speaking with him briefly, the constable spoke to me. Ezekiel would need to front at the police station before 6 pm on Sunday. A responsible adult must accompany him, and if this didn't happen, a warrant would be issued for his arrest. I called the personal trainer Ezekiel admired and respected and who had been a source of calm and knowledge in the past. I told him about our situation and he chatted with Zeke. This kind man possessed the skill needed to reach troubled teens, likely honed through his own journey. Ezekiel looked up to him.

A short time later, Ezekiel got out of bed, packed a bag, and sat on the lounge. He was furious, yet said nothing. Unmoveable indignation. Looking at him, I implored with a trembling voice, "Zeke, you said you wanted to stop using. Buddy, you were unable to do it by yourself, please let us help you. Please!"

Tears welled in my eyes and slid down my face. Ezekiel ignored my pleas, refusing to acknowledge me though blinking back his own tears. His lip quivered. My heart pierced to the core by what was happening. The train had left the station and I was powerless to stop it. Ezekiel left on Friday morning with nothing but his phone and a small backpack. There was no telling where he went or who he would be going with. We let him go. It was terrifying.

So, a few weeks before his seventeenth birthday, he left school. Not long after, he left home.

This was by far the toughest decision to make. Although it was a decision made as a family, the responsibility primarily landed on me. Handing Ezekiel into the police at this time of his life was part tactical, and part sheer exasperation. What else was left to do? How else could we help him? He was only seventeen. I bore the brunt of Ezekiel's anger, abuse, and hostility. I, his own mother, had betrayed him. Ezekiel knew the consequences of his actions would be adhered to according to the prior warning. I don't think in a million years he EVER thought we'd go to the police. For us, it was a last-ditch effort to save our son from himself and the world he'd somehow become a part of. The next few years were the most devastating of our lives and finally brought us to the breaking point.

The quantity of drugs allowing him to admit possession for personal use, instead of supply.

Claiming possession meant he could be part of a Young Offenders Program rather than receive a conviction. Wisely, this was the choice he made. After Ezekiel's interview at the police station, the constable called me. "Ezekiel is not our *usual* offender."

"I agree," I said, "that's why I came to you. I don't want him to become one of your 'usual' offenders!"

The officer assured me we'd done the right thing and said that 99% of kids with Ezekiel's demeanour and background do return to base, eventually... We had to take his word for it!

Our *eventually* took five years. We're only now beginning to see Ezekiel again as he's getting healthy, maturing and wanting to reconnect, but not before we've been to hell and back. Ruby confronted unspeakable distress after tracking him down at a crack house soon after he left home. She had to ask him if he was thinking of taking his own life. We've had crisis calls to lifeline, police, psychiatrists, and we've had to look each other in the eye, knowing we could get a dreadful knock on the door or a phone call that's every parent's worst nightmare to inform us our son isn't coming home.

We've been on the receiving end of horrendous abuse from him. But recognising this is addiction talking, his own pain, shame, guilt and lack of worth doesn't make it OK. We have never given up on him or withdrawn our love from him, but we've had to 'let go', let him make his choices and experience the consequences of those choices. The door always open but not without boundaries. For my own sanity and safety, firm boundaries around what is and isn't acceptable were imperative. Standing firm on truth with love rarely accepted or appreciated. Countless letters and notes written to him, every word filled with love and hope, trusting God over and over with one of our most precious blessings.

Like infidelity, there is not a huge number of resources and support for families who have loved ones caught up in a drug addiction/mental health crisis. Medical practitioners and counsellors are not always helpful in many situations. Friends and family rarely fully 'get it' and, although well-meaning, often give advice they are ill-qualified to give. If they have no understanding of the dynamics or the root of the addiction, they can only assume what they'd do if it were them. The problem is, it's not them. Therefore, words – however well-intentioned – are often spoken with ignorance. I've learned you only need one or two good and Godly friends you can count on to accompany you through dark times. Ones who will just 'be' without trying to 'fix'. Family Drug Support was the most beneficial discovery I made during our painstakingly debilitating ordeal. A godsend. The courses, groups, support and education available through FDS was a game-changer for me. Here was helpful insight from people with a solid understanding of how to support loved ones through addiction and, importantly, how essential it is to nurture oneself during the process.

LESSONS FROM BEYOND

S elf-nurturing differs depending on the season we're in.

Day to day might be as simple as taking time to pause and check where my head and emotions are at. It may be catching up with friends, taking a walk, a bath, or sitting in a coffee shop watching the world go by.

Then there's pampering, a massage, facial, retreat or even a break away by myself or with girlfriends.

At Dave's sickest in 2013, he was hospitalised for six weeks. Choosing to take time out for a week in Bali by myself before he was released may appear selfish to some, but for me it was self-care. I call it essential.

Life can be tumultuous; it is important to continue doing things to find enjoyment despite the storms.

Work hard not to lose yourself in times of calamity.

Stay true to you!

CHAPTER 12

A NEW BEGINNING (AGAIN)

NONI

Dave's health was improving, and each routine check-up returned a positive good report. He was travelling as much for work as he'd ever done while I continued working and juggling home life on the coast.

A local real estate agent piqued my curiosity one morning as he was taking photos of nearby land. Interrupting my stroll to question if the land was being released, he informed me pre-launch was scheduled for the following week. I asked him to send details.

Dave and I perused available lots, securing a small block for the same entry price we paid in 2003, eleven years earlier. Estimating eighteen months or so until the title was released, a reasonable time frame to figure out whether we'd build a new home or flip the block.

The inheritance from Dave's dad helped in purchasing the land. After exploring finance options, we began planning a house to fit the block and our budget.

March 2015, I turned fifty. After the tumultuous years we'd had, all I wanted to do was go to Bali for my birthday. We opened up the invitation to family and friends and celebrated with a stunning dinner at a favourite restaurant. Ezekiel came on the holiday; he was hurting badly in all ways. Cordial and talkative to everyone else, he made a point of showing me nothing but contempt and hostility in a painfully obvious demonstration of his determination to stonewall me.

The moment I laid eyes on him, my heart disintegrated into a thousand pieces. Our beautiful Zeke, swimming in the villa pool, was pale and skinny and there was no mistaking the open gash below his rib cage – a recent stab wound. Gaping flesh required medical attention, but for whatever reason, the laceration had been left untreated. Even though I put on a brave face most of the time, my girlfriends knew how much I was aching. This birthday was my most memorable ever, for all the wrong reasons.

Soon after returning from our holiday, we moved into our new home.

Dave, still travelling substantially for work, was in Sydney while we were in the process of settling into our home. Powering up the Mac to check my email, the large screen opened on an old file. It was Dave's. I had no idea he had any account set up on my computer and it remains a mystery to why this appeared when I powered up. Unsure of exactly what was in front of me I continued scrolling. Exploring a little further, I stumbled across emails from a woman named Susan R. Curious to discover more about this email trail, I found emails between this woman and Dave exchanged over a good eighteen months, years earlier…

Although nothing overtly sexual or blatantly romantic stood out in their correspondence, Dave painted a vastly different picture of himself to this woman I'd never heard of.

His wife and children simply didn't exist. Once I collected myself, recovered from the shock and gathered a chronological timeline of their interaction, I was livid! Sickened this grown 'Christian' man who'd made an oath to love, honour, and cherish me 'till death do us part' could do this again. Already forgiven of two previous marital indiscretions, now he had some sort of infatuated pathetic 'pen pal' relationship with another woman. The timing of their emotional affair was most difficult to swallow. During this time, not only had I been caring for Ruby recovering from CFS, but also trying my darndest to sell our home. Trying to bail us out of the rollicking financial mess of the commercial property!

I was hopping mad, speechless! Sending him one simple text message:

"WHO'S SUSAN R?"

He replied, " ? "

The emails were from beginning November 2009 to mid-February 2011 and Dave had forgotten they existed. Secrets hidden in one's past will always come back to bite, eventually. Dave arrived home from Sydney offering an explanation, downplaying his interaction with this woman. Minimising and explaining it away, rationalising his actions.

Nothing more than an innocent encounter with a musician he met in a bar one night in San Francisco. This did nothing to explain their ongoing communication. He stopped contacting her after waking up to himself, questioning his own motives and asking himself, *why?*

Though outraged by the email exchanges, actually embarrassed for him, I could have almost sympathised if it wasn't so painful once again to be on the receiving end of flagrant deceit.

The only reason Dave's belongings weren't out in the gutter after discovering this emotional affair was because it was in the past. Although hurt, I had no intention of punishing him for something that had occurred almost six years earlier. In hindsight, I didn't ask enough questions at the time nor pry into the identity of this woman or what she meant to him. Accepting his remorse and apology as sincere, I chalked it up to experience and another *error of judgement* on Dave's part.

What I am aware of now is that he met this young woman in San Francisco. The night I flew home to our children, Dave went out and met Susan the singer. Dave was forty-eight at the time and Susan was half his age, a youthful twenty-four. The current age of our own darling daughter.

Susan and Dave made loose plans to meet up the following day. Thanks to phone glitches they missed each other. Perhaps it was a sliding door moment that potentially diverted a different outcome by a whisker. The correspondence alone was enough to reveal Dave's intentions at the time. Once again, though, we put it behind us and moved on...

∾

DAVE

'Pimping tenderness' is a well-versed term in affair recovery that describes overused charm to garner attention and affection from members of the opposite sex. Essentially, this is what I did habitually. Assuming the role of 'rescuer' is another perilous habit. Both behaviours are innocently explained as being helpful, caring and kind, but the major difference is the underlying motive. My self-esteem needed bolstering. I needed to appeal to someone else so I could look and feel 'good' about myself. It took years before I could recognise and unpack this manipulation.

The workplace for anyone is an obvious outlet for extra-marital activity, and my acting out made it all the easier with the distance between work and home granting me control. In the professional arena I could be an expert, a person interested in other people, a person with resources to offer, and I took advantage of this leverage to build myself up in the eyes of others. Although there's nothing inherently wrong with being liked for who I am or how I conduct myself, there is a line I routinely crossed. I compromised my identity by denying my values and presenting myself selectively when it suited me, and this blurred the line.

Example: Dining alone in San Francisco, there was a folk singer performing in the cosy and dimly lit bar. During the break, Susan approached everyone in the room, introducing herself. When she arrived at my table, our conversation lasted longer, likely due to my eager level of engagement. We agreed to continue our conversation after she finished for the evening.

Over a couple of glasses of wine, we shared commonalities; both first-timers in the city, varied musical interests, etc. Omitting the fact that I was married, and my wife had left San Francisco earlier in the day gives a clear picture of how easily I could shift gears. Interaction with an attractive woman who led such a different and exciting life showing interest in me was an intoxicating boost, albeit short-lived.

Attempting to relive a sense of being special, I maintained the relationship via email.

I would curate interest in myself and exaggerate interest in her life, all for the sake of experiencing a rush of gratification and self-importance. Unaware of the game I was playing, I created a fantasy version of me based on a momentary exchange, an adaptation of myself carefully selected and edited that allowed me to indulge in mini escapes with no intention of physically vacating. Rather, I had a desire to distract myself from reality. A reality that at times was stressful and boring. Rather than explore these triggers and vulnerabilities, escapism was my solution.

~

NONI

In September 2015, accompanying Dave on a work trip to New Zealand, I checked a message for him on his phone. This led to discovering a message trail from another female ex-work colleague. There was nothing overtly alarming in the content apart from Dave arranging to meet her downstairs at a Sydney hotel. Farewell drinks were on for a guy Dave worked with.

My husband invited her to the farewell though not the guy leaving the company! This invitation, innocent as it may appear, violated all our verbal agreements. Although a little extreme, because Dave had trouble keeping his word, I suggested we make a written contract.

The goal of our written agreement was to eliminate confusion of agreed safe boundaries protecting our marriage. I asked Dave to write one in his own words, hoping he fully understood the consequences of crossing boundaries. Dave willingly did so. I wish I could say this was enough to finally keep our marriage sacred.

My plea 6th September 2015:

> *"I love you Dave, always have and always will.*
> *I love you with all of my heart and soul.*
> *I've loved you since before we said, 'I do'. I*
> *chose to love you forever when we*
> *exchanged vows. Choosing to love you*
> *whether I have felt like it or not, I have*
> *remained 100% faithful to my decision for*
> *22yrs. This hasn't always been easy, but I*
> *still love you and will continue to love you.*
> *Although I love you, and we have spoken of*
> *our desire and intention to remain married,*
> *there are things we need to be completely*
> *certain of and these need to be absolute.*
> *I can't tell you what to do. I've never wanted to*
> *and won't, but I can tell you what I expect*
> *from our marriage. I expect to be able to feel*
> *safe and confident that I can trust you and*
> *depend upon you to respect and honour me,*
> *to act with integrity when it comes to our*
> *relationship.*

For us to fully enjoy our marriage there are a couple of things we need to be in agreement of.

Your choice to drink alcohol means you will sleep in the spare room. As soon as a drop passes your lips, I will assume you have consciously chosen to do so, and you will respect what this means. I will support you with abstaining from alcohol.

Dave, we placed boundaries around our marriage concerning the contact between you and other women. You repeatedly crossed these boundaries, and, in turn, I am left disrespected and let down. So, can we make one thing perfectly clear? You will not initiate nor accept an invitation to meet with any women outside of immediate work-related business. If you do, and when I find out, this will effectively mean our marriage is over. Harsh? I don't think so. Too many times in our past I forgave you for this. Of course, I would forgive you again, but this would be an absolute deal-breaker for me. I hope knowing the consequence of disrespecting this boundary will be enough for you to fully honour our marriage. I need to trust you will protect the sanctity of our marriage so we can be free to fully enjoy our togetherness.

You know yourself what you want to put in place for yourself. Please, can you respond to this note in writing, so we are both perfectly clear on our expectations of one another?

I want to love and respect you forever.

Xxx"

CHAPTER 13

CHAOS AND CONFUSION

NONI

Our house is one we've melded into a welcoming warm and inclusive home. A humble dwelling yet fully functional and comfortable. The functionality refers to bricks and mortar, every area of land and home well utilised. Relationally, our marriage continued with increasing difficulty.

Negative personality traits Dave held tightly made their way into more settings and he had difficulty keeping 'nasty' confined. I became less and less tolerant, less accepting, and far less understanding. Friends and family not only noticed how ornery Dave could be, but they also began speaking up. No one was bold enough to confront Dave, so their appeals were made directly to me.

He was a true Jekyll and Hyde. One minute completely charming, the next exploding for no apparent reason. An oscillating personality uncomfortable to be around, to say the least. Dave would say one thing to one person and then something completely contrary to another. Double-minded and two-faced, how and what could we trust? If he wanted to impress, he would turn on the charm, if he thought less of someone, he could be dismissive and insulting. The behaviour was narcissistic abusive, and at times, quite bizarre.

In May 2017, we travelled to Airlie Beach for a family wedding. Ezekiel made his way there.

It was heart-wrenching to see him in his current condition, such an angry young man.

An extremely unhealthy skeletal mess. Any attempts at approaching him failed dismally, he wanted me out of his sight. Letting go of the rejection, incredibly saddened then triggered by the overwhelming dysfunction in this family. Too many people ruled by fragile egos.

Holding onto grudges, hostility, and cutting people out of their lives.

Was this really easier than humbling themselves to make peace and restore relationships?

Could they not see how the anger they coveted jeopardised their own happiness? I failed to understand. During our time away, I realised I'd come the closest ever to wanting to disappear. Up and leave everyone to deal with their own sh*^. Life truly is too short!

I voiced my anguish to Dave, adamant that he needed to find the root of his inexcusable poor behaviour. Not that he's a bad person, but he behaved badly and he was getting worse. I felt there must be more to his depression/anxiety; things didn't add up. We arrived home and he made an appointment with a psychiatrist. Accompanying him, we took the following list of alarming behaviours and incidents noted throughout the years:

> *Progressively worsening*
> *behavioural/personality in no particular*
> *order*
> *always had anger issues*
> *problems with being assertive resulting in*
> *aggression, belittling, ridiculing others*
> *snide remarks/comments*
> *mumbling nasty comments under breath*
> *walking away*
> *fear of truth*
> *losing things, e.g., Medicare cards,*
> *sunglasses, prescription glasses, post*
> *office key*
> *people pleaser*
> *talks quickly and interrupts people*
> *(heightened state)*
> *sullen and withdrawn aggressive (depressive*
> *state)*

*exaggerated responses either highs or lows-
    irrational
*heightened state, arrogant proud aggressive
*depressed state, self-deprecating, negative
*build-up of pent-up rage outburst and abuse
    followed by overcompensating for uncalled-
    for aggression and the hurt caused
*We are left reeling; Dave wants to breeze over
    and act as if nothing happened (back to
    extreme overly nice but scary nice
    overcompensating person)
*poor judgement; leading to extramarital
    affairs and other work-related issues
    (compliance issues) Handed over $270k
    cheque with no contract? $800 at casino
*complete lack of clear thinking with alcohol,
    history of alcohol abuse leading to
    aggressive abuse of me, our children and
    rudeness to others *inappropriate
    outbursts/jokes; no filter, lack of judgement
*talking loudly and over the top of people-
    whispering acting secretive in social
    situations
*all behaviours exhibited at both ends of the
    spectrum, extreme ends
*Jekyll and Hyde
*Depression, anxiety, fear and loathing
*father Dementia
*close family member diagnosed Bipolar
*family relationships volatile, unable to have
    healthy conflict, intellectualising and

abrasive smart Alec, sarcastic, caustic but
all in the guise of a "joke"
*cruel and harsh
*smothering and martyrdom
*disorientation
*Sydney Corey abused by a 'madman'
*LA 8.30 pm text, a 15 min walk from the hotel
yet returned 11.20 pm aggressive, the night
before same aggression (alcohol)
*left glasses at a restaurant one night
*wallet at a restaurant a few nights later
*Ruby was going to leave home if he didn't
stop drinking: that week diagnosis cancer
*abusive of both Ruby and Zeke: frustration
not dealt with effectively or early enough
becomes outright rage and angry outbursts
*seeing things that aren't there (night wakes,
looking at "what am I watching" TV
not on)
*running onto a rugby field to swear and abuse
umpire at a junior rugby game
*punching painting repeatedly

Whilst he didn't typically fit into a category, Dave walked away from this initial meeting with a diagnosis of Bipolar 2 and more medication.

LESSONS FROM BEYOND

"THE ABUSER'S MOOD CHANGES ARE ESPECIALLY PERPLEXING. HE CAN BE A DIFFERENT PERSON FROM DAY TO DAY, OR EVEN FROM HOUR TO HOUR. AT TIMES HE IS AGGRESSIVE AND INTIMIDATING, HIS TONE HARSH, INSULTS SPEWING FROM HIS MOUTH, RIDICULE DRIPPING FROM HIM LIKE OIL FROM A DRUM. WHEN HE'S IN THIS MODE, NOTHING SHE SAYS SEEMS TO HAVE ANY IMPACT ON HIM, EXCEPT TO MAKE HIM EVEN ANGRIER. HER SIDE OF THE ARGUMENT COUNTS FOR NOTHING IN HIS EYES, AND EVERYTHING IS HER FAULT. HE TWISTS HER WORDS AROUND SO THAT SHE ALWAYS ENDS UP ON THE DEFENSIVE. AS SO MANY PARTNERS OF MY CLIENTS HAVE SAID TO ME, "I JUST CAN'T SEEM TO DO ANYTHING RIGHT."

AT OTHER MOMENTS, HE SOUNDS WOUNDED AND LOST, HUNGERING FOR LOVE AND FOR SOMEONE TO TAKE CARE OF HIM. WHEN THIS SIDE OF HIM EMERGES, HE APPEARS OPEN AND READY TO HEAL. HE SEEMS TO LET DOWN HIS GUARD, HIS HARD EXTERIOR SOFTENS, AND HE MAY TAKE ON THE QUALITY OF A HURT CHILD, DIFFICULT AND FRUSTRATING BUT LOVEABLE. LOOKING AT HIM IN THIS DEFLATED STATE, HIS PARTNER HAS TROUBLE IMAGINING THAT THE ABUSER INSIDE OF HIM WILL EVER BE BACK.

LESSONS FROM BEYOND continued

THE BEAST THAT TAKES HIM OVER AT OTHER TIMES LOOKS COMPLETELY UNRELATED TO THE TENDER PERSON SHE NOW SEES. SOONER OR LATER, THOUGH, THE SHADOW COMES BACK OVER HIM, AS IF IT HAD A LIFE OF ITS OWN. WEEKS OF PEACE MAY GO BY, BUT EVENTUALLY SHE FINDS HERSELF UNDER ASSAULT ONCE AGAIN. THEN HER HEAD SPINS WITH THE ARDUOUS EFFORT OF UNTANGLING THE MANY THREADS OF HIS CHARACTER, UNTIL SHE BEGINS TO WONDER WHETHER SHE IS THE ONE WHOSE HEAD ISN'T QUITE RIGHT."

— LUNDY BANCROFT: WHY DOES HE DO THAT? INSIDE THE MINDS OF ANGRY AND CONTROLLING MEN

NONI

Mood stabilisers were prescribed as well as a care plan for his preferred counsellor. Dave began taking the new medication in conjunction with anti-depressants. He continued self-medicating with alcohol yet failed to make any counselling appointments. (Was he sleeping in the spare room? No, I'd laid down my role as 'enforcer'. It all got too hard, and I was too tired.)

Seems pills are far easier to take than being accountable for behaviour. I had gone way past the point of trying to monitor Dave's self-care. He needed to show me this was important to him and how serious he was about making the changes necessary for him to be well. I needed him to be a responsible adult that didn't require 'mothering' and I had to stop being the person who kept stepping in to make things right. The white flag well and truly flying now, I sat back and watched and waited…and watched and waited…

Ezekiel continued ignoring me. Anything I wanted or needed to communicate with him had to be done via Ruby whom he had never cut off. This triangular communication did my head in. Although unfair on everyone, the extra pressure on Ruby was especially tough.

During the previous twelve to eighteen months, Dave began reconnecting with Ezekiel, mainly on 'Ezekiel's terms'. Dave was desperate for Ezekiel to like him and strove to be his friend. Dave, the consummate chameleon, regressed to juvenile behaviour and the conversations of a teenager rather than step up to be the respected father Ezekiel needed, or the husband who loved and respected his wife, me, Ezekiel's mother. The lack of maturity absolutely infuriated me, particularly regarding Dave's relationship with Ezekiel.

The duality of the Dave we'd lived with for so many years peaked. Keeping me at a distance from Ezekiel served Dave well to win favour with his son, even if this meant, *being economical with the truth*. Dave would go and spend time with Ezekiel, buying him beers, food, shooting pool, and generally 'chewing the fat'. Just hanging out and seeking approval from our drug-addicted son. Not wanting to confront the truth or unacceptable behaviour, desiring to be with him regardless of alienating me further. The triangle of communication now extended to Dave as well as Ruby. I remained the she-devil, deserving no respect or back-up from the man who swore to love, honour, and cherish me so many years before.

An opportunity arose for me to give Ezekiel a lift home from work. His bargain-basement retail job a short drive from where he was living. A fifteen-minute window, my first chance to speak to him alone. Hardly the ride he would have chosen and I'm confident if he knew I was the only driver available, he'd have found another way.

He greeted me with stony silence and pure contempt in his eyes. Hatred and anger a physical force-shield between us. Attempting to cut through the density, my words fell on deaf ears.

He was interested in one thing only, "Who snitched? Who told you?" I answered that I would not give him a name, it wasn't important. He still couldn't or wouldn't acknowledge his part in the consequences of his actions. As I continued calmly and lovingly speaking to him, his anger didn't subside even one inch. One important question posed that I desperately wanted to be answered.

'Why had he cut me off so intently yet kept loose connections with Ruby and Dave when the decision to go to the police was a family one?'

I wanted to comprehend why, when we had a close relationship, he would he choose to make me the one to bear the brunt of his wrath and fury? It was a genuine question, one that was met with stone-cold silence. I told myself it was because he knew I would never withdraw my love for him, but I think he assumed this the ultimate betrayal. He was still too young to understand that turning him in was our last ditched effort to help him. All else failed, maybe we'd failed again.

After dropping him off, my phone rang as I drove away leaving.

Ezekiel had messaged Ruby asking if what I'd told him was true, she was calling to ask how she should reply. I said tell the truth. Ruby responded to him that she wasn't the 'parent' but yes, it was a family decision, and one she agreed was right. His response?

"That's what Noni said, but David tells a different story."

Ruby was furious.

"What the hell is Dad telling him?"

My heart sank.

Through Dave's need for validation, Ezekiel was most likely getting a lot of mixed messages.

Appealing to Dave, I explained how we may have some crossed lines and suggested that we arrange a meeting with Ezekiel together to clear up any misinformation. It would make sense for us all to hear the same message and do away with confusion and triangular conversations. Dave grew angry, accusing me of not trusting him or his version of their conversations.

His reaction, a definitive "NO".

His reasoning was that it would cause too much anxiety for Ezekiel. Ruby thought getting together would be helpful. Dave was resolute that this was a bad idea and it would be better for him to speak to Ezekiel alone. Once again, I was caught between two fires.

Was it our son who was chemically confused with what his dad had told him? Or was it Dave who liked to control and manage information to keep himself looking like the good guy? Another infuriating battle I had to lay down, albeit begrudgingly.

On one particular day when Dave was meeting up with Ezekiel, I asked two things of him. One, that he asks Ezekiel to unblock my number and allow me to communicate directly rather than via Dave or Ruby. Two, that Dave would not refer to me as 'Noni' when speaking to Ezekiel. Ezekiel had taken to referring to us by our Christian names, I suspect an attempt to broaden disconnection since it was probably easier to hurl abuse at someone you're not akin to. Perhaps a person feels less betrayed, rejected, or hurt by someone they don't consider family. Who knows?

While Dave was content with Ezekiel calling him David, I was not okay with being called Noni, and I took a stand. I owed this much to my own sense of identity and self-respect. In my heart, I am 'Mum' and always will be Mum to our children.

Dave arrived home jovial after seeing Ezekiel. Asking if he had managed to uphold my requests, to the best of my knowledge, he didn't refer to me as Noni. He either forgot or didn't get around to asking him to unblock my number. Apparently, the timing wasn't right, it wasn't appropriate.

∽

DAVE

The trauma of Ezekiel's estrangement affected every member of our family.

Desperate to see Ezekiel, I would regularly park outside the restaurant where he worked. Eagerly waiting, hoping to capture a glimpse of his ponytailed silhouette through the first-floor kitchen window. I prayed in vain that just once he would look out, see me, and maybe even acknowledge me. Seizing any opportunity over the coming years to re-establish contact with Ezekiel, whether taking him items, giving him a lift late after work, or helping him move, any excuse to gain access to our youngest. A library of abusive texts from Zeke on my phone served as a reminder of how tenuous the contact was. Taking such a conciliatory softly-softly approach with him while leaving his treatment of Noni unaddressed became a serious point of contention between us.

Some nights, I would wait up for a text message hoping he would accept my offer to pick him up from the late shift. The forty-minute drive to collect him from work was worth it, it might be the night of relational progress. One evening before dropping him home, we stopped at a nearby public bar, sharing a beer served on soggy coasters atop of sticky tables. Looking into his hollowed pale face filled me with regret. Maybe if we had handled things differently he wouldn't be in this state? At the time, he was defiant about his choice to sell drugs, going to the police was the right thing as it should shock him to his senses. We were wrong. It didn't, that was years ago and here we were. Opening my heart, I broke with the small talk. "Zeke, *I know you have your reasons to be angry with Mum and me, we did what we thought was right at the time and I am incredibly sorry for how this has turned out. I just wish it had been different.*" His response was as cold and flat as my beer.

The nature of my contact with Ezekiel, regardless of his abuse towards his mother, was seen by Noni as a continuation of my people-pleasing, wanting to be the good guy at all costs.

A serial conflict avoider with a history of compromising myself to please others or gain acceptance, it was easy to assume these were my motivations. Although Noni offered Ezekiel the same assistance, her attempts were met with ongoing hostility. In turn, I avoided confronting Ezekiel on his treatment of us, and in particular, Noni. Quick to jump to Ezekiel's defence, I relegated Noni to the status of 'just another person'. Failing to support my wife in this way built resentment and conflict between us for years.

Each occasion to be in contact with our son gradually 'desensitised' him to being near me. I hoped our connection might build a pathway into our lives regularly, as well as meet my yearning to be in his company. I often put myself in the position of placating or negotiating with Ezekiel as I was driven by the fear of losing all contact with him again. I also suffered a degree of guilt over his declining health and active addiction. Erring on the side of trying to make him comfortable, meeting on his terms, the best I could insist on was that he remain civil towards Noni. In pursuing my relationship with Ezekiel, I alienated Noni, sending her the message that I didn't support her.

~

NONI

During Dave and Ezekiel's reconciliation, I stayed in the background. There are over 300 messages of love and support for Ezekiel on my phone. He may not have read any, but it didn't prevent me from sending them. Sometimes nothing more than, "Hey Zeke, thinking of you. I hope you're well." Other times I kept him updated on how his grandparents were doing, what was happening in the extended family, and often simply to encourage him on his journey.

I also wrote him numerous letters; I needed a heartfelt link:

NOV 2014 (six weeks after he left home, he was living on the streets, couch surfing, etc.)

> *Hey, my darling boy, you not being here has left a huge hole in my heart and such heaviness of spirit. I don't only mean your physical absence, but your emotional distance, though the real you hasn't been present for a long time.*
>
> *I want so much for you to see yourself how we all see you. I ache for you to value your true worth and act accordingly, responding to the truth, not reacting to the pain and hurt inflicted upon you. I want you to be able to tear down the walls you put up trying to protect yourself. I want you to be OK to ask for help and to reach out and receive help. You don't have to be tough.*
>
> *You faced hurdles beyond those of most people your age. They started as young as ten when we chose to make the financial decision to move you to a public school. This decision was based on the fact that we thought you were the most resilient of our three children. That decision is one we lived*

to regret. Our first priority when we were
financially able was to send you straight
back to ******. Although we managed this
four years later, it still seemed too late...
Your Dad struggled with personality issues for
many years and this has been extremely
difficult to live with for us all, but it
impacted on you heavily. Maybe I didn't
take a tough stand early enough and you
can blame me for not shielding you all from
his behaviours. The truth is I have been
bamboozled by them for many years myself.
His Jekyll and Hyde personality is a tricky
pattern to negotiate...I tried, failed, tried
again and again and I'm still not sure how
much we've achieved.
Losing Tom... devastating beyond belief.
Add our financial ruin to the mix and to top it
off Ruby's chronic fatigue and then Dad's
cancer.
Any one of these hurdles is enough for most
people. We as a family have been smashed.
Why? No idea, all I'm sure of is every time
I'm knocked down, I will get up again, and
to me, that is winning!
Zeke, you can leave home, that's fine, but the
circumstances you do it under are
important.
Every choice you make carries a consequence.
You must own both the choice and the
consequence. I have no regret with how I

dealt with the decisions I made; I can put my hand on my heart and believe what I did was in your best interests. You can hate me for turning you in to the police, but one day I hope you may see it as a turning point that prevented you from screwing up the rest of your life.

So, I'm going to tell you what it feels like for me, losing you like this, though I know it's the right thing. I miss you. I've missed you for a long time. I miss your jokes, your laughter, your smile your sense of fun. I miss your gentleness, your deep insight into many issues. I really really miss watching you have fun. I miss having you around, I miss your face, I miss your heart. I miss your company. Most of the time I am OK, but when I think of you wandering, trying to find a bed, trying to find company, trying to find where you 'fit', my heart breaks for you and I cry. All I want for you is to be safe and at peace, I want you to believe you have a great future and I want you to have deep hope in your heart. A hope no circumstance can shake. You are such a deep thinker, you are creative, talented, personable. Ruby misses you too. Please don't shut her out, don't turn your back on her. She loves you and has done nothing wrong. She only wants what is

good for you. P.S. I don't miss your
mess. Xxx

JUNE 2017

Hey Zeke,
I'm writing this for one reason only, because I
love you. Nothing more, nothing less.
Nothing you do or don't do will with ever
alter my love for you.
I want only what is best for you though you
are finding this hard to believe right now.
You are such a treasure; you think deep, and
you feel deep. You are creative, you are
exceptional, you have humour, you are
witty, but you are so beautifully
compassionate.
God has created you as he intended, you are
more than enough.
If I could take away your pain, hurt and
disappointment I would in a nanosecond,
but these things are part of our broken
world which we have the power to
overcome.
My heart aches to be able to guide you through
these trials.
Your future is great, life is not always easy, but
it is worth it.
We cannot rejoice on the mountain top unless
we know what it is to be in the valley, the

*climb out of the valley can be a long hard
road but if we persevere, we will get there!
You are more than a conqueror Zeke, I love you
champ. xxx*

*Then there was one I wrote which came off the
back of an extremely hurtful barrage from
him where he told me to F*^% `## and that
he had a loving mother who would never do
to him what I did... At the time he was
living with a friend of his whose young
mother had a different outlook on life to me,
she was a 'cool mum'. He had taken to
calling her 'Mum', and this was my
tipping point...*

JUNE 20, 2017

*I cannot begin to understand the feeling of
hatred you entertain inside of you. You
prefer to allow the loathing to fester rather
than make peace. Holding onto hatred and
anger is like poisoning your soul. It is
impossible to find the freedom to live a full
life while you remain so hostile. You want
to hurt me. You've succeeded. Leeanne is
not your loving mother. Wake up to
yourself Ezekiel, enough is enough. You
want to hold onto the fact that the worst
thing done to you was turning you into the
police for selling drugs under our roof!
Seriously, move on. That was your chance*

*to NOT end up in the state you're in
now... You've made the choices that
determined your health and well-being.
You still have every opportunity to change,
everyone deserves a second chance, even
me. When your misery is greater than your
fear maybe you'll take that chance. Dad
told me you've blocked my number so you
probably won't read this, but on the slim
chance you do, I'm here for you, always
have been always will.
Continually praying you find the help you
need, love Mum x*

And this text message;

NOV 20, 2017

Hey Buddy, I heard you've blocked my
number, I live in hope you'll see my
message. I had a dream last night and I
never dream, or if I do, I rarely
remember them but this one was so clear
and so uplifting. I dreamt we were in a
room with other people, it felt like a
salon and you had gotten to a place
where you tolerated being in the same
room as me. All of a sudden you got up
and ran towards me pushing others out
of the way to reach me, then wrapped
your arms around me and hugged me so
tightly while I held you. You sobbed

NONI YATES & DAVID YATES

and after a while, you stood back
relaxed and calm, you were so soft
gentle and peaceful.

My heart is full of this image xxx I
love you so much, Mum

I held on tightly. At times, my desperation became
unbearable, not much comes close to the agony of
walking this line.

There are literally hundreds more written in the same
vein...such was my hope for complete reconciliation.

LESSONS FROM BEYOND

LIFE DOESN'T STOP WHEN TOSSED THESE CURVEBALLS.

AS MUCH AS IT WOULD BE EASY TO CURL UP AND SURRENDER, WE HAVE THE FREEDOM TO CHOOSE HOW WE RESPOND TO ANYTHING HURLED AT US.

I HAVE A CHOICE, I CHOOSE TO RESPOND WITH FAITH, HOPE AND LOVE.

NOT BECAUSE I FEEL IT, BUT BECAUSE I WANT TO, ALWAYS.

LOVE IS A DECISION.

WHETHER WE 'FEEL' IT OR EVEN FEEL LIKE 'DOING' IT, IS NOT THE POINT.

CHAPTER 14

COUNTING THE LOSSES

NONI

My parents live two and a half hours drive north of us.

Dad began declining in health, and in 2016 when Mum was no longer able to care for him, he was admitted to full-time nursing. We made a point of visiting as much as possible. Understanding how precious time is with our parents, Dave was amazing during this period. Accompanying me on many a trip, he also made it easy for me to go alone.

Dad was a quiet man of great wisdom with a skilful intellect. He was mentally alert to the end; it was his body that failed him on June 5, 2018. Why do these calls always come in the dead of night? Oblivious to which piece of doom would greet me, I reached for the mobile on the bedside drawer. Dad was in ICU after an aortic aneurism erupted. He'd passed away.

Dad had been in hospital with bilateral pneumonia, was recovering well, and doctors planned on sending him home the next day. At seventy-nine with varying health issues, his directive was 'do not resuscitate'. A nurse, unaware of the directive, hit the call button and began resuscitation.

Beautiful oversight on her behalf. Mum had the chance to arrive at hospital before Dad's life support was removed. Though ventilated and unresponsive, as Mum leant over to kiss him goodbye, the flat line declaring the end of this mighty man's life spiked. Dad took his last breath on earth knowing the bride of his youth was with him. Mum by his side until the end.

Fifty-five years married, not all wedded bliss, they rode out the tough times and celebrated the good. Our loss that winter's morning was heaven's gain.

Dave was in Sydney working, Ruby contacted Ezekiel and we collected him on our way to be with the rest of the family at hospital. Ezekiel, dark as the night toward me, was pleasant to everyone else. Drinking heavily in the absence of other substances, I tried talking with him, again to no avail. Dad's passing my priority, I let Ezekiel be. The quality of time spent with Dad in months leading up to this event taught me precious lessons. Live in the moment, live with gratitude, prioritise time doing what's most important. Relationship not regret. Now is all we have to make our moments count!

In winter and spring of 2018 were milestone birthdays for our two sons. Corey was thirty and Ezekiel twenty-one. We began planning a family holiday in Bali to celebrate both boys. Everyone was gladly accepting invitations. Ezekiel filtered a message to Dave and me via Ruby, asking if he could invite a girlfriend which then extended to her partner. Almost twenty-one, a heavy substance abuser in poor health with little regard for anything, Ezekiel was still our beautiful son. Caught up in a world of pain and addiction. He was never a lost cause. We prayed for him, interceded for him, and substituted his name in scriptures, declaring victory over his life.

Faith can appear futile to those without hope, but we refused to give up. I approached this fight like a lioness, Dave concurred, though he was slightly more subdued. This was a spiritual battle. With iron-clad determination, I never stopped believing that God would make a way through this fire. With a close girlfriend, we waged war against an enemy we knew.

The enemy, not Ezekiel but the influence of spiritual darkness!

> 12 For our struggle is not against flesh and blood, but against the rulers, against the authorities, against the powers of this dark world and against the spiritual forces of evil in the heavenly realms.

> — EPHESIANS 6:12 NEW INTERNATIONAL VERSION
> (NIV)

Blanketed by darkness as deep as the ocean, a place convinced light could never shine, I continued believing in a breakthrough for Ezekiel the same way I held onto hope for Dave. When life looks bleak, when black clouds are all we can see, we must dig deep and call into being that which is not obvious to the eye. Faith is confidence in what we hope for, and assurance that God is working even though we cannot see it.

My journal entry at the time reveals how broken I was:

> *Aching, heavy heart,*
> *Loss, distance,*
> *Every day is a choice to go on,*
> *Move forward, release the abuse*
> *It is not my love talking.*
> *The words are from a stranger whose delusion*
>   *ensnares him,*
> *The unwelcome intruder*
> *Deceiving his mind,*
> *In another world, an altered state of thought,*
> *A distorted sense of reality,*
> *All of this, I know..*
> *Still,*
> *I grieve, my heart is heavy, so so heavy,*
> *Lord, please lift this burden from me today*

Throughout Ezekiel's estrangement, he asked nothing from us. Survival instinct kicked in and he fast became streetwise to support his choices. Deserving of great admiration during the absent years was his accomplishment of gaining the title as a qualified chef. I always imagined him suited to a hands-on creative career, but chef? Oh my, the best he managed at home was a bowl of Nutri-Grain. Though surprised, the title suits him perfectly. Ezekiel hasn't made it easy for himself, but then the apple doesn't fall far from the cart. Independent, stubborn, determined, all characteristics Mum and Dad possess. We commend him for bloody-minded grit and determination.

The month before our Bali birthday bash Ezekiel moved home, arranging this with Dave.

Our new housemate took up residence bereft of discussing reconciliation boundaries, forgiveness, or expectations. Ezekiel was moving to Melbourne. His goal for bunking in with us was to save money. How convenient.

He left home at seventeen, a heavy substance user, dark, angry, disrespectful and entitled.

His arrival home heralding the same presence, just a few years older. Dave was stoked to have his son home, me, less than thrilled. I bore the brunt of Ezekiel and Dave's disrespect. The chaos and manipulation accompanying addiction is horrendous. Needless to say, it didn't make for a happy household. I'll leave it there because that's a whole other story.

CHAPTER 15

THE STRAW THAT BROKE THE CAMEL'S BACK!

NONI

Since stepping off that first Garuda flight in 1983, I was in love with Bali. Nostril searing heat and humidity that caused beads of sweat to form on my forehead, underarms, and back before I could acclimatise was a welcome reprieve after the winter chill of Canberra. Thin trails of incense smoke arose from burnt offerings scattered roadside, and the persistent honking of motorbikes issued warning signals to pedestrians and other vehicles. Soulful eyes and smiles wide as east is to west, Balinese people captured my heart. The pungency of open drains was overshadowed by the aroma of spices wafting from warungs, signalling meal preparation. I fell in love with everything. Bali has always been my healing place, though this holiday lacked the serenity and peace I usually appreciated on the island of the gods.

The intensity of Ezekiel's contempt for me (and himself) was evident with his withdrawal. His use of dangerous amounts of alcohol and Valium created an atmosphere best described as ugly and tense. Every so often, there were glimpses of light, but the general mood was dense, dark, and heavy. Adding to this, Dave was more concerned about being liked by Ezekiel as a friend rather than respected as a father. My fifty-seven-year-old partner acted just as juvenile as the two twenty-one-year-old boys holidaying with us. He sat up with them until all hours, drinking and generally talking absolute rubbish. Not once did Dave lead by example. He joined in with the boys. There was nothing about this I found remotely attractive and therefore preferred to keep my distance.

Corey and his companions sourced villas of their own, preferring a rather luxe experience compared to the rustic Bale-style accommodation the rest of us shared.

Two nights before our holiday ended, Dave and I received an upgrade to a private pool villa.

Ezekiel and Dave sat in the pool facing each other. I sat to the side. They were engrossed in conversation, excluding the third person nearby. Me. I tried in vain to contribute, but any attempt made was largely ignored so I remained quiet. Their discussion was about buying real estate, selling items, the move to Melbourne, etc. Beers were consumed but it was a relatively quiet few hours. The topic of conversation moved to whether Ezekiel would take his TV to Melbourne or not. Dave suggested he sell it and buy another once he had settled in Melbourne. Ezekiel said he didn't have the remote for the TV. Wayne might have taken it, or Mum may have moved it. I sat there stunned as Dave kept breezing through the conversation without so much as batting an eyelid. Totally engaged and focused on Ezekiel and self, he didn't flinch at Ezekiel referring to Leeanne as Mum, nor did he say, "Why don't you check with Mum? She's right there."

My heart absolutely sank. I felt as if I was witnessing a stage show of my entire life.

The curtains were finally fully opened, revealing the truth of my reality. Beyond a shadow of a doubt, Dave did not have my back; he had never had my back. Operating true chameleon style, the person he wanted to impress the most receiving his full focus and attention. He was intently engaged with Ezekiel, needing our son to like, validate, and approve of him. I sat there numb, understanding once and for all Ezekiel had no chance of respecting me. His own father didn't respect me.

Everything reached a critical juncture at that moment. Although this may seem an insignificant oversight or small slip up, in the scheme of things it was, in fact, the straw that broke the camel's back. One thing I had asked of Dave during his communication with Ezekiel was to please never refer to me as Noni. I was Mum and asked Dave to support me, Dave gave me his word, agreeing to be mindful.

NONI YATES & DAVID YATES

I said nothing at the time, saving it for later. Before Ezekiel joined us for dinner that evening, I took the opportunity of mentioning my disappointment. Dave denied hearing Ezekiel say any such thing. It bothered me tremendously that he could recall every other minute detail of their conversations. Left flabbergasted, it was blatantly obvious in their exchange who Ezekiel was referring to. Whether Dave did or didn't hear, whether it was deliberate avoidance or an oversight, I could not depend on him to keep his word nor prioritise what was important to me and ultimately us. We were on completely different pages. Something inside of me died.

We survived a dysfunctional two weeks, trying to connect as best we could without a great deal of success. Returning home, I unravelled my thoughts and wrestled with an impending decision. I knew I couldn't go on this way. I'd done everything within my ability to keep this family intact.

On 28 August 2018, the day Ezekiel left and moved to Melbourne, I told Dave our relationship had come to the end of the road. Our marriage was over. Like my decision to leave Corey's father in 1990, I told no one. I had no plan, no roadmap to follow, no GPS of how I would manage on my own. I'd primarily been a homemaker for twenty-five years, but I didn't care. My pain exceeded my fear. I couldn't continue. I was done.

Write it down and make it clear,

— HABAKKUK 2:2

The following letters were written to Ezekiel and Dave.

I didn't want there to be any mistake about how far I'd been pushed.

> *Dear Ezekiel,*
> *I hope you've settled into your new*
>   *environment; an exciting new beginning*
>   *and one I trust will be all you wish for it*
>   *to be.*
> *I wanted to send this on your day off but I'm*
>   *not sure when that might be, and you need*
>   *to hear what I'm about to say. Firstly, you,*
>   *Ruby and Corey mean the world to me, my*
>   *love for you all is indescribable,*
>   *unconditional and I'm very proud of you*
>   *all. I also really loved having you home and*
>   *want to encourage you to keep going well*
>   *and doing your best.*
> *The tears I cried before you left were not*
>   *because you were leaving and even though*
>   *I wished for more healing, connection and*
>   *reconciliation with you, you're doing*
>   *exactly what you should be doing at your*
>   *age, I left Canberra for Darwin as soon as I*
>   *finished my apprenticeship at 18, I'm*
>   *happy for you.*

*I was actually upset because in recent days I
had made one of the biggest decisions of my
life. I decided I no longer wanted to remain
married to Dad. Although I've accepted for
years, it became painfully clear to me in
recent times we view things very
differently, and when it comes to core
values and respect, Dad and I are on
different pages.*

*Over the years both Dad and you treated me
poorly. Mental and emotional health issues
and drug or alcohol abuse are conditions
people can overcome, but, as you're aware,
only if the person affected wants to. I'm
drawing the line for myself and saying
enough is enough. I'm not blaming anyone;
I'm simply saying it is my decision not to
put up with it any longer.*

*Please understand this decision is not your
'fault' nor is it Dads, and in no way is
anything you've done or said responsible
for my choice. Sure, it's hurt, but I own
that hurt and can recognise and address
that, it's mine to deal with as I choose, and
I choose forgiveness and peace.*

*Sometimes no matter how much you love
someone patterns of behaviour erode one's
spirit and leave you depleted and
emotionally drained. Dad and I battled for
many years to stay buoyant in our*

*relationship but it's reached a point where
I'm empty and have nothing left to give.*

*So, like you've needed a father to look up to,
I've needed a husband I can trust and
depend on. Repeatedly I'm left frustrated,
confused, bewildered and disappointed in
the complacency Dad displays, and his
behaviours of anger, aggression, arrogance,
sarcasm, duality, undermining, haughty
and obnoxious or withdrawn, sullen and
disengaged. Sometimes jovial, humorous,
kind and tender...and a desire to make
change.*

*However, words not backed up by action are
nothing but empty promises and there's far
too much of this in our marriage.*

*I'm happy and open for you to talk to me at
any time about this or anything else you
want to talk about.*

*Thank you for letting us meet Daisy, she's a
beautiful girl. I don't know her well, but I
do know you and can tell you care for her
very much, it was lovely to see. I hope
things work out for her. Thank you for
calling Nanna, this lifted her spirits.*

*I love you dearly and am your Mum, I will
always be your Mum and I thank God for
that every day Xxx*

To Dave:
The things I love
I love that we created beautiful children
together, that we hold so many treasured
memories of special times and our strong
bond with each other.
I love that you do possess a soft and gentle
depth that I am sometimes allowed to see.
I love preparing healthy meals for you and
enjoying them together.
I love it when we communicate on a deep level.
I love that we've established some amazing
homes together.
We share a love of good food.
We share our love of travel and adventure.
I love sitting in bed with our morning tea and
coffee, that you support me and allow my
voluntary pursuits.
Always been a great provider, you have a
strong work ethic.
I'm eternally appreciative that you accept and
love Corey and Charlie as part of our
family.
You're generous with finances.
We've built a good level of comfort together.
You've been proactive in planning a financially
secure retirement.
We've supported each other through much loss,
grief and hardship.
I love you, always have, always will.

And even though
I've stood by you and forgiven multiple
*   infidelities,*
I've stood by you and supported you through
*   job loss.*
I've stood by you and supported you through
*   financial ruin.*
I've stood by you and supported you through
*   serious illness and mental health issues.*
I've addressed and faced issues front on, I've
*   not hidden nor pretended that they didn't*
*   exist, I've not backed away from difficult*
*   challenges.*
I'm far from perfect but,
I've devoted myself to our married life, to
*   nurturing our family, tried to share and*
*   encourage a spirituality. The relationship*
*   with our God I deem the most important*
*   relationship we will ever trust and need.*
*   Setting my moral compass on the written*
*   word of God I haven't always gotten it*
*   'right', but my true north is stable.*
I've created a warm home life and been 100%
*   faithful and loyal throughout our twenty-*
*   eight years together. Never once wavering*
*   in complete support of you and your career,*
*   my priority, maintaining a secure home*
*   base for you and our children to come*
*   home to.*
None of the previously mentioned 'mistakes' or

situations left a mark on me compared to the invisible scars, disappointment, hurt and frustration of too many years bearing the brunt of disrespect, anger, inappropriate and passive-aggressive behaviour and underhanded abuse

whether it be opening and eating the whole box of Mum's Belgian chocolates, roping in Ezekiel to take the blame calling my father a 'coward' or leaving me to sleep in a ***** ****** bed while you disappear without so much as dealing with it or having the courage to fess up, or you take photos of me naked, even though just a glimpse of my thigh and not explicit, it's my flesh and you took it without my knowledge then showed it to a dear male friend, what kind of a person does this?

I've addressed and confronted all of these and much more, the majority of the time my efforts are met with a total deflection or justification. And then 'sorry'.

As inappropriate as these behaviours, attitudes and incidents are, they are best left in the past, however, you continue to find more ways to damage the connection and bond between us.

I don't make a habit of revisiting unpleasant incidents, I only list them to remind us both that I really don't walk away easily,

*you and I are the only ones with insight
into the full extent and truth of everything
our relationship endured.*

*Maybe I am at fault for not getting to this
conclusion sooner, and I am truly sorry if
this impeded your own personal growth.*

*But this is now… and this may or may not be
beneficial moving forward.*

*I am done with being undermined; from early
days of you sneaking rice bubbles into a
three-year-old Ruby behind my back.*

*Or you pulling faces and making smart
comments with Ezekiel behind my back to
you blatantly overriding a joint family
agreement regarding Ezekiel's flights to
Melbourne… I am done with disrespect
and manipulation and misdirected
overreactive anger.*

*I won't tolerate abuse in any form, not a foul
look, a foul mouth, profanity nor an
underhanded snide remark, the sorrys don't
make up for the scars left behind eroding
my self-esteem.*

I won't live with the angry smile.

*I'm done with doublemindedness and your
people-pleasing ways.*

*I deserve a husband who respects himself
enough so I can respect him too.*

*A husband who will be a strong dependable
father first and a friend to his children*

second, a father they can look up to and
respect, one who knows how to set clear
boundaries and expectations and is not
afraid to enforce them.
I deserve a solid stable consistent husband who
learned to overcome his fears and can tame
his anxieties and tongue, a man who's not
afraid of the truth (none of this being
'economical with the truth' rubbish), one
who can assert authority with love, not
aggression.
I deserve a man of integrity and of good
character who does not change with the
wind or with those he is with, we need a
man who is true to his word so we can
trust him, and we all know what to expect.
I have no desire for a people-pleasing
chameleon.
I deserve a mature marriage at fifty-three and if
I can't, then I'd rather not have one at all,
and this is the place I'm at.
I still have a great deal of love for you and wish
nothing but the best for you.
Only time will tell if you are serious about
being the man I believe you can be, with or
without me xxx

I spoke to Corey and Ruby individually, letting them in on my decision. I also gave them the letter written to Ezekiel, so they saw exactly what had been communicated. They, more than anyone, understood how our family dynamic operated, both agreeing it was clear and fair.

Ruby verbalised her lack of surprise saying she had been expecting this day would come for many years. Dave, astonishingly, felt "blindsided".

CHAPTER 16

REALITY BITES REALLY HARD

DAVE

ugust 28, 2018, the day my best friend, love of my life, mother of my children and person I wanted to grow old with, tearfully told me,

"Our relationship is at the end of the road; I can't do this anymore."

I was distraught at the prospect of being separated from Noni. Our relationship had been rocky for years. I had hoped our marriage would magically improve with time. Hoping this was just another phase, I begged Noni to give us another chance. I could make it better again (like I had all the other times).

Noni's decision to draw the line and stick to it was the beginning of a road to transformation that neither of us could have imagined.

Spiralling out of control from words that filled me with dread; grief hit me like never before.

In rapid succession, I cycled through remorse, anger, melancholy, rage, hopelessness and defiance making way for erratically inconsistent behaviour. Significant changes had to be made if there was any chance of restoring our marriage. Though efforts were made, the emotional crutches false beliefs and soothing habits I'd relied on my entire life were about to get a major work-out. Quickly and easily, I assumed the role of victim – a familiar and comfortable part I had often played when relationships became difficult and I wanted to avoid responsibility.

Editing the complex cycle of emotional distancing, anger, hyper control and exaggerated compensation down to; 'I can be difficult to live with, have issues with anxiety and anger, but still want my marriage. Noni doesn't.' This misrepresentation of the truth which had worn out my wife and children for decades was a convenient truth for me.

Googling what to do when separating, the first popu-lated answer was to change passwords on bank accounts! The more I read, the more defensive and suspicious I became of Noni's motives and actions. I began using finances as a weapon to exert power over Noni. I withheld the new password to our account for several weeks while I opened another account and had part of my salary paid into it. I tried in vain to find a sense of control and independence. My motivation was not about gaining financial advantage. Rather, it was to control what I could and retaliate where I could. My thinking, 'If you want a future life without me, then this is what it might look like.'

A counsellor I had been seeing sporadically over the years who was familiar with my story was a starting point. Naively, I wanted to be 'fixed' so I could stay married. Despite wanting to 'get better', I was still trying to exert control wherever I could and was being selective with the truth in my counselling sessions by representing Noni's reasons for separation dishonestly, portraying her in a less than favourable light. Professionally counselled to limit 'comfort' contact with Noni during our separation, I applied the advice out of context, using it as a weapon, ignoring Noni or purposely delaying responses to routine issues. Every response was intended to inflict inconvenience or attempt to regain control and power in a situation where I felt helpless, hopeless, and angry. Lashing out in reaction to the pain of having to feel grief, rather than act as a healthy adult. Seeking a way to soothe my suffering at the expense of my wife.

I was a long way from being in good health.

Desperately defending the facade which was crumbling around me, my actions and interactions with Noni in the coming months validated her decision. I, convincing myself how unfair this situation was, filtering everything through a lens of injustice. Any admission of error on my part would always be accompanied by a subtle explanation or excuse. Admitting, yet minimising my responsibility wherever possible. Knee-jerk responses, not calculated nor conscious, a result of habitual defence mechanisms built over a lifetime.

The prospect of losing my marriage and quite likely our family challenged my entire world.

My purpose, identity, and self-worth were all at stake. I simply did not want a future without Noni, though I quickly started considering what might it look like.

I tried to reassure myself of how capable and resourceful I had been in the past and that I would have enough time to build 'another' life, this could be a 'new beginning for me'. These platitudes provided a momentary distraction from the agony I was desperately trying to avoid. On the right day, if I tried hard enough, I could conjure an image of a rosy future after my marriage, but these scenarios were paper thin and without substance. All these exercises were vain attempts to comfort myself with alternate possibilities for my future.

A work trip took me to regional Victoria. I made a detour to the surf coast reasoning that work commitments were fulfilled and I wasn't needed home before any particular time or day. This was a chance to retrace an area that held fond memories from my early twenties. Taking advantage of my new freedom meant I could have this short surf adventure. Driving through the spectacular countryside in the warmth of spring sun, the elements were aligning. My destination in mind, I was full of anticipation. Out of nowhere, I was hit with excruciating sadness and grief. Tears welled up as I pulled the car to the side of the road. My body shuddered and deep-burning groans escalated to loud howling. I was sobbing uncontrollably, almost screaming. Relief was sudden, for in that moment, I embraced true, raw, emotion. In the coming months, similar cathartic episodes repeated themselves without warning. They were moments of authenticity amid chaos and confusion.

I made the mistake of not actively staying in contact with any trusted friends from our marriage. I reasoned they were there to support Noni and I should find my own way. After all, I was the problem. Isolating myself from people who knew Noni's heart and our relationship and history was a bad decision. Perhaps I was fearful of the insights they could offer. Maybe I wanted to avoid the loss of face. It was highly likely I would have reacted defensively, interpreting helpful input as judgment. Either way, removing myself from the familiarity of friends and family placed me in a precarious position. Little access to wise counsel left me choosing instead to ride the roller coaster of my emotions. Each conversation, text, or email from Noni replayed inside my bubble of mistrust and defensiveness.

The people I chose to confide in were visibly shocked when I told them of our separation.

Only having intermittent contact with us since our wedding, a distant memory of the deliriously happy young bride and groom afforded them no clear picture of the current state of our relationship.

In 2017, an ex-work colleague relocated from New Zealand to the Gold Coast. Nancy was a single woman in her early forties who had lived overseas, travelled extensively and pursued outdoor interests.

We began working together in 2010, maintaining inter-mittent contact via email or text after she left the company in 2014 to travel. Like my other co-workers, I enjoyed her company and found it easy to strike up a friendship. Unlike my other co-workers though, I chose to keep this friendship hidden from Noni. Details of Nancy and our interactions were never shared with Noni the same way other colleagues were. After Nancy returned to Australia, we occasionally caught up over coffee and would chat via phone every few months. Although I had no intention of pursuing a romantic involvement with her, I chose to keep everything about this friendship my little secret. (In hindsight, I recognise the danger of my thinking, it wasn't my intention to pursue romantic involvement with the others either. However, intention alone was never enough to stop me.) This secrecy was completely consistent with me keeping a compartment for myself that was separate from our marriage. I didn't wish to give up my interactions with Nancy. They made me feel appreciated and special, and bringing the relationship to the light of day might expose my own selfish motives. In late 2018 Nancy contacted me. She found herself out of work and asked if I knew of any opportunities.

I had my own news of upheaval to share, and as it turned out, Nancy was living just ten minutes away. Having such a narrow window into my relationship, she was naturally sympathetic towards my situation. We both had spare time, enjoyed each other's company and now that I had isolated myself, I began contacting her most weeks. Whether meeting up for a coffee or swim at the beach, time spent with her was a welcome relief from isolation.

Keeping company with a sympathetic and attractive woman also helped soothe my rampant insecurity.

During counselling sessions my therapist expressed concern about how my 'friendship' with Nancy was developing. I assured her I had no intentions of crossing the line into a sexual relationship, it was a complication I could do without and it would have no future. However, this wasn't her point, it was her attempt to highlight my tendency to manipulate people and situations. Missing the mark completely, I continued being selective with facts and taking guidance as it suited. I made the decision to offer Nancy a loan of $1000, figuring this was a noble gesture in her time of uncertainty and financial hardship. At the same time, my behaviour was less than noble where finances with Noni – my wife of twenty-five years--- were concerned.

It made me feel good to be a rescuer when Nancy needed help. I rewarded her 'kindness', toward me, yet where possible, used finances to exercise control and inflict discomfort upon Noni.

Payback for the feeling of rejection.

CHAPTER 17

IF IT DOESN'T RAIN IT POURS

NONI

Informing Dave of my decision brought no relief. How does one end something they fully believed was *till death do us part*? My heart, head, and body ached, eyes raw from crying, and although unclear of how our future looked, confidence in my decision remained.

An hour after speaking with Dave, my mobile buzzed, piercing the gloomy silence which had befallen our home. Mum was on her way to hospital, her condition critical, my personal crisis temporarily shelved to attend to hers. The next two months were all-consuming.

Juggling Mum's health with multiple trips to Brisbane until surgery ensured she was well enough to leave the hospital. One of her procedures sent her into cardiac arrest three times.

Life was hectic.

While my focus was on Mum's health, Dave focused on himself. His present actions were consistent with the past and not surprising. I let it go. One moment he told me he would do everything to make sure we could keep the house and I thanked him tearfully and expressed this meant a lot. He spoke these words to my face, but behind my back he was busying himself to make sure he controlled the finances if he was unable to control me. I knew what Dave was capable of and this could get ugly. My priority was Mum, I had no choice but to trust him to act honourably.

Dave called from Sydney; our conversation didn't end well. A new bank card arrived for him in the mail. Asking if he applied for one, he said yes. I questioned why, he said he would need one when he moved out for paying rent, etc. Left a little confused, we'd had no discussion of how we would move forward.

I told him honestly that I didn't know how to navigate this transition, nor had I thought too far ahead, Mum had to come first. (After Dave moved out, I found account and BSB numbers scribbled on a piece of scrap paper in the office. Suspecting these may be details for the new card, I made a note, filing the information should the need arise to find out what he was doing with our money. He began changing passwords to our online accounts, blocking me from checking any of our finances.)

Dave turned the conversation to the letter I gave Ezekiel, suggesting I was cutting Ezekiel off, that I was distancing myself and withdrawing my love. His perception of what I'd written was far from my intention. I didn't believe Ezekiel would interpret my words the same way Dave did.

After showing the letter to his counsellor, she surmised it was emotionally manipulative and controlling. For the life of me, I couldn't understand how she made this deduction. Suspecting though, Dave only allowed her to see partial content. I've since found my suspicions correct. It was another attempt by Dave to try and manipulate a situation to his advantage. Even though Ezekiel wanted nothing to do with me, my mother's heart believed we still had an unbreakable bond, albeit transparently thin. Our phone call ended with Dave becoming aggressive, abusive, and hanging up on me. Minutes later, he called with an apology, blaming his anxiety as the cause for the outburst. I was sitting alone in my car in the middle of a shopping centre carpark. Left traumatised, my face flooded with tears, lungs gasping for air, I was desperate to find support. Thank God for Google. Dialling a helpline for carers dealing with mental health issues, a lovely woman listened to my story. Quietly attentive, respectful of my grief, gently advising me to call the domestic violence hotline.

What I described to her, whether Dave was Bipolar or had depression or anxiety or not, constituted emotionally abusive behaviour. The psychologist on the other end of the phone confirmed what Ezekiel's counsellors and Ruby, our young adult daughter, had deduced years ago, Dave was an emotionally abusive man.

Dave came home from Sydney and moved out. I couldn't bring myself to be in the house when he did. My choice to spend a couple of days with Corey meant Ruby was left at home while her father packed a bag and departed. This was hard on them both, I was too fragile to handle it.

Dave continued in therapy with his counsellor, and one day, he and I agreed to meet, our first catchup since he'd left the house. Should I pay for my Kombucha? Does he? Whose money is it? For almost twenty-five years, it was 'we' and 'us'. What were we now? This was one of the most uncomfortable times I remember ever having with Dave. Aloof, quite strange, he was extremely detached. Grabbing our drinks, we walked across the road to the beach and sat on a bench in the park. In a cocky tone, he mentioned he'd been speaking to people. They were completely shocked we had separated and offered support and thoughts for Dave to make sense of our separation.

"Maybe I was menopausal," "Having an identity crisis," and then absolute gold from his counsellor; my behaviour, she estimated, was emotionally abusive and I had sought to pathologise him to satisfy my own short-comings. Of course, she deduced this from information fed to her. I sat listening, saying very little. There was nothing to say.

An added bonus from his counsellor was a suggestion that he might need to have his physical needs met, but to just run it by your wife first! Since when has this bit of psychology done anyone any good?

Particularly someone who is confused as all getup and has recently come out of a twenty-five-year marriage and is of Christian faith! I left the park dreadfully uneasy. Who was this complete stranger?

My journal entry:

> *I can now appreciate the suggestion by both specialists that minimising any unnecessary contact is a positive boundary for both me and Dave. I'm sitting quietly, reflecting upon how I feel after catching up with Dave on Sunday. I can honestly say I was coping a lot better for not having contact. I felt uneasy in Dave's presence. Alone I have peace, calm and confidence.*
> *The reactive responses to correspondence and contact since separating is further evidence that I've made the right decision, the best thing for us both. All of the interactions since separating have given greater clarity to my direction and the steps we are taking. The passive aggression, confusion and reactive anger is all that I'm removing myself from. Why have I been so invested in finding out the reasoning behind all of the mean, nasty, spiteful aggressive, and withdrawn*

behaviours, withholding of information,
half-truths, selective memory, duality, in
contrast to the sweet soft gentle side?

Trying to find reasons for the Jekyll and Hyde
mood swings. Could it be because I did not
want to accept the possibility of alternative
reasoning behind the confounding
personality? I was actually blind to the
truth?

Dave is a manipulative, abusive and
angry man.

The signs have been present all along. Surely
there has to be a medical reason for this.
Perhaps not, and this is what I now must
accept.

For many years, I encouraged. Best Counselling/Psychological outcomes are totally dependent on how transparent/vulnerable a client is prepared to be. Honest truth is at the core of success. Dave viewed many things through a distorted filter. He needed to maintain control in every situation, even counselling.

During this time I sought counsel from the dear couple who cared for Dave when he had his hiatus following the abusive episode in 2013. They were a safe, mature Christian couple who pass no judgement. They are strong in faith and walked a mile in many shoes. I trusted these people implicitly. They love Dave and I equally and understand the frailties of humanity. I needed their support.

From our moment of separation, Dave had zero contact with people who had been our friends over the fifteen years we'd lived in our coastal community. Disappearing up the coast he began catching up with old friends and acquaintances. None who possessed any insight into our situation or marriage nor had particularly healthy relationships themselves. This allowed him to create his own story, his own version of events, and to savour support from people manipulated into thinking their advice was helpful.

He would come down for a visit and call to chat, most often, this was pleasant. He continued counselling, his therapist advising him to limit the amount of unnecessary contact with me.

I agreed with her. It was too easy for us to be together. These visits and connection provided him with false comfort. Very unwise considering I determined our relationship done and dusted. I could see the pain in his face, my agreeing hurt him terribly. Although I loved him this wasn't healthy at all. It wasn't right to have the comfort of couple conversation when we were no longer a couple. Sadly, it went incredibly pear-shaped from here.

Dave took limiting unnecessary communication to an extreme level. He wouldn't reply to the simplest of questions, e.g. Could you please tell me how to back-wash the pool, I need to let water out? He began stonewalling me. Responding passive-aggressively if he chose to reply via email or text, often not bothering to reply at all. A blunt message received one day asking me who had changed the Netflix password piqued my curiosity. I certainly hadn't and no one else had access so I decided to check his viewing history. His 'continue watching' list included titles such as Nymphomaniac, Hot Girls Wanted and other sexually explicit movies he'd been viewing. This shocked me considerably. We've previously discussed what we consider appropriate viewing. Fearful I'd be accused of snooping; I filed this information away and said nothing.

This maddening time ended up quite costly. I had seen a solicitor for advice on how to go about moving forward. He suggested Dave and I speak to a therapist who assists couples navigating their way through a separation process. Author of the book Separating Respectfully, Lynne Clark's specialty is strengthening relationships to function in an adult manner, regardless of whether the marriage survived. Our financial settlement up for discussion, we needed mediation. Dave was not the slightest bit interested in seeing anyone, who, in his mind helped people separate.

Adamant, he would prefer receiving our settlement proposal in writing rather than sitting down and discussing it with me. On my instruction, the solicitor complied with Dave's request.

I'm not sure what Dave expected. When the legal document was emailed to him, he absolutely hit the roof. My phone lit up with a barrage of aggression. (This had less to do with the terms of settlement and more to do with six jarring words in the standard opening line, 'the marriage has irretrievably broken down'.)

Occurring on a balmy November afternoon, I was with friends when the first message came through. My heart started racing and my breathing grew shallow. It's hard to explain this type of fear and panic. How can words in a text message strike like a fist? The person is not even present and you feel like you've been whacked again.

What Dave failed to realise was that every angry email, text, and unpleasant encounter only serving to remind me of what I was removing myself from. Every single incident was reassurance that I was making the right decision.

Dave received the solicitor's letter on the eve before I flew to Las Vegas on a whirlwind trip with Corey to see Cher at Park MGM. Living on tenterhooks, Dave wasn't present, but it was difficult escaping the wrath of his anger. My solicitor helped settle my nerves, helping me to understand Dave's reaction, explaining it's normal that one partner is emotionally further down the track of separation than the other.

After weeks of not wanting to see me to discuss our separation, weeks of stonewalling and hostility, the morning I was to leave for the USA, Dave asked if I would like to meet with him. I declined.

Wishing me a safe trip, he asked me to make an appointment to see the relationship specialist on my return. On

Wednesday, December 5, we had our two-hour meeting with her.

This was the beginning of a drastic catalytic change neither of us anticipated.

∼

DAVE

When I received a letter from Noni's solicitor, I couldn't move past the first paragraph. WHAT? Our 'marriage has irretrievably broken down.' NO! She must be kidding!

That phrase, stark and unyielding, sent a shockwave reverberating through my body. I could barely stand. The room shifted in and out of focus and I was engulfed in so much anger I thought I would explode. My mind was racing. *WTF!* I thought we were both hoping reconciliation was possible, but now, right before my eyes in print on a legal letterhead, it says our marriage was 'irretrievably broken'! When did Noni decide there was no hope for our marriage?

'I thought…', yes, they were my thoughts.

Although Noni had told me we were finished, I still refused to listen. A close friend who had practised law confirmed the phrase was routine legal language in divorce procedures!

Pinballing between flight or fight primal responses, the weeks ahead had me alternating between obstructing communication with Noni and striking out with short staccato-like barbs when I did talk to her. Most of the time I was confused and lost. If our marriage was broken beyond repair, maybe I was too. Keeping up with the unpredictable flood of emotions was exhausting. On the back of my confusion and agitation from the legal correspondence, I reluctantly agreed to a mediation meeting.

CHAPTER 18

ANOTHER NEW BEGINNING

NONI

Lynne Clark spoke to us individually at first and then together. Her question to each of us,

"What would be the best possible outcome for you?"

My response was the same I'd given to Dave months before. I considered three possible outcomes.

"Best case scenario; we sort our financial ties out now, do the work each of us needs to do on ourselves. In time, we reconcile, two different and whole individuals; Our marriage is stronger than ever.

Next Best:

We don't get back together but are two solid healthy adults who love and respect each other and are able to function independently. The financial necessities completed early; we can both move on with our futures however we choose.

Either outcome a win for both of us even though excruciatingly painful at present.

Worst case scenario, we give in to fear and return to repeat the same patterns of behaviours"

At the time, Dave agreed number three was not an option. This was good news. I gave her my number one best outcome. After our meeting, Dave and I left agreeing to the 'process of a possible reconciliation whilst not being attached to the outcome.'

Although sounding like an okay plan in her office, growing fear in my belly had me walking away questioning what the hell I agreed to! Dave left amazed by my number one best-case scenario. Despite me communicating this option with him months before, he remained in disbelief of my truth. What would it take to convince this man? My apprehension and fear can only be attributed to the memory of every past negative, hurtful, and abusive interaction within our marriage. ALL were flashing before me now.

~

DAVE

Anxiously waiting with Noni in the lobby of the separation specialist, my stomach was churning, blending resignation and trepidation. Arriving separately, I figured we would depart even more so. Our situation had become so volatile that professional assistance was essential; in my view, the objective was to help Noni exit from our marriage. After speaking to us separately and then as a couple, we reconvened, the counsellor sharing her observations and recommendations. When told Noni's best-case outcome, I was at first astonished and quickly delighted. There was some hope after all. Hearing a third party analyse specific behaviours impacting our relationship with Noni present, illuminated the incredibly unhealthy cycles I had created over many years. The puzzle began taking shape. All of the small pieces kept distinctly separate, once camouflaged, now laid out on a table before me. Her recommendations gave us a roadmap, one that might just pave the way to reconciliation

The suspicion and scepticism I had been harbouring regarding Noni's motives and feelings started to dissolve. My demeanour towards Noni changed, softened. I'd also run out of steam. Remaining angry, reactive, and combative is exhaustive.

Tackling the roadmap, I decided to start with Ezekiel. Noni felt completely disrespected by both of us and our treatment of her. Now was the time to step into my responsibility, husband first, father second, and friend to my son last.

Undertaking to make amends with Ezekiel on my next visit to Melbourne, it was a chance for me to share revelations on how I had mistreated his mother for years. My conversation with Ezekiel, "I know you feel hurt and disappointed with us from decisions we made years ago but enough is enough. You know in your heart your mum never deserved to be treated as badly as you have done. I know you're a sensitive person, you have regrets as well, so please for your own sake, it's time you put the past aside. Apologise to Mum for the hurtful things you have said."

Holding my gaze, contemplating the suggestion, he responded that he would "think about it".

I added, "That's good, but don't wait too long. In the meantime, can you start by unblocking Mum and acknowledging her messages?"

Ezekiel agreed.

We parted and I was hoping he would start reflecting on his relationship with Noni. For the first time in years, Ezekiel witnessed his father stand up for his mother. He didn't lash out as I feared. I was able to show Noni I am for her and not against her. For once, I didn't succumb to my fear of rejection and, instead, did what I knew was right. It was a small but significant step for me, and I believe that moment evoked a new beginning for all three of us.

~

NONI

The specialist instructed us on five absolutely impera-tive steps that needed to be adhered to before any couples counselling began. They included we remain living separately.

The binding financial agreement put in place. Dave would address Ezekiel and stand firm that I had done nothing wrong warranting Ezekiel's behaviour toward me. He was to tell Ezekiel he owed me an apology. Another which I assumed went without saying, we remain one hundred per cent monogamous throughout the process. Finally, we return to see her a few months later to check in on our progress.

Immediately after our meeting, Dave started sending me couples counselling information. Quick to bounce straight into reconciling, it seemed he forgot the other important steps before counselling could happen.

Recalling I had bank details for the new account he set up after our separation, on a hunch I logged on. I was instantly alarmed by a $1000 transfer to a Nancy K. I almost couldn't breathe. I had never heard of this woman and why the heck was Dave giving her $1000?

Sickened not only by the fact that he had given to another woman financially while I was trying to exist on a measly amount, but also because I couldn't believe how I'd stooped low enough to hack into his account. Feeling like I'd been reduced to a new level of crazy, I was insecure and desperate.

Looking a little further, the timing of this transaction was Wednesday, December 12. Precisely one week after the mediation meeting I had to borrow money for so I could pay half the fee! This left me questioning my sanity as I tried wrapping my mind around what felt like evil manipulation.

I shared my findings and fears with my safe couple and heeded their advice. Once over my guilt of hacking into Dave's bank account, I convinced myself God allowed me to find the transaction for my own safety. To prevent me from returning to a place I was no longer meant to be. There had been countless starting points before, and they all led to the same place we were currently at.

With a multitude of red flags staring me in the face, I was absolutely certain of this.

I still had to face Dave though and needed to be smart when I did.

I asked Dave to meet me the following Saturday afternoon to discuss our agreement.

Saturday, December 15. On advice from my counsellor and solicitor regarding safety, I met him in public. Wanting to make certain we both had the same understanding, points needing clarification were documented. Hyper-vigilant, there was no letting my guard down. I'd been here too many times. We needed to contact the mediator during our discussion with Dave questioning the necessity of finalising a financial agreement.

Repeating matters discussed during our previous session with her, although less than pleased, he agreed to follow her advice.

Broaching the question of monogamy, Dave bristled. I questioned his therapist's suggestion of having his physical needs met, he reiterated this wasn't his desire. We've always held comparable interpretation of what constituted infidelity. Prone to weakness in this area, our boundaries were acutely defined. Although keeping 'mum' on the name of the unknown woman in his bank transaction, he became incredibly defensive when I asked who he'd been spending time with. I left more certain than ever he was lying to me.

Momentarily, I believed I would go through the process set out by the mediator in a last 'ditch effort' to prove we'd done everything possible to salvage our marriage.

My inner voice was roaring, "Noni, you're a lousy pretender."

What is the cost of gain when compromising truth and authenticity?

Uneasy about the situation, on Tuesday, December 18, 2018, I bravely approached Dave with the following letter. This letter was written mainly on gut instinct and snippets I'd discovered.

(When we were first dating twenty-eight years before, Dave was the first person I'd heard use the term *being economical with the truth.* In my eyes, this was lying or omitting the whole truth to hide something. When questioning why he thought this, he answered, "Telling the truth never paid off for me". This was another quandary in our complex relationship.)

> *Dearest Dave,*
> *Since making our commitment to each other and to the process of a possible reconciliation, many thoughts and past insecurities arose in me. I'm processing them as they surface and want to be as honest and transparent as possible with you and myself.*
> *You mentioned on Saturday your counsellor suggested you see other people both sexually and relationally. That may be the choice for some, but certainly not for me.*
> *The depth of intimacy I desire in my marriage is one that is at the complete exclusion of all others. I want to feel safe enough to be vulnerable so I can give my heart and body completely and freely to my husband, it's a non-negotiable for me. This is my choice though, so I need a partner who shares this choice and one who will guard this sanctity at all costs.*
> *My trust has been broken on many occasions throughout our relationship.*
> *No one can simply say I'm sorry, move on and expect trust is restored. One MUST*

*continue to prove themselves trustworthy
and reliable.*

*I need to be able to completely trust someone to
share this depth of intimacy.*

*Each time you do something behind my back or
withhold the absolute truth, no matter how
you justify it, my trust is broken again.
Changing passwords without discussion,
giving large sums of money without
discussion, etc. makes me feel like I don't
matter, I'm not worthy of consideration in
important decisions and you don't love or
respect me It sows a seed of mistrust and I
start to wonder what it is you're up to?*

*When I ask a question, I'm asking for absolute
honesty. Only then can I regain my trust
in you and lower my guard.*

*Even now when I ask you whether we share the
same understanding with regard to
monogamy, I'm uncertain as to whether
you told me the full truth (and I'm not
talking about having sex). I'm talking
about women you spent time with alone.
We're both aware that infidelity begins
with a thought and not an action. You said
yes to "work dinners" but when I asked
who they were with you wouldn't say. This
leaves me questioning why and doubting
your transparency. You say I don't know
them, but Dave, plenty of people you speak*

NONI YATES & DAVID YATES

*about I've not met, yet you use their
names...*

*I'm not saying this to make you angry, but to
help us establish clarity going forward to
remove obstacles of doubt.*

*If we agreed to commit to the process of
reconciliation this is vitally important to
me for establishing trust again.*

*So, I am being vulnerable and openly asking
you again, and please, I need the absolute
truth, because if anything comes to light in
the future, I'm not sure I will ever be able
to summon the strength nor courage to
trust in you again. So please Dave, I'm
begging. This is so important to me. Take
this opportunity now to divulge anything
hidden which will cause us harm if
discovered. You're aware of the boundaries
we set around this issue previously.*

*Have you had connection, kept company with
or communicated with (text, email,
Facebook pm) or spent one on one time
with any women including your
immediate work colleagues outside of
direct work business?
Coffee/dinner/drinks/beach or any other
activity? Calls? Texting?*

*If there is something, please tell me. If there is
nothing, great. If something comes to mind,
please text or email me later but please,
please, please do not let it be kept secret*

> *leaving me in the dark for devastation*
> *further down the track.*
> *Weeding out the seed of mistrust needs to be*
> *prioritised for me to move forward if we are*
> *to be one and this only begins with 100%*
> *honesty and transparency.*

I knew I had to accept whatever truth he offered. I had to gear myself up for and steady myself for whatever may come.

Truth, this is what I wanted, hungered for.

Only when I had the whole truth would I be empowered to make clear calculated decisions for myself.

I was terrified that giving him this would invoke an angry outburst and frightened that the nasty, controlling, mean person I was so close to escaping would rear his ugly head. I was also fearful, particularly because I wrote mainly from intuition and not fact. What if I was way off the mark?

∾

DAVE

Remaining monogamous was accepted with the same state of double-mindedness that had operated in me for decades. Rationalising that if I am not having sex outside marriage, I am monogamous. When Noni pressed me about spending time with any other women, she found herself on the receiving end of a pointed, prickly and defensive reaction.

With the soft-tipped subtlety of a cactus thorn, Noni had experienced these responses far too many times to be fooled. The idea of facing the truth about myself caused incredible irritation. Reacting to discomfort the only way I knew – avoid at all costs.

When Noni handed me a letter asking me to give a true account of my movements, I looked into brown soulful eyes and experienced her distress. Distress created by my evasiveness. Hers was a genuine loving appeal. Though her plea moved my heart, I was torn between needing to control how I would be perceived (image) and responding legitimately in my love for Noni.

Over the next few days, I spent hours debating how much truth to share. Surely all of it would be too much and derail any chance of reconciliation. Neither was I prepared to admit the extent of emotional involvement I reserved for outside of marriage.

~

NONI

Instead of rage rising, he read the letter quietly and contemplatively. Folding the A4 sheets of paper, he placed them in his top pocket and gently said,

"Could I please answer this thoroughly later?"

My heart pounding, relieved he showed no anger, inwardly rejoicing I was going to finally receive a clear answer, not lip service.

Thankful and appreciative of him taking this seriously, what followed next is beyond my comprehension. For the first time in years, my heart softened, holding extraordinary tenderness toward Dave. How was it possible for my heart to do a complete one-eighty?

Where did this love come from, and where did my fear, pain, and anguish disappear to? The protective barriers, inches of thick, steel walls melted in a flash. How does a state of mind bordering on contempt become akin to compassion? What was happening?

This instantaneous change was not of my doing and was nothing short of miraculous. An overwhelming feeling took me completely by surprise. All because Dave was going to answer truthfully, or so I thought…

Once again, God had shown his hand in a mighty way, bringing me to my knees and revealing His power within me. Overarching grace and mercy flooded through me, lifting me to a higher place.

Arriving home later that morning, I wrote a reply even though he hadn't answered yet. Presumably gearing myself up for the worst…

> *Thank you for your honesty, I appreciate it.*
> *I will need time to sit with this and process. I'll*

*also need wise counsel to help me clarify
everything around it.*

*I'm sure I don't need to tell you I'm shattered
and grieving all over again.*

*My initial thoughts are, your choices and
actions do not reflect a man determined to
fight for reconciliation with his wife, who,
in your own words, is the greatest love of
your life.*

*The choice you made to see other women is not
the choice of a man honouring his
marriage, even in separation. The desert
period is the wisest choice in my opinion,
but I'm no expert and we can all exercise
free will.*

*Though your psychologist encouraged you to
explore other relationships and sexual
encounters, my understanding is that this
is discussed with the spouse first. I don't
agree with the psychology behind this for
anyone who is broken and straight out of a
relationship, but I'm not the professional.
You also told me it was not what you
wanted so why did you do it? You still
went forward and crossed every boundary
we had put in place to guard our
relationship.*

*Yes, Dave, we separated, but we are not
divorced, and you said you will fight for
reconciliation.*

I've been completely honest with you Dave

*every step of the way, not made false
promises or declarations. You are free to
pursue whoever and whatever you want,
but I'd appreciate a single-minded stance
on this and closure of our marriage first.*

*There is no room for these extras in the depth of
intimacy I desire for my marriage. It is
wrong for me to ask this of you if it is not
within your ability. I'm one hundred per
cent certain of what I want.*

*Please remember we're modelling what
marriage is to our adult children, I trust
you're comfortable with your choices and
can share openly with them, I will too.*

*So, whilst I am hurt and confounded right
now, I am still open and committed as we
both agreed, to the process of a possible
reconciliation further down the track. This
disclosure, although sincerely appreciated,
most definitely pushed me back
considerably. I agree it is best for us both if
we keep our distance. Keep communication
to the absolute necessities until such a time
as we're both ready to move forward one
way or another.*

Dave's email response later in the week shed light on matters he knew crossed boundaries.

Although there was plenty to work through, there were no absolute deal-breakers. I felt no need to show him the response I'd written, confident I could save my concerns for later.

~

DAVE

Over several nights, I carefully crafted my response. It was a struggle between my heart's desire to be open and the overwhelming need to deny my stupidity. Selectively including information I deemed relevant, I asked that any further questions be saved for counselling.

Reasoning I would have to reveal more damaging truth, there may be a better chance of navigating the minefield in the presence of a professional.

Guilty for not mustering the courage to seize the moment and honour Noni's request completely, I instead opted to avert what I believed would be a disastrous revelation.

The following week, Noni shed much of her tentativeness and I, my defensiveness.

Each day filling with a little more hope. When Noni called by to see me on Thursday before Christmas, I could barely contain the pure joy of just being near her. Staring at her, filled with wonder and tenderness just like when we were first courting. Life was going to be much better even though I was terrified of the secrets still hidden.

∾

NONI

Here's what he disclosed:

> "Dear Noni,
> I am going to answer your concerns
>   regarding interactions with women in the
>   last three months - by detailing all people
>   and context.
> I hope this will put your mind at ease. If it
>   doesn't,- we should save it for future
>   couples counselling.
> When I said I have enough female social
>   interaction through work activities - I
>   meant socializing at group dinners or
>   lunches at educational events such as
>   seminars and dinners and internal
>   company meetings. Again, not one on
>   one time with female work contacts.
> The only female work colleagues I confided
>   re our situation are Lucy M – Lucy's been
>   with **** since I started. Similar age to
>   me and in the industry the same length
>   of time, not had much to do with her
>   before ****. Lucy married to D (it's their
>   second marriage for both with adult
>   children). A bit in common, but ZERO
>   attraction, mutual respect and trust
>   which makes me comfortable in her

NONI YATES & DAVID YATES

presence. I never had one on one meal
or drinks etc. with Lucy. During a group
dinner in the last month, she asked
how's the family and what we were doing
for Christmas. I told her of our separation
with not much detail other than my
sadness and that it's a work in progress.
Jen P calls me every 3-4 months for a chat,
check-in on who's doing what back at
****, how my health is, how long either of
us has till retirement, stuff like that. I
haven't seen Jen in person since before I
was sick. Jen called for a catch up about
two months ago, I told her what had
happened, she was shocked but
provided some useful insights from
friend's experiences and her own -
(before her current husband A- she had
apparently been in a physically abusive
marriage.) She was able to give me a
perspective of the separation process
and what to expect from the legal
process - which was helpful.
Noni, two exceptions:
I did have a coffee alone with the following
women. Both already known to me via
work in some capacity. Both contacted
me via LinkedIn wanting to speak
regarding potential sales roles, the ones
we are now currently interviewing for.
• Nancy K - an ex **** representative

• *Val G - a ***** representative*
*Ended up telling both the role would likely
    be filled with an internal candidate, but
    there would be a vacant sales role in the
    New Year (which will be created).
    Motivation for me, I can refer both for the
    now vacant position and if either is
    successful receive a $1000 bonus.*
*Noni, none of the stuff above should alarm
    you. I am happy to unpack my initial
    responses to your questioning last
    Saturday during counselling - as there
    were probably some complex dynamics
    going on, part of our bigger
    communication picture.*
Next page;
*When you read the following Noni, please
    remember the context of where we were.
    I am being very open and trusting.*
*Following you saying you have no desire or
    capacity to try and salvage our marriage,
    and the lawyer's letter confirming my
    marriage is irretrievably broken, I sought
    professional advice from psychologists
    and lawyers. I didn't want to hear it, but
    the opinion from them after reading all
    correspondence was, in their experience,
    I needed to get used to the idea of my
    marriage being over.*
*In the weeks following, as a way of getting
    my bearings for what the future might*

*hold for me, and to get some vague
level of comfort for what that future
looked like, I started scanning the
papers for information on single
bedroom units for sale on the coast,
looking at future developments and
plans.*

*With the same motivations as the real estate
search actions above, but with some
trepidation, I joined an online dating site
Tinder, not to seek sex (as suggested as
an option to consider by my counsellor).*

*• I was initially and superficially comforted
by the number of likes or whatever
they are.*

*• over about four weeks I did 'chat' to about
three women - not explicit stuff (like
members of parliament) just what you
do, where are you from? Where have you
been etc.*

Confession;

*I did agree to meet a fifty-five-year-old
woman for a coffee and chat at Surfers,
a twenty-minute conversation, someone
else with recent experience of
separation. (This is about five weeks
ago). It was like talking to a stranger, no
connection - except one who had gone
through the marriage breakdown. I
realised quickly I didn't want any new
friendships or relationships, plus the grief*

*I was feeling was not a good basis or
motivator for seeking them.*

*Upon reflection, i.e., asking myself WTF are
you doing Dave? I realised*

* *I found the whole process tedious and
superficial - my heart was obviously not
in it.*
* *I do not need the diversion, attention or
entertainment of strangers to make me
feel better/good about myself.*
* *I do not want to pursue a relationship,
physical or emotional encounter with
another woman while ever there is hope
for my marriage (even if it's just my
hope), deep down I still had hope for us.*

Account/profile deleted days later.

Noni,

*I have opened as you wanted - and hope it
is received with the trust it was intended.*

Love Dave xxx"

Revealed in his reply, the name of the woman he'd
given the money to. Although still at a loss as to why he
gave her $1000, I deduced there must be a rational
explanation seeing that there would be the same amount
paid to him should she get the position. I decided I
would save my questions for couples counselling as he
requested. I also knew it would be wiser to have a third-
party present when I disclosed to him that I'd logged
into his account. I felt like a criminal! The Tinder business did surprise me. Nevertheless, I figured his revela-

tion around this whole process was a learning curve for him. It didn't stop me from feeling like the exercise showed real weakness of character though. Annoyed as I was, the way Dave explained his lapse allowed me to excuse what I considered flawed behaviour.

Dave had been working in Melbourne when he sent me his reply. Assuming he would be anxious about how his email was received, I responded, thanking him, reassuring him of my love and hopefully alleviating some anxiety. I knew what it would have taken for him to allow such transparency. On Thursday, December 21, Corey was arriving on a late flight from Sydney. There was time to fill while waiting for Corey's plane to land. Dave was back on the coast. Wanting to be near Dave, I drove to his place. Rather than arriving unannounced, I sent a simple SMS asking if he would like me to call by. Without hesitation, his response 'yes.'

Facing each other on the lounge, sharing intimate conversation, we reconnected most lovingly.

Even though actions disclosed in his letter were out of bounds, I embodied genuine and deep love for him and, as his wife, wanted to express this love. Yearning for him to be free from binding fears, desiring as always for our love to be light and liberating, not bound by secrets and darkness.

Two nights later Corey, Ruby, and I met Dave at a Japanese restaurant up the coast.

Dave and I wanted to reassure our two eldest of the progress and hope we had for our marriage. Both adults deserved to be privy to updates. Nothing worse than shifting goalposts; they'd witnessed calamity leading to our separation as well as the meltdowns following.

I worried my swift change of heart might confuse them. More than likely though they couldn't care less, being a 'let's be clear' type of person, I thought it was important they knew. Dave awkwardly brushed over the Tinder business, Ruby and Corey thought that was amusing if not a little weird. Taking the information in their stride, neither one showed any great interest, eager to resume check-ins on their social media.

The Zashiki seating arrangement on tatami flooring was considerably more uncomfortable than our table conversation. We enjoyed a tasty Japanese meal before parting ways. The weather turned bleak in the time it took us to finish dinner. A true Queensland summer's evening, wet and humid. Walking hand in hand, we side-stepped puddles until we reached the corner and kissed goodbye. Ruby and Corey walked ahead, turning right towards where we had parked the car. Dave pushed the button at the pedestrian crossing, signalling he was turning left.

The kids continued walking until I called out to them. Caught up in their own world, they were oblivious that their dad and stepdad was heading in the opposite direction. My heart ached to watch Dave cross the road alone. We'd see each other tomorrow though. It was the day before Christmas...

Little did I realise the week's disclosure would simply be the tip of the iceberg, 'trickle truth'. The beginning of one earth-shattering revelation after another. A decidedly rockier road lay ahead.

CHAPTER 19

AN UNEXPECTED CHRISTMAS GIFT

NONI

We briefly caught up on Christmas Eve and made plans for Dave to join us early on Christmas morning to celebrate the day. We would all enjoy breakfast together, exchange gifts, swim, surf, lunch, etc. Everything was in place and felt great. It had been a tumultuous journey, but things were finally looking up.

Dave left our home early afternoon, love and kisses until tomorrow. Noticing a missed call from him at five, I retrieved the message and almost died...

He had pocket dialled me when he was talking to someone and inadvertently left me a five-minute voice-mail. His voice and the voice of a woman. Through muffled words, I discerned the conversation was not overly intimate. I strained my ears to listen and could hear him consoling her.

"I know, I know…" as she gently protested at whatever news she didn't want to hear.

The call continued along these lines until it cut out.

Frozen in disbelief; HOW COULD I BE SUCH A FOOL!

I called him immediately but the line was busy, so I shot text after text to his number, crazed with fear, anger, disbelief. I was furious!

"WHO ARE YOU WITH?"

"I GOT A FIVE-MINUTE VOICEMAIL, YOU POCKET DIALLED ME!"

"WHO ARE YOU WITH? LET ME GUESS. NANCY K!"

"SICK!"

Dave was driving while I was madly texting, no doubt nauseous when he finally read them.

He called back. I absolutely lost my s***. I don't think I've ever used as many profanities in one conversation, ever. Dave continued pleading with me as I let fly, bombarding him with my hurt and anger. Screeching at him not to bother coming on Christmas Day. Bile rose in my belly. There was no way I wanted to see or hear him. End of story, the red receiver was the only button to push at that moment. He tried calling back a few times but my phone was buried under piles of pillows. Too wild to engage with him, unable to function, Christmas Eve was over for me at 6 pm.

~

DAVE

Christmas Eve 2018.

The mental contortionist, verbal gymnast and relationship juggler residing in my emotional circus who had sought to hide the truth and limit damage was about to be outed. The years of practising and perfecting all of the above, a wasted effort. Almost 'home' after spending a lovely afternoon with Noni, my phone exploded with text messages. Bringing the car to a screaming halt, I thumped the steering wheel and cursed myself out loud.

How could I be so stupid to risk so much… for what exactly? What were the chances I would unknowingly pocket dial while leaning on the doorway of Nancy's apartment? There was no good answer and it didn't matter. Despite my efforts to 'manage' the situation to protect Noni, and of course me, the truth came down in torrents, raining a flood of agony for Noni.

When I finally managed to speak to her, the pain and fury in her voice was palpable. I was incredibly concerned. I had nothing to comfort her. More than crushing Noni, I disregarded her grace, kindness, love, courage, and spirit. I deserved everything thrown at me and much more. Emailing my apology and a partial explanation preceded a sleepless night.

During the evening, I messaged Ezekiel in Melbourne.

He asked, "How are things?"

"Ezekiel, I've really f**ked up, Mum gave me the chance to be honest and I blew it! She trusted me and I lied."

"Wow, yeah you sure did Dad, how is she?"

We talked a little longer, there was some consolation knowing he was genuinely concerned for his mother.

~

NONI

Dave emailed the following explanation, my responses in capitals:

> *Dear Noni,*
> *I am so angry with myself for letting old habits and irrational fears keep me from completely seizing the opportunity we had last week.* AS YOU SHOULD BE!
> *Fear - you would imagine the half dozen catch-ups (which did start with the one initial career discussion) for something much more than they were.* BECAUSE YOU KNOW THIS IS OUTSIDE OF THE GUIDELINES WE HAVE HAD IN PLACE TO PROTECT OUR MARRIAGE. THESE ARE NOT THE ACTIONS OF A MAN WHO IS SERIOUS ABOUT WANTING RECONCILIATION WITH HIS WIFE.

*Afraid our talks of rebuilding our relationship
would be wiped out. No doubt now that
lying when given the opportunity is 100
times worse.* AND THEN SOME!
*This was beginning to weigh on me
yesterday,* WEIGHING ON YOU SO
MUCH YOU HAD TO GO AND VISIT
HER???????? AWESOME!
*I started to wonder when or how I might be
able to complete my disclosure to you.
During the challenge?
During couples counselling? I just knew I
wanted it out.
I want to be in a place where I can
understand 'why' I couldn't be an adult
from the outset.
I have a way to go.
Probably no consolation to you,
· There has never been and never will be a
romantic or physical aspect of the
interactions.* YOU FORGOT TO
MENTION EMOTIONAL.
*I had not seen her since you and I sat down
at Tweed last weekend.* OH, BUT YOU
HAD SINCE OUR DEC 5 MEDIATION
WHEN WE AGREED ON ABSOLUTE
MONOGOMY AND WE WERE
COMMITTED TO THE PROCESS OF A
POSSIBLE RECONCILIATION. YOU
DAMN WELL KNOW WHAT THAT
MEANS!!!!!! IT IS NOT ABOUT SEX; IT IS

ABOUT BETRAYAL OF TRUST AGAIN &
AGAIN & AGAIN……..

*None of this helps the fact that I chose to lie
last week.* NO, IT DOESN'T!

fyi today;

Today I was feeling sad for Nancy WITH NO
REGARD TO ME OR US. YOU WERE
ONLY THINKING ABOUT YOU! ABOUT
HOW YOU CAN LOOK GOOD IN THIS
WOMAN'S EYES. YOU'RE SUCH A
HERO DAVE, SO KIND AND CARING
AND THOUGHTFUL, EXACTLY WHAT
KIND OF MESSAGE DO YOU THINK
THIS LITTLE GESTURE AND ALL OF
YOUR MEETINGS WITH HER CONVEYS
TO HER????????- *knowing she is
distanced from family, spending
Christmas alone and is stressed about
looking for work for what is now an
extended period.* THAT IS A SHAME,
BUT HOW IS THIS YOUR
RESPONSIBILITY?

*I took some moisturiser I purchased for
myself but hadn't opened yet (I started
taking care of my skin a bit), wrapped it,
and, on the way back dropped it by her
place. That's the conversation at the
front door you heard.* YOU'RE WORRIED
ABOUT CONFUSING RUBY WITH
MAYBE STAYING OVER, I'D SAY THIS IS

A LITTLE CONFUSING, WOULDN'T
YOU??????

*Noni, I feel so stupid for not telling you
about my meetings with Nancy when I
should have.*

*I wouldn't have put you through this horrible
episode and probably set off an
avalanche of emotions and memories.*

*I wish somehow I could take the hurt and
anger from you. All I can do is pray.*

*The last week has been the tentative
beginning of a new season for both of
us, one I could not have imagined. I
completely stuffed it up with old habits
and underlying fears.* YEP!

ALL I CAN SAY IS YOU HAVE ABUSED MY
TRUST AGAIN; YOU WILL ALWAYS GET
CAUGHT OUT DAVE. AND I FEEL LIKE
AN ABSOLUTE FOOL ALLOWING
MYSELF TO BELIEVE YOU AGAIN. I
HOPE YOU'RE SATISFIED. GO AND RE-
READ THE LETTER I WROTE, AND
THEN, JUST KNOW THAT YOU HAVE
ABSOLUTELY S*** ON MY HEART AND
RIGHT AT THIS MOMENT YOU DO NOT
DESERVE THE PERSON I AM.

~

NONI

I felt like I'd walked into a propeller, lacerated body parts thrust into orbit, no safe landing place in sight. At a loss as to what to do, my head was spinning.

This didn't make for the best of Christmas spirit. My mind was in overdrive hatching a crazy plan. Dave could come for lunch and I would prepare our usual Christmas feast. On his arrival I would leave him to it and take a chilled bottle of Veuve Cliquot down to the beach for my own private Christmas cheer (or in my case cheerless), announcing to him that he could explain to our family why things were as they were. Complete madness made complete sense to my betrayed self.

After receiving my raging words early Christmas morning, he messaged wanting to speak.

At 6 am, with the household still sleeping, I agreed he could come down and meet me on the beach. Within half an hour, we were facing each other on the shoreline.

This was no Mexican standoff, there were no more hiding places for Dave, it was game on!

Out of the trench, my guns were loaded. Dave stood, offering an explanation for his actions.

Limbs flailing in the air, my hands expressed the rage burning inside. Infuriated, I delivered him a long-overdue and well-deserved serve. A little more truth dripping from his lips.

An hour or so later, I told him he could explain to our adult children why their mother was in bed curled up in a foetal position with her cup of tea at 6 pm on Christmas Eve. I was no longer going to cover for him and was sick to death of this charade. As much as Dave cringed at the thought of facing Ruby and Corey, I left him no choice. If he wanted to be with us today, the only option he had was to man up and own this.

~

DAVE

Accepting an invitation to face Noni and my own deception early Christmas morning filled me with fear and relief. The drive to our family home took too long and, at the same time, not long enough. Gingerly, I sauntered down a partially shaded path towards the beach where the sparkling clear ocean met white sand. Waves rolled in gently, lapping around Noni's feet. In the distance was the deep dark blue horizon. Any chance of me rescuing our relationship was even further away, light years beyond the horizon. There were buckets of tears and righteous anger.

Beachcombers needn't have heard Noni's words to understand her agony. Toe to toe on the sand, I really didn't know what to do other than give up with the band-aid explanations and do whatever was needed to get us both through this day. The prospect of facing Ruby and Corey terrified me. Baulking momentarily, there was nowhere left to run. Although Corey stands six-foot-five and Ruby a tiny five-foot-nothing, Ruby was the one I feared telling most. Six years earlier, I hurt Ruby horribly with a nasty, unnecessary retort. That had been an absolute low point in my relationship with the entire family.

Ezekiel, protective of the sister he adored, wrote me off and wiped me completely. Ruby, already frustrated with my selfishness and arrogance, wanted nothing to do with me from that moment on.

That incident proved to Noni I was emotionally unsafe for her and our children. Over the following several years, I worked hard and slow at being consistent around Ruby, hoping to gradually build a relationship. Noni advised – don't expect anything, just build trust one day at a time. A few years later Ruby gave me a Father's Day card. It was the only card from any of my children in the past nine years. A statement more about me than my children.

> *Dear Dad*
>
> *First & foremost, Happy Farter's Day (not a misprint)*
>
> *We certainly had our ups and downs over the years, but I am extremely grateful that you never stopped trying to be the best possible father you can be. Your efforts have really shown, particularly in the last year or two and I'm very proud of you for that. Thank you for all that you do for us*
>
> *Love Always*
>
> *Your Favourite Child*

I cherish this card. It reminds me I am not a hopeless screw-up. There were plenty of frustrating slip-ups in the years following, and now, on Christmas morning, I was going to be shredding it to pieces in front of her.

Telling Ruby and Corey was tearful and fearful for me, but I didn't have any other options. The disdain, disgust, and anger that flew across the kitchen bench didn't surprise me. I deserved it. An unexpectedly slight sense of relief accompanied the disclosure, my world didn't end.

At that moment, I admitted betraying Noni and my family without resorting to defending my brokenness. Ruby was in a fresh world of pain I had no remedy for. Making my way through the day, feeling awkward opening presents Noni had lovingly purchased and wrapped for me, I wished I had opted for a much more luxurious weekend getaway for my girls than the one I purchased. Noni's heart continued softening towards me as a result of the kitchen confession. A burden had unquestionably been lifted, but also shifted, and guilt fluttered within me for this shift. Each detail tentatively revealed during the day drew Noni and me closer; the exact opposite of what I had feared and expected.

~

NONI

Back in the house, Ruby and Corey were in the kitchen – Corey cooking pancakes and Ruby making gingerbread. I remained silent. Dave gave it his best shot. Details were kept to a minimum as he apprehensively relayed the gist of what transpired. Casting him a stony glance, Ruby declared, "And I thought you were supposed to be an intelligent person."

Dissolving into tears, she retreated to her bedroom. Corey continued flipping pancakes. Dave wept. I was motionless and numb but pleased. For the first time ever, Dave faced the kids truthfully. I would be able to tolerate this day, champagne helped...

We manoeuvred our day reasonably well even though Ruby spent most of it in her bedroom. This wasn't the first Christmas Ruby's absence formed a statement directed at her father. Our day went on. Dave and I spoke calmly about his interactions with Nancy. He divulged loaning her $1000.00 and explained she had been out of work. My lips remained sealed, not confessing I already possessed this knowledge.

Under the impression we were strolling down a path of truth, I questioned him about the Netflix viewing. He strenuously denied watching the titles, so I had to assume there'd been a mistake in his profile. ASS out of U and ME. To be continued.

Showing him the pre-emptive note written weeks earlier, the one I completed in preparation for the devastation I was currently experiencing, he commented, "Maybe you should give it to me now."

Despite the horrendous fallout, Dave expressed that he felt relief for the pocket dial. The call forced him to face the truth and the lies he'd been telling himself and us. My trauma took considerably longer before transitioning to relief.

The most amazing phenomenon concerning this recent bombshell was that despite the pain, my heart was surprisingly very soft and warm toward him even though it was badly bruised. I could see he was hurting too, and I loved him deeply. Thinking back, my ignorance astounds me. I'm humbled yet again.

Mistakenly believing that Dave's Netflix history exposure and the money given to this woman was actually God's way of warning me against returning to my marriage. Nothing could have convinced me otherwise that this wasn't God's revelation. Why else would I be so certain?

My thinking prideful, how wrong I was.

The light shone on hidden secrets had less to do with me and everything to do with God, about who HE is, and what only HE can do. My miraculous change of heart mid-December '18, and the love I still had for Dave despite this latest calamity revealed more of God's divine nature.

Our all-powerful, all-loving God.

> Now to Him, who is able to (carry out His purpose and) do superabundantly more than all that we dare ask or think (infinitely beyond our greatest prayers, hopes, or dreams) according to His power that is at work within us.
>
> — EPH 3:20 (AMP)

I am eternally thankful for the Christmas Eve pocket dial. A call which became the catalyst for my husband to begin telling the truth.

CHAPTER 20

SILLY, SILLY ME

NONI

Early in the New Year, I suggested contacting Nancy and providing our account details so she could repay the money. Writing the following letter, Dave read it and agreed I should send it.

I was writing, woman to woman, with the understanding she had been mates with Dave, not intimately involved. Dave shared with her we were working towards reconciling, she wished him well. From information which has come to light, my assumption was somewhat gullible and naïve. This letter was probably a foolish gesture, but too late, I did it. When a man tells his 'friend' that he and his wife are committing to the process of reconciliation and the friend responds, "So, I guess that means we won't be hanging out together as

NONI YATES & DAVID YATES

much anymore," it tells me this 'friend' was no friend of the marriage. Hindsight is a wonderful thing!

I wanted her to know the truth, my own little bit of self-justification. I shouldn't have bothered. Regardless, after sending her a message via Facebook and receiving no response, I contacted her through LinkedIn.

> *Hi Nancy, sorry to contact you on here but I wanted to be certain you received this message. You've no doubt been given Dave's version of truth and events that led to the breakdown of our marriage as you've been spending time with him. No doubt this filtered through his charming but distorted sense of reality and truth.*
>
> *As a 'friend' to Dave you possibly had no intention of the friendship progressing into anything further, though any friendship which must be covered by lies and secrecy has no place within a marriage. (BTW, this is not the first letter written along these lines, although the first, which at the moment, I'm led to believe is still in a platonic state.)*
>
> *Dave's truth to me when I laid my heart bare to give our marriage another chance was yet another lie.*
>
> *Because of his inability to be a man of his word and one who is trustworthy, we've had strict boundaries in place to protect*

our marriage and rebuild my trust. One of these is that he does not spend one on one time with women or contact them outside of the necessity of immediate work business.

On Dec 5th we had a mediation meeting where we both vowed and committed to the process of a possible reconciliation. One of the conditions set out by the highly skilled and highly paid mediator included we both are 100% monogamous. Aware of our previous boundaries around this, I assumed Dave and I were on the same wavelength.

After reflection though, my gut instinct issued red flags and I knew if ever I was to trust him with my heart again I would need to ask some questions. I penned a letter openly and vulnerably asking for him to disclose anything which crossed our boundaries and would cause harm if discovered in the future. Below is part of his reply.

Noni, 2 exceptions:

Coffee alone with the following women. Both already known to me via work with **** in some capacity. Both contacted me via LinkedIn wanting to speak regarding potential sales roles, the ones we are now currently interviewing for

Nancy S - an ex **** representative

Val G - a **** representative

*Ended up telling both the role would likely
be filled with an internal candidate, but
there would be a vacant sales role in the
New Year (which will be created).
Motivation for me is I can refer both for
the now vacant position and if either is
successful, receive a $1000 bonus.*

*Obviously, this is a lie regarding the one
coffee with you. Motivation for the lie, no
idea, not sure he does; all I know is it's
destructive in a relationship and causes
incredible pain.*

*The mediation cost $700.00. I told him I
would pay half and borrowed money to
do so. The reason I mention this is
because I understand you borrowed
$1000.00 from Dave. You wouldn't be
aware, but while I'm trying to live off my
small income of $300.00 a week and
anything else I can rustle up, Dave
chipped me for needing to use our credit
card for fuel and medical expenses.
However, he can loan you $1000.00. Not
cool in my book! None of this is your
fault or responsibility, but it is a reflection
of the state my husband of twenty-five
years and partner of twenty-eight years
is in....*

*Included are bank details for you to deposit
the $1000.00 when you're able to.*

BSB ******
ACC ******

Christmas Eve he accidentally pocket dialled
me when with you, I received a five-
minute voicemail. Only that week he
promised he would not cross this
boundary again. Glaringly, this was yet
another lie exposed.

I hope you haven't had to live this reality and
I hope you never do. Please understand,
boundaries are not in place to restrict or
control a man's freedom, but rather, they
are a necessity to regain trust from his
wife and family. When betrayal
repeatedly occurs in a relationship, it is
the betrayer's responsibility to prove
themselves worthy of the trust and
respect from the ones hurt. I trust you
can and will respect these boundaries.

Cheers, Noni

Her response, not to me but Dave...

Hi David. Sorry to bother you.
Can you please let your wife
know I received her long
message but don't wish to
engage with her, thanks,
Nancy.

This absolutely floored me, not only did she disregard the courtesy of replying directly to me, but I didn't even deserve a name, referring to me instead as "wife"! Fellow travellers on the infidelity road will understand how this kind of response adds serious fuel to the fire. It cast enormous doubt over Dave's version of events. Every question I could possibly think of flooding through me, Dave copped the lot of them. All I could think was if she is just a 'friend', why would she not reply to me and say something like,

"Great news you guys are working on things. I'll repay the money as soon as I can. All the best Nancy."

After reigning myself in, I flicked her another message.

> *Thanks for your reply via Dave, the intention behind contacting you was purely to give you some insight, an alternative perspective, and our joint bank account details rather than seeking to engage with you. So, my apologies if you thought I was looking for something other than maybe an acknowledgement and respectful understanding? Dave read and appreciated what I'd written to you before I sent it. No hidden agendas, truly. I wish you well, Noni*

To this, no reply. In May 2019 I sent her this:

> *Hi Nancy,*
> *I trust you're doing well. Dave and I are*
>   *closing the CBA account which I*
>   *previously gave you details for. When you*
>   *have the $1000 to repay the loan Dave*
>   *gave you in December could you please*
>   *deposit it into the following account?*
> *DD and NA Yates*
> *BSB ******
> *ACC ******
> *Many thanks*
> *Noni*

And to that, she actually replied to me. This was five months after my initial contact in January.

> *Hi Noni,*
> *I had no intention of repaying the money*
>   *back into your personal account after the*
>   *discussions I'd had with David regarding*
>   *why you were separating. I will pay the*
>   *money into the account he originally*
>   *used unless I hear otherwise from him.*
> *Nancy*

Now I was absolutely seething. The maddening thing was, I felt like I'd been so terribly deceived over and over again. WTH had he told her? Obviously his 'version' of circumstances. If fuel had been thrown onto the fire before, the whole oil well had now been added. My attempt to be matter-of-fact with her blew up big time.

I was hoping to communicate necessary facts without Dave reconnecting with her.

Trying to remain as calm as possible, my response to her was simply:

> *I'm not sure what kind of discussions you had, but he's sent you a text message to clarify any misunderstanding. Kind Regards Noni*

In the time I pressed send, Dave received the following text, she was plainly annoyed I dare contact her.

> *David, don't appreciate you giving my number out to your wife. I was nothing but nice to you over your separation and have refrained from communicating with your wife as I don't wish to lie to her. I feel sorry for you both. Will deposit the money into the second account she has suggested soon. Nancy*

WTH! I still didn't deserve to be referred to by name and now I was questioning WHY the heck she would think she needed to lie to me. This correspondence once again cast shadows of astronomical proportion over the story Dave had told me! Now I was really raging and asked Dave to reply.

> *Hi Nancy,*
> *There's no need to fear replying to Noni and no need to lie to her. I've botched up a sh****** of stuff over the years but we're moving forward most healthily. Noni has access to all of my contacts and we both agreed to give you our account changes. I've got no secrets and yes you were a support during my separation.*
> *Thanks, hope you're well.*
> *David*

A few days later, we received $1000 into our account. I sent one final message.

> *Hi Nancy*
> *The money is in our account, much appreciated, thank you. I sense by the nature of your response to my contacting you, your opinion of me and us (i.e., Dave and I) is based on the*

> *distortion of facts you were*
> *given. I can understand. And*
> *whilst my flesh wants to*
> *shout the truth, wisdom*
> *whispers don't bother.*
> *Please let me acknowledge I*
> *am truly sorry you were ever*
> *placed in this awkward*
> *position. I wish you well. I*
> *won't contact you again. I*
> *wanted to say thanks. Noni*

Nor have I made any contact. There has been no need, the correspondence served its purpose, the money was in the bank. We could move on with doing the work we needed to do to resurrect 'us'.

~

DAVE

This was the beginning of a long and painful (unnecessarily so) process of disclosure and discovery. No one could have dreamed what would come to light in the coming months, not even me. Despite many years earlier agreeing with Noni that hidden female friendships had no place in a marriage, I continued to maintain and cultivate them for years afterwards. Reasoning my twisted theory to suit, 'It's alright for me, I'm not doing anyone any harm, and I am certainly not having an affair'! Christmas 2018 blew my warped rationalization to pieces. My wife and daughter – the two women I vowed to protect were heartbroken. All because I placed a need for validation first and my marriage second. I began to realise and admit an emotional affair is just as much a betrayal as sexual infidelity. Betrayal is betrayal. None of it can be excused, and comparisons are a dangerous foundation on which to build a relationship framework.

The disclosure on December 25, 2018, started a process and journey neither of us could have anticipated. Noni could never have imagined the extent of my double life that was about to unfold and I still didn't have a plan on how to divulge my secrets.

~

NONI

Along my new education pathway, I discovered an interesting characteristic common to someone caught out in a lie, or several: the deceiver's ability to skilfully downplay or minimise the extent of their deception. A friend who is a dietician once said, when discussing with an alcoholic how much they drink, the professional might multiply the amount the patient has admitted to by three. The same can be said for our situation. Dave deceived himself, struggling to cover the shame of what he is capable of and continued doing, regardless of how harmful and wrong. Lying to himself, tipping the scales of justice in his favour.

A more palatable version of events pushed down and hidden, or so he thought…

Unfaithful partners are well aware of atrocities they've already inflicted upon the betrayed spouse and mistakenly think withholding information protects their spouse from more pain. This misconception couldn't be further from the truth. Like many betrayed partners, I was more than capable of handling the absolute truth. Selective drip-feeding of information is far more destructive and resembles death by a thousand paper cuts, a cruel and agonizing death.

Being 'economical with the truth' is a saying I'll forever detest. Call it what it is, LYING LYING, LYING! It may be lying by omission, but it is still LYING!

The week after Christmas, we decided to go bush for a couple of nights. Over the New Year's Eve holiday, we would take time out to recalibrate and be intentional about transitioning into 2019 and our future. It was a wise decision. We played cards and spent hours talking about our dreams and desires for ourselves and our marriage. It was amazing. Our hearts tender and gentle towards one another, the depth of our love evident and undeniable. It felt good, but as we know only too well, 'love is a decision', not just a feeling.

Christmas came and went, I googled madly trying to find answers and support for what I thought had to be a unique situation. Dave moved back home in January. Our reconciliation gaining forward momentum at a miraculous and accelerated pace. Both of us fully acknowledged how much work and healing lay ahead.

A counsellor I had seen, whilst not particularly remarkable, enlightened me with a significant takeaway. The old relationship Dave and I had was over, but our marriage was not. Any new relationship would look completely different. As a starting point, I suggested we put pen to paper, write down exactly what we desired for our future as we reflected on the pastor's question asked of us early in married life,

"Do you want this marriage to work?"

This is what we wrote:

> *Noni to Dave: I want to be married to you for the rest of our days. I want our marriage to begin on a whole new foundation, a foundation of truth - complete honesty and transparency. Pride and arrogance have no place in the relationship - replaced by respect, humility and honour.*
> *I want to sleep next to you and wake up with you for as many nights as is possible.*
> *I want our communication to be deep and authentic always.*
> *I want to travel together, experience new adventures, share as many intimate moments together as we possibly can.*
> *I want you to trust me with your deepest fears*

and emotions - I won't think you weak, this
shows strength and builds intimacy.
I want you to be a man of your word and a
husband I can always depend on to do the
right thing.
I want to be able to trust you again so I can feel
safe.

Dave to Noni: I want for us
A life of moderate financial freedom allowing
us to pursue interests together,
Assist our children where needed,
Have the time to make contributions to
communities and causes.
A respectful, passionate loving relationship
bound by shared faith and taking priority
over all else
Supporting each other in a joint and individual
pursuit of God's will, protecting time
together and being, not necessarily doing -
yet looking to deepen the bond that exists
always.
A life sharing what we establish through time -
friendship- talents – finances.

~

NONI

It was painstakingly clear that both of us wanted more than anything to be married to one another for life. We had to learn how to do it well, to make a new beginning with a solid foundation.

As I delved through a plethora of daily plans on the Bible app, I discovered a reading plan from Cindy Beale, a pastor's wife betrayed by her husband. It does happen, we're not alone. We're not freaks and I'm not crazy for still wanting my marriage! We personally knew of no Christians who had overcome and survived an affair. Hoping to find a holistic recovery plan, Cindy's message reflected our core values and beliefs.

It wasn't enough to merely survive; our goal was to thrive. This meant we needed resources aligned with our spirituality. Exploring her website, I found the Affair Recovery recommendation. This discovery unlocked the vault to invaluable information and expert advice on infidelity.

We'd been tossed around by every piece of flotsam and jetsam from the shipwreck of adultery. The AR website uncovered a community of people just like us.

Gaining access to articles and videos in the Affair Recovery Library was the beginning of making sense of this madness. For the first time in decades, everything I had experienced in the past was validated. My feelings, thoughts, and reactions were all completely normal. I was not crazy. I was not unduly suspicious, and I had every right to question Dave. My voice gained confidence even as I walked through this battlefield.

My biggest question was "Why?" Why did he do this? How could he do this?

At the time, Dave truly didn't have the answer.

One morning as I was leaving home for an appointment with my therapist, Dave had waxed his board and was strolling down the driveway hoping to catch a wave. We'd enjoyed a coffee in bed, watching an affair recovery video and spoke more about his affairs. Everything was calm, there was no apparent tension. I had asked him again "Why?" and again he answered that he didn't know.

We left our conversation there. I hopped in the car, put it in reverse and waved to Dave as I began to leave. The next minute, a switch flicked in my mind and I ripped up the hand brake, flew out of the driver's seat, and stood face to face with him.

"If you don't know WHY you did this in the first place, HOW are you going to make sure it never happens again?"

Dave remained stunned and speechless. I turned about face and jumped back in the car and continued to my appointment. He needed to get to the bottom of his 'why'.

∽

DAVE

I watched Affair Recovery videos and was amazed and encouraged listening to men speak candidly of their history of cheating, speaking without pride, yet free from any signs of lingering shame. Men described how they reasoned with themselves, deceived themselves and used the same distortions I had for years. I recoiled in discomfort for identifying with these behaviours but was comforted that I wasn't alone. Maybe there was hope for me. It became apparent that total disclosure was a cornerstone in the recovery process, a consistent message throughout the AR resources. In previous weeks, I made significant steps facing entrenched fears.

I had talked to Ezekiel about his treatment of his mother, plus my part in modelling disrespect towards her. I abandoned any attempt at the 'just friends' defence of my relationship with Nancy and called it what it was, a long-standing emotional affair. I took responsibility and faced my children, owning the Christmas Eve bomb-shell. Gradually I removed layers of a well-worn protective mask. I was failing forward. To my utter disbelief, instead of each reveal repelling Noni, it drew us closer, proving many of the fears held were false or grossly exaggerated. I grew less defensive of the image I thought so important and fought hard to maintain. Massive betrayals needed to be disclosed. The idea of sharing the detail of sexual affairs I had buried in a 'vault' filled me with dread. My anxiety could not be quelled.

~

NONI

I emailed the AR team hoping they might provide names of counsellors in Australia.

We were desperate for specialist care and advice. We needed people to guide us who had walked this road, people who really understood our pain, ones with street cred rather than academia alone. It turns out our Great Southern Land is lacking in affair-specific services.

After explaining a little of our situation, their reply suggested Dave may have some kind of addiction. This surprised me. I had never thought of it this way and knew little about sexual or approval/validation addictions. However, I knew Dave's behaviour appeared excessive.

During our separation period the word 'narcissism' kept cropping up. I was still looking for reasons for Dave behaving as he did. My research led me to a book titled *Why does he do that? Inside the minds of angry and controlling men*. Insightful reading by author Lundy Bancroft gave me a glimpse into abusive behaviours. Addiction clothes itself differently, yet there are common threads. I took my highlighter to many a page and at times had to lay the book aside. The confronting and overwhelming content ticked far too many boxes. Dave has since read this book and much of the information is more than he'd like to be comfortable with. It resonated with him. There is no way I could have mentioned this book had he not had significant self-realisation and revelation. Six months earlier, the mere suggestion of narcissistic behaviour would have been met with catastrophic denial and aggression. Highly recommend reading if you find yourself in a relationship wondering, *he says he loves me, so why does he do that?*

We took a free 7-day online Bootcamp offered by Affair Recovery. A brilliant starting place for anyone unfortunate to have had their relationship napalmed by infidelity. The Bootcamp helped us unpack essential steps and begin our recovery journey.

Amongst the AR recommended reading was *The Monogamy Myth* by Peggy Vaughan, a widely referenced resource. Googling further I stumbled upon BAN, Beyond Affairs Network, an organisation for betrayed spouses that originated in America. Peggy founded BAN after discovering her husband's affair. Continuing my search for the right professional support, I found an Australian contact listed on the BAN site and, to my absolute delight, they were located in Brisbane. A little over an hour drive from home, the shot in the dark I needed. I sent an email with the reader's digest version of our situation and awaited her reply.

Consistent throughout recovery resources is rule number one, spouses have access to each other's mobile devices, passwords, emails, social media etc. In the past, I assumed this was an invasion of privacy. Although I've nothing to hide, Dave has always been extremely protective of his mobile, iPad, and laptop. Rarely leaving them lying around, with good reason as I've since learned. Allowing access to this personal space was a huge step for Dave. The changes demonstrated to me he truly wanted to be free. I believe he was prepared to do whatever needed to break habits and patterns of behaviour holding us back from having a healthy, mature marriage.

Midway through the 7-day online program Dave flew to Sydney for work. I picked up the spare iPad at home for one of many check-ins and was surprised to see he had also emailed Affair Recovery. Surprised in a good way that he, too, was reaching out for help, and was also appreciative of how he'd referred to me in the correspondence. Kudos to Dave for this, however, my gratitude soon gave way to horror as another disturbing revelation was disclosed…

∼

DAVE

Preparing for this journey of disclosure, I sought the advice of an AR counsellor online. How do I break the news of an affair fourteen years earlier? The question quickly became redundant after Noni discovered the email. The disclosure completed for me, pre-empted at least. When Noni demanded I rip the band-aid off, she could not have imagined how big and sticky that band-aid was.

Hi Troy,

I have been married for twenty-five years to Noni - my best friend.

My marriage started with me continuing a sexual relationship with a work colleague. Within several months this was discovered and terminated. I was forgiven.

It was this fall that brought me back to an active relationship with God and I pursued my faith life. I again engaged in an emotional/physical relationship with a work associate several years later which was discovered after several months. My wife is a woman of extraordinary faith and love I want to be with her all my life.

About five years later I found myself flirting with a woman (again, a work colleague) and this ended in a sexual relationship-consummated twice. I intermittently stayed in contact but with no sexual activity.

This was the last physical betrayal (fourteen years ago).

However, I did meet someone while travelling to the US in 2009. We talked and shared a glass of wine one night - I found her life interesting - no romantic involvement, I did maintain hidden intermittent correspondence (eventually discovered of course). I maintained

*contact and friendship (no romance real
or implied or physical relationship yet
hidden) with another ex-work mate after
they left the same company in 2011.*
*We corresponded intermittently and met up
a couple of times a year in recent years.*
*I am committed to healing my marriage
and restoring our relationship, as is my
wife.*
*I struggle with sharing the past with Noni,
and how much detail is right.*
*One of the affairs above she does not know
about, but I need to tell her.*
*We are starting the Bootcamp this week.
Any advice for me would be awesome.*
Dave Yates

∼

NONI

WHAT THE HECK!

I could hardly believe my eyes.

Another affair I knew absolutely zero about, how many now? How many others?

Completely beside myself, I sent him a message before he'd had a chance to disembark the aircraft. I wanted a name, nothing more. Just a name. I wasn't chasing an explanation, merely wanting to know who else he chose to betray me with. His evasiveness did nothing but stoke the fire.

I texted: `RIP THE BANDAID OFF!`

Far out!

How many more of these discoveries would I have to deal with? When was I going to get to the bottom of the full extent of his deceit and betrayal? It seemed each time I got close to landing somewhere safe, I was tossed out of a plane again without a parachute by the one I loved! How much could I survive?

I was horrified. The only thoughts scrambling through my mind were,

WHAT ELSE? WHAT'S NEXT? HOW MANY MORE LIES HAVE I BEEN FED? NOTHING'S REAL!

I was in heart-pounding shock, breathless with nowhere to turn…

~

DAVE

In 2004, my underlying vulnerabilities coincided with an opportunity in the form of an encounter with another employee at an overseas meeting. She too was married with children. What started with flirting soon progressed to sexual. Here was another woman bolstering my ego and desire for recognition, she offered this boost free from commitment or expectation.

Freedom to act on our mutual attraction was limited. Living interstate from each other, our 'hook-ups' were restricted to intercompany conferences held biannually for the next eighteen months.

The separation from Noni and the kids, or loneliness caused by interstate travel was not a catalyst for the affair. It was my desire for affirmation, the excitement and sense of entitlement combined with the opportunity to indulge myself in what I considered relatively 'safe' circumstances. 'Safe' referring to my chances of being caught out since the meetings with Ann were a long distance from my family home and always out of sight. Familiar self-explanations used to justify this affair were a well-worn record. I should be entitled to some 'space' for myself, I'm working hard and sacrificing so much with the time away from home. It's not like I am seeing her each week, it's only 'occasional'. I am going to be careful the relationship won't escalate into anything more.

Returning home after eighteen months and leaving the job that provided the periodic contact with Ann allowed me to end the physical aspect of this affair, also the lack of travel in the new job removed access to further opportunity.

Though I had no plans to continue sexual infidelity, I still chose to stay in touch with Ann.

It was too much of a challenge giving up the easy ego boost available from her attention and the favourable image of me she reflected. I enjoyed a sense of power or importance by maintaining the contact, thinking I could manipulate circumstances to recommence a physical relationship... if I wanted. Eventually, I went for a year or more of no contact, then for no particular reason, I touched base to catch-up and chat under the guise of friendship.

Deep down, it was to prove to myself that I was someone special, still had 'something'.

～

NONI

This was the second week of February 2019.

That same day, I received a call from Catriona, the Brisbane contact for Beyond Affairs Network. Catriona is a licensed social worker and specialist couples therapist, herself having walked the path and worked through the devastation of her husband's betrayal. It was the first time I had spoken to anyone who knew, understood and was still married to her husband after unimaginable trauma. Through tearful conversation, I told her of my most recent discovery.

Heaven answered another prayer that day. Listening attentively before calmly advising, she said Dave was not currently a safe person for me.

'Safe' is a well-utilised word in the affair recovery vocabulary since we understand its importance. We humans all want to feel safe; it is paramount to healing and essential for both partners, betrayed and unfaithful. If we cannot be safe with each other, how will we ever learn to trust one another?

Catriona suggested we book intensive counselling. Two full days conducted over two consecutive days. Twenty-eight years of unravelling required an intense approach, would two days be enough? Once I composed myself, I said I'd speak with Dave and get back to her. Sending Dave a text giving him dates, beginning of March or end of March.

"Please book for the earliest possible."

He couldn't wait until the end of the month. Wanting this over and out, to begin repairing the damage as soon as possible. Regardless of the cost, he didn't want to lose our marriage.

I made an appointment.

Three weeks to wait, three weeks wading through quicksand. We were in unknown territory and decided to keep things that had come to light private. Only Dave and Noni knew what secrets the darkness kept. Desperate to find our way, navigating uncharted waters with a broken compass and right or wrong, judgement or speculation from others would not receive invitation. We also had no idea how this was going to play out and knew of no one equipped and able to direct us. The well-meaning opinion of others, intended out of concern, would serve no purpose in our unholy mess.

Unfortunately, trying to protect 'us' placed ourselves in isolation. Still seeing friends but only allowing superficial catch-ups meant we weren't being authentic. Being there in person yet having such distress right beneath the surface was almost an out of body experience, operating on a different plane but not in a good way. I hated it. Totally surreal.

Returning from Sydney on Valentine's Day, Dave handed me what I thought would be full disclosure. Sitting in bed, he asked if I wanted him to stay while I read his truth.

I'm not certain if I wanted him there or not but I said yes.

~

DAVE

Unable to imagine uttering the words I needed to say, while away, I drafted a letter to give Noni on my return. The letter not only revealed the affair with Ann, but also the fact that I reengaged with Karen a couple of years after the first discovery. I carried on in that affair for years.

Noni was waiting upstairs for me to arrive. Tiptoeing into the house, I quietly climbed the carpeted stairs. Noni was sitting on our bed deathly quiet. Passing the summary of my sordid history printed out felt like passing a bomb. I knew not to bother unpacking my bag.

I remained standing and watched the bomb explode. Time was moving for no one.

Then, in slow motion, as Noni read, her face froze in horror and disgust – eyes screaming, HOW COULD YOU?

I concentrated on breathing, staying in the room, remaining upright. I had been running away from the truth and consequences for decades. It was time to be still, strong, and witness the fruit of my choices. Standing there powerless to fix anything, there was no image of myself to rescue any longer. The battered heart of my wife and the mockery of my marriage remained.

I was exposed completely, the framework of the false identity I had carefully constructed was demolished. Over the next few months, I would sift through the debris, occasionally knocking down hidden remnants of the structure in search of the answer to, "How could you, Dave?"

~

NONI

With Dave watching as I read, grief and numbness permeated my body.

"I recommenced a physical and emotional

relationship with Karen within the first year of our marriage. We did sleep together/have sex. This was during the times we were at the same offsite meeting/conferences or work trips. This affair continued up until the day it was discovered. As you know I hid the extent of the relationship at the time of discovery. From then the relationship with her was as a work colleague and emotional distances were put in place.

A few years later (I do not recall the year exactly) I met Beth at a Sales Conference in NZ (all business divisions attended the same venue. She worked in a different division). We sat next to each other at a dinner and I was a bit flattered by the attention she showed me (flirting). There wasn't a sexual or physical encounter. When back in Sydney we would occasionally (maybe once a month or few weeks) catch up for lunch somewhere near the office. There was kissing, but not sex. This was discovered via a flirtatious text message (these communications were the nature of the relationship). All contact ceased.

The only contact since was when I saw her in a surgery she worked at (around 2009), a polite chat ensued, that's all. I think I recall getting and declining a FB friend request a bit later. I looked at her FB profile back around November last year with no intention of contact, just curiosity and boredom, I think.

Around 1998-9, I don't recall exactly when, I completely crossed that boundary with Karen and the relationship became emotional and physical again. Sexual activity was not regular, it did take place during offsite conferences (not all, but that's zero consolation). The affair ceased in 2000 (I believe she became involved with a department manager). After leaving the company the only contact I had with her was an occasional email or LinkedIn message (I think you saw the last one around the time of a colleague's death). I did actually see her by coincidence while having breakfast at a hotel in Sydney about two years ago. I said hello as I was leaving.

In 2003-4 while working at **** I met Ann P who was a rep out of Brisbane at the time. We flirted at a conference in Fiji and kissed one night which escalated to having sex at the next two meetings (one in the Blue Mountains and one in Port Douglas).

We did remain in intermittent contact via email. I recall a year or two later she contacted me about being a referee for different jobs in the industry. At that time, she said we should catch up. I did agree to

*meet her for a coffee and chat (in public
places, once in Brisbane and on the Gold
Coast) three-four times over almost ten
years. No physical or sexual content on
these occasions or ever since. Just talk
about colleagues, work and family. The last
contact was November last year. We met
for a coffee and chat. I was looking for
sympathy (not romance) and she did share
some of her separation/divorce experiences,
some of which was encouraging (she
admitted she wished they had tried harder
to work on their marriage).*

*She now works for another company and has
not been at any conferences I have
attended.*

*In 2009, when I remained in SF after you left, I
went and had dinner at Blues and Biscuits
near Union Station. Susan R was playing.
During her break she walked around and
introduced herself to everyone (probably
twenty - thirty people). We talked for a
while and agreed to continue the
conversation when she finished the show.
We did just that, talked - I did find her and
her life very interesting No physical
contact or sexual innuendo. Subsequently
stayed in contact as you know (likely some
escapism on my part but the whys etc. are
for later). I remember asking myself at
some stage wtf and stopped.*

In 2009 I started at ****. Nancy K was a representative. She presented as a well-travelled person with diverse interests. I did like her as a person but did not feel a strong attraction beyond a friendship. There was no overt flirting innuendo or other physical contact ever.

The contact I had with Nancy was in the context of a colleague at a sales meeting and together at two customer dinners, around 2013. No flirtation or contact of a sexual nature. She left the company to travel shortly after I returned to work (sometime in 2014). We stayed in touch via email no more than twice a year. Late 2016-17 Nancy started work on the Gold Coast. In time we did meet, probably twice in person and by phone or email three-four times a year. No flirtation or contact of a sexual nature. We have never attended the same conferences.

A month or two before you and I separated we made contact around the subject of current and future employment prospects (she had been made redundant and gone back to a company, but it wasn't working out). We met to discuss, I took her CV and gave it to HR.

When you and I separated I would meet Nancy once a week, have lunch, a coffee or go to the beach. During this time I found myself

*getting comfort from her friendship,
conversation and companionship. No
flirtation or contact of a sexual nature.
I realise that I hid this relationship and lied to
you - tells me I knew it was wrong."*

∾

NONI

Like Dave's previous attempts at disclosure, the extent of this most recent confession was also played down. It was only after making a list of 'tell me more' could we get a little closer to the truth. I accepted partial reason being the time frame twenty-five years of memory recall, and partial fact, feeling such disgust and contempt when facing the truth. Dave was still trying to maintain control to protect both himself and me. Often the hardest person to confront 100% honestly is yourself!

When I finished reading his disclosure, I think what floored me the most was discovering he had reignited his affair with Karen. What kind of f****** self-respecting woman would do this? Especially after I extended her an olive branch, stepped up in forgiveness, and made peace with her after she'd had an eighteen-month affair with a man who was in a relationship, engaged, and then married. THAT man was my boyfriend, my fiancé, and my husband! I showed her love she most certainly didn't deserve. WTH! She was at our farewell in Sydney in 2003 and she kissed me goodbye! This was more than betrayal and abuse of my grace and kindness; this was an unspoken betrayal of womanhood. In my opinion, crossing the line like this was something only a bottom feeder would do. I wrote her another letter. This one I kept. It will never be sent. The letter served its purpose by allowing me to vent. It is included at the end of the book. To inflict pain on another person is never motivation to act, no matter how hurt we are. I wanted to berate and insult her, to show her my pain. Goodness knows I wanted revenge at that time like I have never wanted in my entire life. Thoughts crossed my mind about what I might do if she was unfortunate enough to cross my path. I prayed I would have the self-control and grace I've grown appreciative of.

It did leave me wondering...This letter was for me to release the agony and anger I felt in my heart, to give expression to all my hurt, a landing place that would cause no one injury.

Once again, though, I had been made to look like a fool. Someone too trusting, too quick to forgive, too naïve. Was I a doormat to wipe their dirty feet on? Am I really that dumb?

God, Jesus was my best friend and stabiliser, my even keel and peace through this kind of crazy. He loves and knows me intimately. None of us deserve His love but are shown love anyway. Knowing how much forgiveness I'd received for my own mistakes and shortcomings and understanding I am as broken and flawed as the next person, I know holding onto anger is like wearing a weight around my neck and trying to swim. There but for the grace of God go I. His word being written on my heart, ultimately, I had a choice. My choice was not to be ruled by emotion, but instead, to trust in Him.

> Do not take revenge, my dear friends, but leave room
> for God's wrath, for it is written, "It is mine to avenge;
> I will repay," says the Lord.
>
> — ROMANS 12:19 NIV

God never tells us to not be angry, he admonishes us to take care when we are.

> "In your anger do not sin."
>
> — EPHESIANS 4:26 NIV

Primarily, numb and silent was my reaction. Where do we go from here? I felt defeated.

LESSONS FROM BEYOND

DID I WANT TO FORGIVE KAREN? *HELL NO!* INITIALLY I WAS AS ANGRY AS A HORNET.

WAS SHE ALL OF THOSE NASTY THINGS I SAID ABOUT HER IN THIS CHAPTER? MOST DEFINITELY NOT.

HAVE I FORGIVEN HER? YES, I HAVE.

DOES SHE DESERVE MY FORGIVENESS? MAYBE NOT, BUT FORGIVING OTHERS IS OBEDIENCE TO GOD'S WORD AND A GIFT I RESERVE FOR MYSELF.

WOULD I GO OUT OF MY WAY TO AVOID HER IF WE CROSSED PATHS? I DON'T THINK SO.

WOULD I GREET HER? YES, PROBABLY IN PASSING.

NOT EVERYONE WANTS TO RECEIVE FORGIVENESS, EXERCISE THE POWER WITHIN AND GIVE IT ANYWAY.

Our appointment with Catriona was booked for early March, we needed to keep this.

Days after Dave's written disclosure and before our intensive, we retreated to a quaintly refurbed dairy bale in the Byron Hinterland. It was necessary to work through this disclosure, plus, it was vital that I acquire more detail. Intentionally, we set about doing what I needed for clarity; what we both needed. We created another list:

> *Go through every contact/friend/photo/event*
> *on all platforms, face to face with you*
> *present. Retrieve any deleted or archived*
> *messages to women and have you explain*
> *to me who these women are and what you*
> *have to do with them,*
> *then delete and block any potentially risky*
> *connections.*
> *Both of us together, in agreement.*
> *This is so I'm fully aware and know what*
> *you're capable of.*

And this we did! Through this arduous process and the many, many discussions that followed, I learned how Dave has always sought affirmation, validation and relationship with other women in one form or another. Even when the physical aspect of a relationship ended, he needed to continue his association as 'friends'. Special friends, friendships hidden from the marriage and always conducted in complete secrecy. The balancing act of juggling secret relationships over many years prevented him from being 100% present. Dave was never fully available, not to me, our marriage, or our family.

During our weekend away, we watched a movie called *The Heart of Man*, a cinematic retelling of the parable of the prodigal son juxtaposed with interviews of real people, men and women struggling with distractions from their faith and the shame accompanying addiction. It's a brilliant movie that highlights the shame of sexual sin, pornography, and hiding/running from God. It exemplifies the intensity of our Father's heart, His enduring love and relentless pursuit of us. Dave and I, unguarded, let tears roll down our cheeks throughout the movie. It was useless trying to stop them. We were humbled and prostrate. I realised my love wasn't the tool wearing away, melting and chipping the icy walls around Dave's heart, it was God. God was pursuing Dave back then and it was God pursuing him now. My role was simply being committed to the process thereby allowing God to do the work.

LESSONS FROM BEYOND

TWENTY-EIGHT YEARS; SO MANY BETRAYAL QUESTIONS.

INITIALLY, I NEEDED TO GET MY HEAD AROUND HOW, WHEN AND WHY. NOT THE INTRICACIES OF THE SHARED PURSUITS, BUT I NEEDED DETAILS. WHICH MEETINGS, HOW OFTEN, WHERE ETC...

THE QUESTIONS CHANGED OVER TIME.

I ONLY ASKED ABOUT ONE COMPARISON. "DID YOU WISH I WAS MORE LIKE ANY OF THE AFFAIR PARTNERS?"

AFTER A LONG PAUSE HE SAID, "I WISH YOU LOOKED AT ME IN THE SAME WAY."

"GIVE ME A REASON TO LOOK AT YOU LIKE THAT."

WHO WAS IT THAT FELL IN LOVE WITH THEIR OWN IMAGE REFLECTED IN STILL WATERS?

HMMM...

～

DAVE

The term narcissist is generally associated with someone in love with themselves. How could this apply to me when I really hadn't liked myself for eons? There are many variations on the fable of Narcissus. One commonality was that Narcissus was inconsiderate and dismissive of others; as punishment, he became obsessed by a reflection of himself in a pond. It was the image he was obsessed with. An obsession that resulted in death when he realised the image was not real or achievable. Just like Narcissus, I became enslaved to an image I desired yet could not attain. A favourable image reflected by the affair partners. None of them knew the real me.

Like a spin-doctor during a crisis, I was often in damage control even when there was no obvious damage done, bending and contorting situations and interactions into positive reflections of me. The people closest wondered why I needed to keep proving myself right when I was plainly wrong. In my mind, I created a world where my intentions stood for who I am, not my actions. Intentions to love and care for my family; to be kind, gentle, and thoughtful; faithful and wholesome. Intending to be patient, tolerant, sober, and moral.

I fully intended to be all of these things and therefore I was. I identified with the created image, not the actions. When I was treated per my actions rather than my intentions, I claimed to be judged poorly and unfairly and wondered why everyone couldn't see the good things I was. Why did they focus on small aberrations? My hypervigilance against perceived attacks, challenges, feedback, or simple questions arose from insecurity and a poor sense of self. My responses were prickly

and judgemental, insisting I was right and everyone else had it wrong.

Extreme fragility disguised as the height of arrogance.

I didn't think more of myself, on the contrary, much less. Grasping at anything to prove a sense of control or certainty, anything to feel better about me, I exerted so much energy trying to capture and preserve that perfect image. This led to incredible weakness and a blemished character. These days, I acknowledge my weakness and am thankful.

I will boast all the more gladly so that Christ's power may rest on me.

> "My grace is sufficient for you, for my power is made perfect in weakness."
>
> — 2 Corinthians 12:9 (NIV)

CHAPTER 21

NEXT...

NONI

Surgery kept me homebound for a few weeks at the end of February. With time on my hands, I checked Dave's Facebook history and was astounded by the illumination of more discovery. In the space of weeks following our separation in 2018, Dave looked up not only his previous affair partners, including Karen, but also a friend of one of my significantly younger girlfriends who had recently separated from her husband. She was a neighbour on our street! This sent me spiralling again into an abyss of uncontrolled emotions. It was another WTF! It seemed like there was a never-ending list of women he needed and sought after to soothe him.

Fury and rage escalating, yet again, he was away travelling. I was a mess. I confronted him about this over the phone. He offered excuses – all lame and lacked plausibility. Nothing could make sense of his neediness or ease my pain.

A close and trusted girlfriend sensed something happening. She turned up with a coffee and croissant in hand, sat at the end of my bed and I told her everything. Nothing surprised her. We sat talking for hours and I was filled with enormous relief after finally sharing my burden. Entirely certain that she would keep our confidence, I proceeded with caution, still unsure of what we needed and what needed to be told.

The night before our two-day counselling session with Catriona, Dave gently and lovingly said, "Non, if you don't want to stay with me after this weekend, I wouldn't blame you, I totally understand if this is too much and you've had enough."

This was one of the greatest acts of love Dave had shown. Instead of fighting to gain control over me and our relationship he demonstrated honour, graciously allowing me to make a choice without coercion. He was genuinely offering me freedom from this tangled web. He was exasperated that he had inflicted so much pain on me and despised himself for causing unfathomable destruction.

What he failed to grasp was that I needed to heal from this devastation whether with him, or alone. My choice was clear. We reread the notes we'd written previously and I reminded him exactly how we wanted our futures to look.

Despite massive heartache and pain, beautiful moments existed simultaneously.

We relished our newfound vulnerability which provided more opportunities for us to offer ourselves physically and emotionally to one another. I felt all the joy and passion of the new bride I had been twenty-five years before. Unlike the young bride who had been hoodwinked, this time, I was going in with my eyes wide open. Dave and I booked an Airbnb in Brisbane for our intensive with Catriona, and yes, it was intense. The ground covered over these two days was arguably the most beneficial investment we'd made in our marriage. The cost of us not separating or divorcing was around $15,000.00. This sum included a relationship program on the west coast of Australia, solicitor's fees, mediation, and the infidelity intensive with Catriona; nothing by comparison to how costly divorce would be. (BTW a mere 10% of this total reflects our two-day intensive, worth it and more!)

We left with a greater understanding of the how's and why's of affairs, tools for communicating effectively and respectfully, as well as action steps to take moving forward. We also dug deeper, differentiating between what is actual, factual, and what might be 'the story we are telling ourselves'. Equipped with our 'conquering infidelity arsenal', we headed home.

Although fatigued, the future looked promising, filled with greater confidence and hope.

We found our bearings. A follow-up session with Catriona was planned for early May.

One of the steps agreed upon (Dave albeit apprehensively), was the need to be completely vulnerable and transparent with our adult children. Determined to move forward in truth and love, we agreed that they, too, had the right to be kept in the loop. The three siblings each in their own way, were damaged by tiptoeing through this minefield.

Concurring also, it was time to tell a select few of our trusted friends. We chose to meet with three spiritually mature couples as well as our pastor. They would support us prayerfully and be a safe haven when we needed one. Meeting with each couple privately, we decided to share with them before telling the kids. We would need God's wisdom and protection when speaking with Corey, Ruby, and Ezekiel. Our confidantes would shelter us with prayer. Rather than verbalising and risk losing direction when opening the dark caverns, I scripted a brief yet succinct draft we would use to convey the main gist of our message.

> *For our children:*
> *You've all read the message I sent Ezekiel*
>   *explaining how I arrived at the decision of*
>   *separating from Dad. I wrote Dad another*
>   *one with a lot more detail. You don't need*
>   *all of the details, but you do need to*
>   *understand the source of a lot of the*
>   *dysfunction, confusion, anger, aggression*

and hurt we've all lived with for twenty-eight years. The reason we want to tell you is because we love you. We love each other deeply, and we don't want to go on living with secrecy and lies. We don't want to pretend we're OK when we're not. We want to be fully transparent, authentic, and most of all we don't want to continue with this destruction in our lives or see any of you repeat our mistakes in your own lives.

This is not going to be easy to hear. It's been excruciatingly painful for both of us, but we're both committed to our marriage, to each other, and to you all. We will do whatever is necessary to safeguard against this ever happening to us again.

Mum xxx

Although I love mum from the depths of my being, our entire marriage has been clouded by a web of lies, betrayal and deceit. I was having an affair with a woman I worked with at the time Mum and I got married and I continued that affair after we got married. Mum found out, forgave me and the woman, but I chose to re-engage with this woman emotionally and sexually from 1998 until just before we moved up here.

> *I have been unfaithful in our marriage to Mum*
> *and yourselves in one way or another ever*
> *since.*
> *I have kept secret relationships with five*
> *women over the past twenty-five years,*
> *three of those were physical/emotional and*
> *out of these, two included sexual*
> *encounters right up until 2005. I*
> *maintained contact with one of these*
> *women and saw her as recently as Nov of*
> *last year.*
> *Mum knew and suspected snippets of my lies*
> *but she showed me love as much as I would*
> *let her. She had no idea the extent of my*
> *double life until I disclosed to her on Feb*
> *14th, 2019.*
> *Dad*

Conveying the bare bones of our story, we watched as each dear couple and the pastor read quietly. Bordering on disbelief, although speechless and heavy of heart, our brokenness was received without judgement. The utmost grace and love was extended to Dave and me. Embracing our trust, offering their support in any way we needed. Our dear friends were visibly distressed for us and me, of course, and they all demonstrated respectful curiosity. No one required details. None were able to extend insights from their experience, but they could offer their love, prayers, support, and of course, their confidence.

NONI YATES & DAVID YATES

This is all we needed.

With each disclosure, Dave became lighter in spirit and demeanour. This, in itself, was a good thing. We truly rejoiced in his new-found freedom. The freedom I asked of God right back at the beginning of our courtship! Who knew this would take so long and be this hard?

Infidelity betrayal, when exposed, has an insidious way of transferring its weight off of the unfaithful spouse squarely onto the shoulders of the betrayed. We at no time requested or deserved this burden. It's simply another one of the many unfair realities of adultery!

CHAPTER 22

HOW MANY MORE SKELETONS ARE LEFT IN THIS CLOSET?

NONI

One more discovery left me questioning my own judgement of Dave's character more than ever. Gasping for air, I wondered, "Who the bloody hell is he?"

April 1, 2019, April Fool's Day, but I was no fool!

Dave had been an active member of an online surfer forum for many years. Harmless enough, I thought, surfing and sport, blokey stuff. Flicking through his current emails during a semi-regular check of his iPad, one popped up titled 'Babe of the Day'. Now THIS caught my attention and I decided to follow the trail. WOWSERS didn't that open up a whole new 'Pandora's box'. On this forum, some threads are public, others you must subscribe to.

No guesses for what Dave had subscribed to. 'Babe of the Day' was one, but there were more.

I set about finding every comment and every contribution his alias made over five years and was disgusted, embarrassed, humiliated, and repulsed by the puerile derogatory nature of who he portrayed himself as on this forum and alarmed at his distasteful regard for women. The insulting discovery left me flabbergasted. Disgust percolated toward his other Neanderthal 'mates' hiding behind their avatars and keyboards.

$\sim$

DAVE

Surfing was my passion. I frequented different websites for information on travel, forecasts, reports, board design, and everything associated with the sport. Beginning on one page as an observer and occasional anonymous forum contributor (as are 99.9% of participants), I restricted my comments to moments I thought I had insight worth sharing.

Over the years, I gradually participated with greater frequency, realising I enjoyed the sense of recognition directly associated with responses to my contribution. My participation continued to increase. Like many online platforms, the forum was a place where a shared interest and familiarity created a sense of community. Unlike real community though, the anonymity provided freedom from the restraints of conventional social interaction.

There is only so much content and discussion relevant to the sport that can be generated at any time. I began reading various tangent threads and discussions and these often descended into online feuds, 'flaming' competitions with escalating put-downs, sometimes amusing, at other times extreme and offensive. Considering myself quick-witted, I soon became a regular participant in these threads. Starting with twisting words or taking them out of context, using double entendre and jumping on board a 'joke' that was escalating. A combination of entertainment, attention, and acknowledgement fuelled my new routine. I was like a schoolboy trying to impress by outdoing the previous kid's act of bravado or vulgarity. Whether making offensive, derogatory, and inappropriate comments or applauding the efforts of others, I was in boots and all. This guise of humour was driven by recognition and acceptance. It was an online game of sport played anonymously with no contact, no accountability, and no consequences until exposed. Leaving my own standards and boundaries at the login screen, misogyny, sexist, and crude humour was rampant.

I, a willing participant, enjoyed the gratification of being acknowledged or belonging.

$\sim$

NONI

I was ropeable.

I was too enraged to speak, and seeing how Dave was in Sydney, I let my fingers do the work.

They almost bled as I furiously sent messages conveying my ire.

Dave asked me to please stop looking, a request I denied. He contacted the administrator asking for his profile to be deleted. This happened, but not before I took screenshots of the rot so he could not deny and minimise. No more 'gaslighting'. He had to face himself again.

Journaling was the avenue to unleash my pain.

> *"How much do I have to suck up? How much*
> *do I have to get over?*
> *Is it possible???? Can I do this?*
> *Am I crazy for wanting to?*
> *Am I such a faulty human being that I have to*
> *hang onto someone who is using me?*
> *Am I hanging onto someone who doesn't want*
> *me or want the pure relationship I*
> *hope for?*
> *Is my self-worth in the gutter?*
> *Do I not deserve the marriage I desire?*
> *Am I kidding myself?*
> *Am I expecting the impossible?*
> *Should I let it go?*

Should I walk away?

Am I keeping Dave from being where he wants to be and doing what he wants to do?

Am I an idiot?

Dave has had affairs during our entire marriage (twenty-five years) including sex with at least four other women (that I know of) since we met in 1990 (twenty-eight years) and continued a relationship with at least one of the sexual partners until Dec 2018.

Plus, he had several other emotional affairs right up until Christmas 2018, that I'm aware of (there's at least two but could be more).

He's viewed and masturbated to pornography, enjoys rugged, visually erotic sex, yet struggles to make tender love to me.

He is an active member of a surfer forum where smut is the norm and he actively views and participates in threads called 'Babe of the day' (which comes with a 'work warning' because of the explicit nature). It's not hard-core porn exactly, but a sexually arousing soft porn thread. He previously commented on this thread saying he is 'as stiff as a board' and he tells me his comment was a joke, some joke! (He visited it again today and erased the last two days of browser history.)

It's no joke when…

> *He comments on a public forum he's 'crossed*
> *the border to chase waves and escape*
> *domestic tension' and he's disappointed*
> *he's not seen any 'cougar action'.*
> *WTF! WHO IS THIS GUY I'VE BEEN*
> *MARRIED TO FOR twenty-five years?*
> *I feel humiliated, undesirable, disrespected and*
> *devalued.*
> *I AM NOTHING TO HIM AND I'M A*
> *F****** IDIOT FOR BELIEVING THE*
> *B******* HE SPINS ME TO KEEP ME*
> *HANGING ON!!!!!"*

Yes, I was wild...

When he came home, we sat down to discuss yet another hidden side of him. He was slowly seeing how detrimental this online interaction was, how subtle the slide from innocence to smut. Once again, this was a man without boundaries. Desensitised from years spent venturing into different compartments of his life. The forum was another secret hiding place finally exposed for what it was, now; no longer as enticing as he once thought.

"Who keeps company with the wolf will learn to howl." Vietnamese proverb.

It's a little like placing a live frog into a pot of cold water on the stove. Bringing the water to boil slowly, the frog doesn't jump out. It swims around until it gradually dies.

Now that we'd dived into this abyss, I supposed it's timely to go back and revisit the Netflix viewing history. The history he'd previously denied. Turns out maybe he watched those titles after all… he wasn't entirely clear. What did become clearer was his appetite for pornography, and like every other secret that had found its way to the surface, the full truth of this compulsion came trickling out over time.

The assemblage of every agonising revelation injured me more, yet concurrently allowed deeper access to him. Authenticity matured in our relationship more than previously possible, and yes, I still loved him. This didn't mean I didn't hate what he'd done, I absolutely hated every single despicable act. By April 2019, I finally considered myself close to knowing the extent of who my husband was and what he was capable of doing. It was now time to tell the kids.

CHAPTER 23

COMING CLEAN WITH
THE CLAN

NONI

W e'd had some discussion around how we would approach the kids. Dave needed lots of encouragement, I was confident that our honesty would only serve to strengthen their relationships, not weaken them. They too had only ever known part of their father, so it was impossible to love him completely while he tried to control what they saw.

I wanted to respect Dave, reassure him that I had his back, that he had my unreserved support and love. Ideally, we wanted to talk to them together, but logistically, this was impossible since all three resided in different states. We spoke of whom to tell first, mindful of not placing too big a burden on any of them without the others knowing. We'd likely never procure a perfect or easy solution.

Dave had a work trip to Melbourne and caught up with Ezekiel over dinner. I didn't realise he was going to divulge his secrets that evening but I'm glad he did. I wasn't with him, so he had to fill me in on how that went down.

Ruby would be the toughest cookie to crack, not only because her relationship with Dave was constrained, but because she'd lived with us the longest and witnessed the most toxicity. Plus, I'm her mum. She is a young woman and this man, her father, has disrespected both of us big time. We would need to broach Ruby with extra sensitivity. I spoke to Rubes, telling her we would like to chat, said it was important and asked when would be suitable. Dave and I scheduled our 'appointment' with Ruby the following week. Dave led, managing to communicate most of our 'script', even though he was extremely anxious.

Stony faced and silent she remained, sitting on the lounge facing us. Asking if she had any questions, we reassured her of our intention.

Her only question, "Have you finished?"

"Yes."

She stood up and left the room. I guess it went as well as could be expected.

She has never asked any questions; Ruby is a strong-minded young lady with her own independent thoughts. We respect that. She has been less than impressed by us, we are not perfect.

Corey heard the news over dinner one night in Sydney. In true Corey fashion, he quietly looked at us and said, "Hmmm…" It was as simple as that. SUMO; Shut Up and Move On.

None of the kids asked further questions. Not sure if this is healthy or not. Nothing catastrophically consequential about any of the conversations eventuated.

In fact, Dave's internal dialogue, "How can anyone love me if they know the truth of who I am?" has proved to be the exact opposite. There has been significant healing in all relationships.

Dave was unmasked and practising being true and authentic so surely there were no more stones left unturned. Both of us were relieved to be past this hurdle. Now we could move on and do the work needed for our recovery.

CHAPTER 24

MOVING PAST THE PAIN

NONI

I flew to Bali mid-April and Dave joined me a few days later.

During 'quiet' time, my subconscious recalled a photo I had seen in one of my many periods of 'social stalking'. A photo of Nancy grinning from ear to ear, her lovely, young, fresh-faced self was perched cross-legged in front of a brightly coloured café backdrop. Something about this did not sit well within my spirit. Logging in, I revisited her Instagram profile.

The photo was taken at Byron Bay on December 5. My gut churned, and instinctively I knew who the photographer was.

I sent Dave the photo with a caption that read, "You took this, didn't you!" It wasn't a question.

He confirmed my suspicion. Yep! You bet, I was off and racing! OMG, I was raging!

The most bothersome part for me was not only did he take time off work to be with this girl, hang at the beach, buy her brunch, all the while I was f****** scraping together $$$ to exist!

The greatest insult of all, wait for it... is that he did this TWO DAYS AFTER we left the specialist's room where we agreed to 'the process of a possible reconciliation'. What kind of person does this????

A NARCISSIST! That's who! I don't think words exist to describe this insurmountable pain. Alone in my resort room, I penned my emotional anguish.

> *I'm sorry*
> *I have never been enough for you*
> *I will never be enough for you*
> *My love is not enough for you*
> *I'm sorry*
> *That you didn't mean 'I do' the same way I did*
> *That I assumed you and I shared the same*
> *   moral values*
> *For giving myself so totally to you*
> *I'm sorry*
> *That I've been robbed of safety in our marriage*
> *That I have become insecure beyond anything*
> *   ever imagined*
> *That I am threatened by every sideways glance*
> *   you cast at an attractive woman*

That your wandering eye is the first step in
*   you betraying me again*
That my self-confidence is shattered
I'm sorry
For the years lost
For the many days, nights, calls, texts, emails,
*   thoughts, fantasies, feelings and passion*
*   you shared with your many affair partners*
For my naivety in believing all your lies and
*   trusting you*
I'm sorry
That our children were deprived of an
*   honourable marriage commitment by their*
*   father*
For all the anger, angst and manipulation
*   they've had to live through*
That they too are the collateral damage of your
*   double life*
I'm sorry
That these wounds run so deep
That my heart and mind are scarred forever by
*   your betrayal*
That I'm really really frightened of how
*   unpredictable this journey is and am scared*
*   we won't make it*
And I'm also hurt beyond belief and so very
*   very sad*
My heart is aching, I feel like an anchor and
*   chain are around it and I've been tossed*
*   overboard into deep water.*

Arriving at midnight and while I slept, at least pretending to, Dave quietly crept into bed careful not to disturb me. When the morning sun peeked through the window covering, we lay facing each other. Recognising the now all too familiar sadness in our eyes, we began wading through another round of hurt. Without trying to explain or justify, Dave simply remained 'present', holding a safe place, listening to my pain. The simple act of not recoiling, justifying, defending, or blaming is the most soothing action we've discovered in healing after betrayal. Showing up in this way communicated to me that Dave 'gets it'. He understands how his actions caused inconceivable damage. He's prepared to own his actions as well as the consequences. He's willing to be present for me, not to fix or change, but just be there, one hundred per cent. With balm applied to the wound, we were now free to enjoy our holiday.

From Bali we flew to Sumba, both excited for a new adventure at a very cool simple surf camp. One of us a tad more excited than the other.

Our storytelling journey originated in this camp. Plenty of spare hours while Dave surfed allowed me the freedom of unfolding my inner world. My only distraction, every fine element of nature.

Breathtakingly beautiful, Sumba's landscape is pristine. Crystal clear water meets white cliff outcrops. In April, the flora is still green in the wake of the wet season. A perfect combination for us. Sumba is remote and less inhabited in comparison to Bali, Lombok, and Java. We had an amazing couple of weeks, glowing with positivity and hopeful we would be able to move beyond the pain. Dave nailed some good waves and fish and both of us enjoyed the much-needed rest.

Although Dave is fit and healthy, he'd had a persistent cough for a month or so and now that I was with him 24/7, I noticed it more. He seemed to be struggling slightly with shortness of breath when walking inclines. Fine in the water and on flat ground, we ignored other symptoms as being unimportant at the time.

Our adventure came and went, and we returned home refreshed and loved up on Saturday, May 4.

Amongst our pile of mail was a letter from the government with the results from the bowel screening test Dave submitted before we left. Traces of blood were found in either one or both samples tested.

Nothing alarming in and of itself. When coupled with fatigue, shortness of breath, coughing and weight loss, we realised this could be a much bigger deal. As Dave and I walked down the beach, he looked at me and said, "Well this is a real s*** sandwich!"

As soon as business hours rolled around, Dave booked a colonoscopy for the following Monday, May 13. He scheduled a GP appointment for Friday, May 10 to pick up the referral. Dave's GP examined him, not overly concerned with the lab results until we mentioned Dave's other symptoms. The doctor casually suggested a chest X-ray and blood tests, routine measures to rule out anything more sinister. More than six years since his stage IV SCC, Dave was officially in remission. Not wanting to waste time, Dave's blood tests and X-ray were completed that same afternoon. The colonoscopy procedure culminated in the removal of a few polyps, fairly standard for someone his age. While resting at home in the afternoon I noticed several missed calls on Dave's phone. The medical centre had called more than once.

Dave returned the calls and his doctor informed him of a mass in the left lung. He should have a CAT scan to find out more. Dave was going to Sydney in the morning for work.

Away for two nights, he told his GP he'd have a scan the following week. With a degree of urgency, his doctor told him not to wait until next week, that he needed the scan done sooner.

A CAT scan was booked for Thursday as soon as he returned from Sydney.

Dave caught the first flight to Sydney on Tuesday morning. By Wednesday afternoon he was extremely unwell and decided to retreat to his hotel room. It appeared he was coming down with a bad case of 'man flu'. We spoke briefly, he was sick.

Next morning, I called to check in on him, but his mobile diverted to message bank. I tried calling the room. Becoming increasingly concerned, I contemplated calling a work colleague to ask whether he would check on Dave. I can honestly say this is one of the few times in our history my mind and heart did not race to suspicion after calls went unanswered. Heaven knows plenty rang out purely because he was with other women. Another stark reality of how crazy infidelity can make you. Unfortunate, but true.

It wasn't long before my phone rang, Dave had been in the shower and was preparing to leave for the airport. Instant relief, he's on his way home.

He felt like death, as bad as he'd ever felt, and he had been close in the past.

Ample hydration was necessary for an efficient CAT scan which was to be done at 2.30 pm.

His throat was excruciatingly painful and he'd only been able to sip fifty ml of water in the past twenty-four hours, which wasn't going to be enough to hydrate him properly. I called his doctor to ask if we should postpone the scan or take him to ED for intravenous hydration.

There was no hesitation, we headed straight to the ED. Once triaged, Dave went in for examination. He was running a fever. We explained he was actually scheduled for a CAT scan in a couple of hours. The doctor checked the X-ray results asking us if we'd seen them. Had Dave's doctor explained them to him? Replying "No", we perceived it couldn't be good. The doctor asked for Dave's phone, took a photo of the X-ray, and came back with a picture.

He pointed at the mass, "You know what this is, don't you?"

Staring silently at each other, he announced the dreaded C word and instructed the nurse to pump fluid into Dave as quickly as possible.

We spent hours in Emergency before Dave was moved to the oncology ward. Memories flooded back as we found ourselves amidst familiar surrounds. The cancer diagnosis failed to explain the fever or man flu symptoms. Turns out this illness was entirely coincidental. He had septicaemia and could have been dead within days if we hadn't acted when we did! If there was any good news associated with Dave having blood poisoning, it was this; Dave's specialists from 2013 were all on-premises so everything about his upcoming C treatment was expedited.

Stable, though still hospitalised, we arranged a leave pass, a day out for Dave.

Removing cannulas and electrodes, Dave swapped hospital gown for boardshorts and we escaped the regular buzzing of call bells. The sterile hospital stench soon was forgotten as fresh salt air filled our nostrils – the sweet solace of the beach and ocean. Dave's happy place. We sat, emotionally closer than we'd ever been. We both conceded that if this is what it took to arrive at the place we were, and this is all we had, then it's all been worthwhile. Every uncomfortable discovery, disclosure, and heart-breaking detail. Every tear shed, every sleepless night. Every single grief-stricken moment. Worth it.

~

DAVE

Some might say cancer is the toughest challenge they've had to face. I can honestly say my two bouts pale in significance to the personal battles I brought upon myself.

After Christmas, a series of events propelled me into confronting new and sometimes excruciating truths. Clothing myself in decades of shame, a cheap substitute for humility.

Shame allowed me to remain self-focused and self-centred when faced with my unpleasant character traits. Exploring new ways of managing discomfort, I began empathising with my family instead of blaming them. I sought to understand how my actions impacted Noni, the kids, and others, rather than minimising and deflecting responsibility. Instead, I forced myself to lean into those thorny moments. It wasn't easy; every instinctual urge told me to run from conflict. There was plenty of opportunity for practice. Each time I resisted the temptation to flee I gained strength and restraint I'd not known previously. Just like the shedding of secrets and shame, undoing my defensiveness and fragility was a gradual process. A process that released a burden I was unaware existed until it lost its grip. For most of my life

I strove for perfection over authenticity. As a consequence of aiming for an unobtainable measure, I could never love or be loved unconditionally. While ever I controlled and permitted Noni to conditionally know me, she was only able to love that version.

How could she possibly love the 'real' me? Conviction of my worthiness had nothing to do with a newly perfected upgrade of the old version of Dave. Noni loved me and continued loving me despite being fully aware of each flaw and imperfection. More than this, Noni chose to love me when she had every reason not to. Her love demonstrated to me how God has loved me my entire life. It is only through my failures and weakness that I could experience this love. A revelation indelibly marked in my memory.

Late May 2019

Taking advantage of day leave from the hospital, Noni picked me up for a few hours respite.

I was ready and waiting, eager for the sunlight to greet my body. Winding down the car windows, craving the feel of fresh air and breeze on my face, we headed to the beach.

It felt so good to be out of the circulated air-conditioned ward. The feel of soft warm sand between my toes, how I'd missed this. Procrastinating where I could, attempting to delay the unavoidable return to Oncology, I asked if we could swing by home so I could pick up a form which I didn't need. Anything to stall going back to hospital. Walking into my office to grab the unneces-sary document, I was stunned at what greeted me. Above my desk on the white painted wall, filling space between desktop and louvred windows were eighteen handwritten post-it notes from Noni.

1. I'm so grateful that we are on this journey together
2. love love love
3. Thank you
4. You are so brave
5. You're my hero
6. You are more than enough
7. Thank you for loving me
8. You make my heart sing
9. I choose you
10. I love you I adore you
11. I appreciate you
12. My heart belongs to you
13. Thank you for being courageous
14. I love you like I've never loved anyone
15. Thank you for being gentle
16. Thank you for helping me become the person I am today
17. I'm a better person because of you
18. You are all I want and need

Clasping both hands to my mouth, I read each loving expression through a multitude of tears, barely able to contain my joy at that moment and overwhelmed by the depth and breadth of this love. If this is what Noni believed about me after everything I had subjected her to, it was high time I started to believe this of myself. The gravity and uncertainty of what I was about to endure physically faded into a different perspective compared to the reality of who I had become. This is pure, unadulterated truth. I am loved as I am, weak and imperfect. This is who I am, and I am enough! No longer did I need to chase a better image nor seek approval from others. The only way was up, it was time to fully embrace the love I'd been denying for more than half of my days on earth!

~

NONI

Without a doubt, the anguish of the last six months taught us to love each other completely.

It sucked that this bloody cancer showed up. Us and our relationship though, our love, was more than enough. The incredible blessing of this timing, we were well on the path to healing and reconciliation. Doing everything within our ability, creating a brand-new relationship.

Rewriting 'our story'. In all honesty, had God not changed my heart towards Dave five months earlier, I doubt this cancer would have been reason enough for me to reconcile with him. I was heading in one direction and one direction only. Subscribing to emails 'Divorce Care Daily', girding myself with tools to go it alone, and as far from Dave and his anger as possible. Sure, I would care for him and do anything required to look after him, but this care would be more out of sympathy than the deep love which was now transforming us both daily.

So, when we thought the biggest battle ahead was our relationship recovery, another almighty curveball was hurled our way (justanothercurveball.wordpress.com our blog keeping everyone up to date through both death-defying bouts with cancer). The size of the tumour in Dave's left lung meant he would need a pneumonectomy. The whole lung had to be removed since the position of the tumour increased an already complex procedure. While not entirely clear on scans, the tumour appeared dangerously close to Dave's aorta. Dave's surgery carried significant risk. Ruby was with us, but I thought it a good idea if Corey and Ezekiel came home so we could all be together before the operation.

Ezekiel was still fairly non-communicative with me, although sometime earlier in the year he unblocked my number from his phone. I might get an occasional reply when I sent a message. He came home a few nights before Dave went back to hospital. It was obvious he was self-medicating heavily with alcohol. At twenty-one, he was an adult who'd been out of home for almost five years. Although we were still extremely concerned for him, I had bigger giants to slay.

Ezekiel's second night home, he followed me to my room asking respectfully if he could talk to me.

"Sure, what's up?"

Walking into my room, he sat near me on the bed.

"Thank you for never giving up on me, I'm sorry." And then he said, "I kept all the letters you wrote to me."

Neither of us expressed any great flood of emotion. Thanking him for the gesture, we chatted briefly though I doubt he would remember any conversation.

I've anticipated a day would eventually come when we would have full reconciliation.

This was not that moment, but perhaps it was the first step. Survival when loving someone caught in addiction is to hope for the best yet steady ourselves in preparation for the worst (a true statement, not intending to sound pessimistic). Addiction is often a vicious cycle and long, drawn-out process. This moment in our timeline was a beginning I was more than thankful for.

On Thursday, June 6, 2019, Dave underwent a five-hour operation to remove not only cancer, but his entire left lung! Initially, the surgeon attempted to remove the cancerous lung laparoscopically. Two hours after surgery commenced, Dave was placed on a heart/lung machine and the operation was completed through a fully opened chest cavity.

Cancer had attached to the aorta.

My beautiful, strong husband pulled through. High as a kite on Ketamine and Morphine made for plenty of humour in serious surrounds. After a few days in ICU and a couple more on the ward, he was allowed home. Twelve weeks of chemotherapy followed once his body recovered from the surgical trauma. Recovery was slow. At times, Dave was as weak as a kitten. His strong, muscular physique had been ravaged; he was at the bottom of a steep incline.

Bearing in mind also, this major event occurred while we were only two months out from D-Day. Only a handful of people knew of the other challenges we were facing privately.

Understandably, from May until November, all care and concern was for Dave. He lost a lung through the most intrusive procedure. Throughout this period, it would be nice to imagine all was wonderful on the home front. There were many sweet moments, but we were still struggling through the atrocities of Dave's secrets. Our recovery needs didn't supernaturally vanish with the resurgence of cancer. While we were still trying to wade through the mire of duality, we had to fight for dear life again! Sweet and sour is the best way to describe this period. We were gifted with hours, days, and weeks to be fully present, grabbing a hold of time and claiming the power of 'now'. In the same instance, I was clambering. Trying to work on my own healing after betrayal as well as supporting my beloved emotionally, physically, and spiritually. At times, I felt like Dave's cancer trumped my pain and I voiced my truth. For most of our married life, Dave had leaned on me, Noni the grown-up, the mature responsible one. Noni, the glue who held it all together. Noni, strong, dependable, emotionally stable.

Once we embarked on the affair recovery process, balance shifted. For the first time in twenty-eight years, Dave was learning how to be an adult. It seemed the scales were tipping, allowing me to feel safe. To lean on Dave, permitting me to take my hands off the wheel.

Trusting him to man up and be strong and dependable. Taking up his mantle and covering us, protecting his family. This bloody cancer, though, destroyed Dave's flesh, leaving me with a frail skeletal shell requiring close observation. Noni morphing into nurse, meeting Dave's every need. Until you're a betrayed, you won't understand this feeling, words hardly convey what this is like.

Many times, I had to literally talk myself back from the ledge of stepping into crazy town.

Much of our recovery had to sit on the backburner. We were moving at a much slower pace and depending on Dave's health status often at a complete standstill. I needed to recover with or without him, my energy and love was stretched to the max. My capacity bordered on overload.

I erected walls, stopping any outside invasion no matter how well-intended. Wisdom told me what I could and couldn't handle. We leaned on our close Godly circle.

They were the ones who would ask, "Noni, how are you?"

Beyond Betrayal

They *got* the enormity of our battle. God bless them. I am forever thankful we decided to trust the few.

Weathering the months, we moved through the fog until it began to lift.

Once again, we could see the road ahead.

LESSONS FROM BEYOND

RAVAGED BY CANCER AND CHEMO, DAVE WAS PHYSICALLY AND EMOTIONALLY TRASHED.

UNDERSTANDABLY, THE ILLNESS LEFT LITTLE TO GIVE TO US.

PUSHING ON THOUGH, MOVING THROUGH EACH OBSTACLE, HE BECAME STRONGER AND STRONGER.

HIS PHYSICAL APPEARANCE ONLY A SHELL OF HIS FORMER SELF, THE INNER MAN ROSE AND CONTINUES TO RISE.

THE MAN DAVE HAS BECOME, IN MY OPINION, IS MORE ATTRACTIVE THAN EVER.

WE ARE ALL OUTWARDLY WASTING AWAY...ARE WE ALL STRENGTHENING INTERNALLY?

16 THEREFORE WE DO NOT LOSE HEART. THOUGH OUTWARDLY WE ARE WASTING AWAY, YET INWARDLY WE ARE BEING RENEWED DAY BY DAY. 17 FOR OUR LIGHT AND MOMENTARY TROUBLES ARE ACHIEVING FOR US AN ETERNAL GLORY THAT FAR OUTWEIGHS THEM ALL. 18 SO WE FIX OUR EYES NOT ON WHAT IS SEEN, BUT ON WHAT IS UNSEEN SINCE WHAT IS SEEN IS TEMPORARY, BUT WHAT IS UNSEEN IS ETERNAL.

— 2 CORINTHIANS 4:16-18

CHAPTER 25

THE PRODIGAL RETURNS

NONI

Only a few short months from the last discovery day, Ezekiel asked Dave if he could move back home. Although welcomed news, I was apprehensive of what the return of our prodigal would mean for 'us'. Did we need an extra challenge when our plate was already full?

Ezekiel displays many of his father's traits and characteristics (good and bad).

I was determined not to place myself in a position where I could be subjected to verbal or emotional abuse ever again. There was nothing unclear about my determination, Dave understood completely. That ship had well and truly sailed, our future had to look different, very different.

It was time for Dave to read *Why does he do that? Inside the minds of angry and controlling men,* the book I'd read following our separation in 2018. Perhaps the lessons and information might be beneficial for Dave to help Ezekiel make sense of his own actions, behaviour, and feelings. In giving Dave the book to read, I reminded him of the importance of remembering, behaviours discussed in the book are what he's known, learned, and done.

They are not who he is. It's crucial that we discern between what we do and who we are.

The things we do don't define us. Our past doesn't define us, our jobs and bank accounts don't define us, nor does the car we drive, the clothes we wear, the house/street we live in, or the person we're married to. Thank goodness!

The Bible says God knew us before we were formed in our mothers' womb, we are fearfully and wonderfully made, we're made in the likeness and image of Christ himself.

It is our choice to decide what, who, and how we want to identify ourselves.

Often, we believe lies, robbing us of our true identity rather than believing what God says about us. Lies like, you're not good enough, you're undeserving, you'll fail so don't try, etc.

An endless list of negative self-talk on replay in our minds. Lies like the one I told myself at sixteen, "I'm unlovable." The one job of these lies is to trap us in destructive cycles of bondage and fear. No need to remain stuck though, we are free to make choices.

Choices like Dave began making. Decisions that strengthened and lifted him higher as opposed to dragging him downward.

Dave read and accepted truths from that book as applied to him, which resulted in greater revelation and light shining into dark secret places. He was ready to face his demons, and the desire to bravely confront himself only served to help me love and respect him more.

∾

DAVE

It was very confronting to find much of my acting out fit into the category of abusive behaviour.

I would never have identified myself as being an abusive man and certainly not towards Noni. Yet, after reading *Why does he do that*? for the second time, there was no denying it.

My behaviour was consistent with being an angry, controlling, and at times, abusive person. Never would I have previously accepted this truth; such was the extent of deceit, self-preservation, and fear I lived with.

∾

NONI

As Dave continued to overcome his fears, practice humility, show transparency, and learn how to be assertive, my admiration and attraction for him grew to a whole new level, as did my feeling of safety. Day in and day out, we developed healthy patterns and rituals that improved ourselves and our marriage. Each incremental advancement was a step closer to restoring trust...

A monumental feat.

Ezekiel returned home in September 2019. Although it's been a transition involving a measure of discomfort for everyone, the biggest difference has been in Dave. His ability to stand firm and assert his authority whilst supporting me at the same time has demonstrated a new strength to our son. Respect given is respect earnt.

LESSONS FROM BEYOND

A SMALL OBSERVATION: EVER SINCE I HAVE KNOWN DAVE, HE HAS HAD A 'NERVOUS HUM'.

NOT A TUNE OR A SONG, A VERY AWKWARD HUMMING. HE WAS UNAWARE HE MADE THE NOISE UNLESS I BROUGHT IT TO HIS ATTENTION. THE HUM WAS SO ANNOYING I WOULD TURN TO HIM AND ASK WHY HE WAS HUMMING; DID HE WANT TO SAY SOMETHING? HIS RESPONSE WAS ALWAYS, "HUH? NO, I'M JUST HUMMING..." GRRRRRR!

ANYWAY, THE HUMMING HAS STOPPED. COMPLETELY. NO MORE SECRETS, NO MORE HUMMING! GO FIGURE!

CHAPTER 26

ARE WE THERE YET?

NONI

Affair Recovery.com describes infidelity as the keeping of secrets.

I couldn't agree more. Dave kept plenty of secrets in the shadow of darkness for decades.

His modus operandi; to be economical with the truth, aka, lying by admission.

The cost of living inauthentically is colossal.

Beyond Betrayal is our story from brokenness to wholeness. We continue moving forward.

We don't boast about arriving anywhere, we're just a little further down the path. Retaining a firm grip of our Father's hand, walking humbly with God, holding each other and our love in a safe space.

Though one may be overpowered, two can defend themselves. A cord of three strands is not quickly broken.

— Ecclesiastes 4:12 (NIV)

We highly recommend Harbouring Hope and Hope for Healing Affair Recovery courses

Dave and I completed in 2019. Experts who comprehend the intricacy of affairs share precious wisdom in these insightful, educational, and supportive programs. Packaged with a non-judgemental delivery, revival is possible whether you are the betrayed or the unfaithful. Hope and life do exist beyond the crushing pain of infidelity.

Building new daily rituals enriches our marriage. Watching video blogs offered freely in the Affair Recovery library keeps us mindful of where and how far we've come. This practice prompts fresh and invigorating discussion regarding where we're at and where we are headed.

Most days, we share revelation and thoughts from scripture with one another. Passages reveal more of the nature of God, with some relating to infidelity, addiction, anger, marriage, work, family, and relationship. All of them are about how to live our best life, not a perfect one.

We enjoy a restored, healthy, and beautiful physical and emotional intimacy. In summary, we are intentionally focusing forward and reaping the benefits tenfold!

For the most part, Dave and I are great. We might not agree on everything, but we know how to fight fairly and respectfully. We're constantly learning to live and love better, all the while striving to keep our own sides of the street clean. I can't do Dave's recovery work for him any more than he can do mine for me. What we can do is continue being safe people for each other. We can continue to show up, be present and vulnerable with each other, and allow nothing to fester when relapse occurs – relapse not referring to Dave 'acting out'. Relapse may be an attitude, hint of disconnection or miscommunication. We keep very short accounts of any wrongdoing and offence.

Through our experience, we've come to the realisation that far too many people walk the excruciating path of infidelity and not enough emerge healthily. We believe our pain has a purpose. Our purpose is to be a testimony of hope for others.

If you find yourself reading this and can relate, if you need help, if you want to communicate with others who understand both sides of the coin, please reach out. We will offer what worked for us and what did not.

Email us, send an Instagram or Facebook message, even if you just need to share your burden, don't do this alone.

On October 24, 2019, we received the great news that Dave's PET scan showed no cancer present. Physical recovery with one lung delivers daily challenges. We learn as we go.

"Tomorrow is promised to no one."

— WALTER PAYTON

Taking our days one at a time, we spend precious moments together trusting God with our tomorrows.

"Therefore do not worry about tomorrow, for tomorrow will worry about itself."

— MATT 6:34

At the time of writing, Ezekiel is living back with us, employed in a great restaurant.

He works toward his own healing and recovery; this is an evolving story and his to tell if ever he chooses. Ruby spread her wings and is spending six months of her final study year in the U.S.A. (edit, this adventure ended prematurely due to the Covid-19 pandemic). Corey continues to land on his feet no matter what is thrown his way.

Whilst 'our story' is just that – a very personal glimpse into our life – we do hope it might offer encouragement and support when healing from affairs. If our story can help others feel like they're not a complete lost cause, it's worth it. If one marriage can be restored by our transparency, then it's worth it. And if our marriage can be restored, we believe yours can be too.

Dave and Noni xxx
OH, AND GUESS WHAT!

It turns out Dave isn't Bipolar. He doesn't have depression, and he's discovered some roots of his clinical anxiety were misdiagnosed and he was mis-medicated all because of the shame that kept him bound for too many decades.

The truth truly set us free! But first, it made us angry...

Sergey Chayko/Shutterstock.com

God's promises never fail:

"And we know that in all things God works for the good of those who love and have been called according to his purpose."

— ROMANS 8:28

"to bestow on them a crown of beauty instead of ashes, the oil of joy instead of mourning, and a garment of praise instead of a spirit of despair."

— ISAIAH 61:3

LESSONS FROM BEYOND

- LOVE; THE ONE THING WE DESIRE AND NEED THE MOST IS OFTEN SOMETHING WE FEAR THE MOST...
- AFFAIRS HAPPEN IN GOOD MARRIAGES, BAD MARRIAGES, AND CHRISTIAN MARRIAGES.
- ALTHOUGH NO ONE IS PERFECT, AN AFFAIR IS *NEVER* THE FAULT OF THE BETRAYED PARTNER. IF THERE ARE ISSUES/DEFICITS WITHIN THE MARRIAGE, THERE ARE PLENTY OF OPTIONS AVAILABLE, HAVING AN AFFAIR IS NOT ONE OF THEM.
- IT TAKES TWO PEOPLE TO MAKE AN AFFAIR HAPPEN, THE UNFAITHFUL PARTNER AND THE AFFAIR PARTNER, NOT THE BETRAYED SPOUSE.
- BAD MARRIAGES DON'T CAUSE AFFAIRS, BUT AFFAIRS DO CAUSE BAD MARRIAGES.
- I LOVE THIS QUOTE FROM AFFAIR RECOVERY, NOTHING TRUER... "YOU CAN NEVER BE LOVED UNCONDITIONALLY IF YOU ONLY LET YOURSELF BE CONDITIONALLY KNOWN."
- IT WAS NEVER DAVE'S INTENTION TO DELIBERATELY DECEIVE ME AND DESTROY OUR MARRIAGE.
- I DON'T BELIEVE THE MAJORITY OF PEOPLE WHO HAVE AFFAIRS ARE MOTIVATED BY THE INTENT AND DESIRE TO HURT THEIR SPOUSE. HOWEVER, THIS DOESN'T NEGATE THEIR RESPONSIBILITY OR DIMINISH THE ENORMITY OF THE RESULTING DEVASTATION.

LESSONS FROM BEYOND continued

- FEELINGS ARE NOT FACTS. FEELINGS ARE VERY REAL, BUT REGARDLESS OF HOW VALID OR INTENSE THOSE FEELINGS ARE, THEY MAY NOT ACTUALLY BE THE TRUTH...

- LEARN TO DECIPHER THE 'STORY' YOU'RE TELLING YOURSELF; YOU CAN REWRITE IT. WE ARE NOT RESPONSIBLE FOR ANOTHER PERSON'S ACTIONS, BUT WE ALONE ARE FULLY RESPONSIBLE AND HAVE THE FREEDOM TO CHOOSE HOW WE RESPOND AND REACT TO THE ACTIONS OF OTHERS.

- INFIDELITY IS THE KEEPING OF SECRETS. (FRANK PITTMAN)

- NOT ALL AFFAIRS INVOLVE SEX; FINANCIAL INFIDELITY AND PORNOGRAPHY MAY ALSO BE CONSIDERED UNFAITHFUL. OTHER AFFAIRS INCLUDE THE ONE-NIGHT STAND, FALLING IN LOVE, SEXUAL ADDICTION, EMOTIONAL AFFAIR, WANTING THE MARRIAGE AND THE AFFAIR, LOVE / APPROVAL / VALIDATION ADDICTION.

- IT IS POSSIBLE FOR AN UNFAITHFUL PARTNER TO FALL INTO MORE THAN ONE OF THE ABOVE CATEGORIES.

- VULNERABILITY + OPPORTUNITY = AFFAIR (BRIAN BERCHT)

LESSONS FROM BEYOND continued

- TIME ALONE DOES NOT HEAL ALL WOUNDS; HOW YOU CHOOSE TO SPEND THE TIME WILL DETERMINE HOW YOU HEAL.
- "PAIN WHICH IS NOT TRANSFORMED *WILL* BE TRANSFERRED." FR RICHARD ROHR
- AFFAIRS THRIVE IN SECRECY; THEY MAY LOSE APPEAL ONCE THE SECRET'S OUT.
- BETRAYAL TRAUMA IS ONE OF THE MOST INSIDIOUS CHALLENGES I HAVE EVER EXPERIENCED, SEEK PROFESSIONAL HELP!
- 'GASLIGHTING', LOOK IT UP. THE UNFAITHFUL ARE ABSOLUTE MASTERMINDS AT THIS ABUSIVE FORM OF CONTROL, MANIPULATING FACTS AND YOUR EVERY GUT INSTINCT. THEY NEED TO USE THIS TO THROW YOU OFF THE SCENT. THEY WOULD SOONER YOU THINK YOU'RE GOING CRAZY THAN EXPOSE THEIR LIE.
- COGNITIVE DISSONANCE IS WORTH EXPLORING. "THE STATE OF HAVING INCONSISTENT THOUGHTS, BELIEFS, OR ATTITUDES, ESPECIALLY AS RELATING TO BEHAVIOURAL DECISIONS AND ATTITUDE CHANGE." OXFORD DICTIONARY IT IS ESSENTIALLY HOLDING TWO OPPOSING VIEWS SIMULTANEOUSLY.
- NOTHING SURER THAN INFIDELITY TO PUT THE 'IN' INTO 'SANITY'.

LESSONS FROM BEYOND continued

- FAR MORE DAMAGING THAN THE AFFAIRS IS THE ABUSE, LYING, BEING ECONOMICAL WITH THE TRUTH, MINIMISING, DEFENDING, OR JUSTIFYING BAD BEHAVIOUR. I DON'T SEEK PERFECTION, GIVE ME REAL, GIVE ME AUTHENTIC. PROVIDE THE OPPORTUNITY, SHOW ME RESPECT AND ALLOW ME TO MAKE A SOUND CHOICE FOR MYSELF BASED ON THE TRUTH, NOT DECEPTION.

- MY CURRENCY FOR LOVE IS HUMILITY, INTEGRITY, HONOUR, AND RESPECT, GLADLY GIVEN AND GLADLY RECEIVED.

- HEALING IS POSSIBLE, WITH OR WITHOUT YOUR PARTNER, *IF* YOU DO THE WORK!

- LOVE IS A DECISION.

- IT IS POSSIBLE TO BE STRONG WHILE KEEPING A SOFT HEART. ALLOWING THIS INSURMOUNTABLE PAIN TO TURN OUR HEARTS INTO STONE ONLY ROBS US OF EXPERIENCING THE MANY BLESSINGS OF LIFE.

- EVEN WHEN YOU'RE WALKING THROUGH HELL, DON'T LET THIS HEINOUS ASSAULT STEAL YOUR JOY.

- WE WILL BECOME BITTER OR BETTER; THE CHOICE IS OURS.

LESSONS FROM BEYOND continued

- Forgiveness is not the same as reconciliation, you can forgive a person without reconciling with them, but you will not achieve reconciliation without forgiveness.
- Forgiveness is "Giving up the hope of ever having a better past." (Affair Recovery)
- Forgiveness is obedience to God and a gift that you give to yourself.
- Forgiveness is not saying that what happened is OK. It is not letting the other person off the hook. Forgiveness means what happened or what has been done will no longer have any hold over you.
- Holding onto unforgiveness is like drinking poison from a cup and expecting the rat to die.
- We can forgive people whether they've asked for it or not, even when they don't deserve it.
- Forgiveness is entirely our choice; forgiveness empowers us to move forward.

LESSONS FROM BEYOND continued

AND FINALLY,

NONE OF US HAS ARRIVED ANYWHERE THIS SIDE OF ETER-NITY, SO KEEP WALKING IN THE DIRECTION THAT YOU WANT TO END UP. DON'T LIVE YOUR LIFE LOOKING IN THE REAR-VIEW MIRROR. YOU'RE NOT GOING THAT WAY! MY BIGGEST LEARNING BY FAR THOUGH, THROUGHOUT MY TWENTY-EIGHT YEARS WITH DAVE, HAS LITTLE TO DO WITH ME OR WHO OR WHAT I AM, BUT IT DOES HAVE EVERYTHING TO DO WITH WHO GOD IS AND WHO/WHAT OUR IDENTITY IS IN. MY SENSE OF SELF-WORTH IS NOT WRAPPED UP IN MY PARTNER, MY APPEARANCE, MY SUCCESS, NOR IN MY FAILURES. I NO LONGER LOOK SIDEWAYS FOR APPROVAL OR VALIDATION. THE OPINIONS OF OTHERS DON'T CHANGE HOW I FEEL ABOUT MYSELF. JESUS IS MY FOUNDATION, HE IS FAITHFUL, GENTLE, KIND, THE SCRIPTURES TELL ME HOW HE FEELS ABOUT ME AND WHAT HE'S DONE FOR ME. THE SAME IS TRUE FOR ALL, WE'RE CREATED FOR A RELATIONSHIP WITH GOD AND THE CHOICE IS OURS TO ACCEPT HIM OR NOT. EVERYTHING CAN BE STRIPPED AWAY, BUT WHO I AM IN CHRIST REMAINS. WHO HE IS AND WHO I AM CALLED TO BE ARE ETERNAL AND UNCHANGEABLE. I LEARNED TO TRUST IN A MANNER I THOUGHT WAS BEYOND IMPOSSIBLE. I LEARNED TO BE CHILD-LIKE WHEN IT COMES TO TRUSTING JESUS.

LESSONS FROM BEYOND continued

I DON'T NEED TO UNDERSTAND WHAT HE'S ASKING OF ME, I JUST NEED TO TRUST HIM. ON DAYS I DON'T TRUST MY HUSBAND, I OPEN MY HANDS, LET GO, AND CHOOSE TO TRUST GOD WITH HIM.

UNDOUBTEDLY, THIS HAS SUSTAINED ME AND US THROUGHOUT THE ENTIRE JOURNEY. THIS IS WHERE VICTORY LIES!

ALL GLORY AND HONOUR MUST GO TO HIM, EL ROI, *THE GOD WHO SEES.*

WHAT DOES RECOVERY LOOK LIKE?

NONI

In our experience, the recovery road is made up of potholes which often feel more like sinkholes! The grieving process is not linear, but it would be awesome if it was. If we knew that once we'd ticked off ABCD we'd naturally progress to EFG and eventually arrive at XY&Z... VOILA!

It's been twelve months since I began writing our story. While waiting for Dave to complete his writing, I thought I'd share a few insights into the reality of our recovery. Behavioural patterns developed over a lifetime won't change overnight.

Rest assured they take time to undo and reconfigure.

No secrets, complete transparency, and a hundred per cent honesty when answering questions are essential ingredients to healthy healing for both partners. Reluctance in embracing these necessities is a sure-fire way to set recovery back a few notches if not all the way back to the start. Providing passwords and access to his electronic devices allowed Dave a greater sense of freedom and safety while enabling me to see if he is telling the truth. In the early days of hypervigilance, I made it my mission to keep a regular check on Dave's online activity and interaction. I wanted to see if there was anything else hidden that I needed to know. As betrayed, we need absolute honesty around even the smallest of things.

Example: Dave and I agreed that if he saw any of the affair partners at conferences or they contacted him via any platform, he would tell me so that we could formulate an appropriate response together.

Following the disclosure of Nancy, I was checking Dave's emails while he was in New Zealand. There was a notification that his referral (Nancy) had submitted her CV for a position within the company Dave worked for. (Nancy was the woman he loaned money to during our separation.) When he called later that night, I didn't let on that I'd seen this email, but I asked if he'd heard anything about her application. He answered hastily,

"I'm not sure if she ended up applying for the job."

Silently, anger welled up, readying myself for the impending eruption! I knew his kneejerk response came from a place of fear and insecurity. At the same time, I was furious because of the lie. If he could lie in this instance, we both knew he could lie about anything.

After this setback, I told him he should know that sometimes I might ask questions I already knew the answers to.

As horrible as this version of trickery is (I hated it), when you've lived most of your adult life with a compulsive liar and someone in addiction, trust is not given easily and nor should it be. Right or wrong, this was a way of testing for truth on the way back to trust.

Another gut-wrenching behaviour that sabotages the best chances of recovery and derails hard-earned gains is when an unfaithful spouse minimises the impact their actions had on the betrayed.

One particularly unpleasant incident occurred fairly early on in our recovery, within the first three months. (Our first three to six months was probably the most treacherous, even with Dave 'doing the work'. None of it is easy, but it changes. Pain does dissipate over time.)

Trauma presents differently for all, often correlating with how we've learned to process painful experiences throughout childhood. Dad was a cool, calm, and collected man, one who faced physical and mental danger courageously during wartime and natural disasters, consistently appearing fearless and unshakeable. As a child, I knew exactly where I stood with my father. I knew the lines not to cross and knew that he had the strength and resilience to go any distance.

He was a man of quiet disposition, never overly up nor down. He was a good, kind, and safe man. I think I'm a little similar to Dad. If I had to describe my personality with one word, I'd call myself a 'flatliner'. Neither given to extreme highs or lows, life is mostly taken in its stride. Sounds super boring, but it's true. Perhaps this inherited trait buoyed us when circumstances rocked me to the core. However, no such inheritance was rendered the night I came closest to losing my mind.

We had just finished a lovely meal, on a beautiful autumnal evening in March 2019 when Dave asked me if I had seen a friend of mine.

(After allowing me access to his iPad, I delved into Dave's Facebook history and timeline activity.) Within weeks of our separation in 2018, he began looking up numerous women. These women included two previous affair partners, my girlfriend he was now inquiring about and one of her close friends, a neighbour of ours who recently separated from her husband. Dave previously mentioned he had run into this woman in the beach carpark and had chatted with her. Although I'd never met the woman and at the time of him telling me thought nothing of it until I found that he'd searched her Facebook profile. Questioning their interaction, he told me he confided in her that we had separated etc...

We had a calm conversation about this being inappropriate and continued discussion about the other searches. His explanation was that it was out of "curiosity", not to actually connect.

Lame, lame, lame but it was what it was.

A person with an addiction will default to whatever soothes their pain.

So, my reply to Dave's question was:

"No, I haven't seen Tracey, she might feel awkward after you caught up with Peta." With that, Dave got up, got angry, and stormed off. This left me sitting alone and hurt. There was nothing accusatory in my tone. I stated a fact. He didn't have the decency to stay.

Once again, this became all about him. His shame, his guilt, his sorrow, etc. This may not seem like a big deal to most. For me, it demonstrated his unwillingness to accept that my no contact with a friend might be yet another consequence of his choices.

That night was probably one of the worst nights in our recovery. It was impossible for discussion with Dave. He gaslighted, deflected, defended, and minimised his actions. In one fell swoop, Dave made almost every mistake in the Affair Recovery Bible. Altogether distraught, I locked myself in our bathroom and stood under the shower for what seemed like an eternity. Bellowing, crying out to God over and over, asking, "WHY?"

This was just too much to bear. I was sobbing great heaving sobs, clawing at my skin, pulling at my hair and pounding my body. Never have I felt such despair.

He just doesn't *get* it and he's not going to *get it.*

This was unlike anything I have experienced and definitely not something I'd ever like to experience again. Without thought, I ended up wrapped in a towel on the bathroom floor. The door was still locked. I lay there for hours, trapped in my grief. Unbeknownst to me, Dave sat right outside the bathroom door listening to my heartache, wanting to run, but needing to stay.

He needed to hear, to witness and sit in my pain with me even though I wanted nothing to do with him. As painful as that night was, it was actually the moment Dave truly understood how deep this pain went. He understood with no uncertainty that his selfish choices had significantly damaged me and us.

This was the moment when he finally began to own his choices and quit the blame game.

It was huge. REALLY UGLY, but huge!

~

DAVE

The night I triggered the tripwire that hurtled Noni into betrayal oblivion has been one of my biggest wakeups in recovery. It was the moment I saw that I pushed my strong wife over the edge of sanity and continued to kick her while she was down (*figuratively speaking*). Her innocence and honesty became my shame and disgust. When Noni needed me to remain adult in our conversation, I regressed to the self-centred tantrum-throwing adolescent. In a huff, storming off under perceived attack, I removed myself from the discomfort of the truth. Yes, I made Noni's honest observation all about my pain, my feelings, my-self. I had a choice in that moment, I could retreat and repeat, or I could man up and do something I'd never done before, no matter how painful it was for me. Sitting outside the bathroom door listening to the wailing of Noni's grief, knowing that I was the one who caused the heinous injuries was excruciating, yet I knew I had to feel as much of Noni's torture as I possibly could. I sat, I remained, and something inside of me changed.

No longer was this injustice about me, all concern was now with Noni.

~

NONI

Probably around six months into the recovery timeline, I found myself feeling the need to check Dave's iPad less and less. This was largely due to the fact that I could see tangible changes in Dave's behaviour and countenance, his responses and openness to discussion were encouraging.

Triggers are another unwelcome but completely normal part of the post-traumatic stress response. The ghastliest factor about these triggers is that you never know when they might invade your day. There is no five-minute warning that informs you of incoming shrapnel. Literally, a split second exists between the sound of incoming and point of impact. An actual physical response to fight, flight, or freeze. It could be a word, a song played on the radio or broadcast in the middle of a shopping mall. Maybe it's a car of a particular colour or the bell tone on their mobile phone signalling a new notification. The list is infinite.

For a short time after discovery, profound sadness accompanied me when looking at photos, knowing that almost every moment and visually recorded piece of our history was marred by Dave's deceit. Was anything real? A question haunted me momentarily. *Yes*, the smiles were real, the holidays, birthdays, Christmas's, picnics, the fun, love, and laughter were all real, secrets were there lurking, but that didn't negate the rest of our lives as being true. My choice became to focus on the good, if I only fixated on the affairs and lies, then I would be saying that all else about our lives was invalid.

Two weeks after Dave's full disclosure in February 2019, we attended a relationship workshop, an exercise that included partnering up with another attendee as our 'buddy' for the weekend. We were required to eat lunch with these buddies in order to get to know one another. Although the unknown affair was a fresh revelation and I was still delicate, I'd completed significant work with a therapist specialising in PTSD.

During the first lunch date with my buddy, a four-lettered word spoken mid-sentence hurtled me full thrust into a cerebral obstacle course and time travel.

My voice was the starter's gun, 'Fiji' the signal and I was off and racing. An onset of rushing palpitations, chest booming, heart pounding faster, louder, and harder, sweat building on my forehead, parched mouth and clammy hands, were they trembling? The physical response preceded an avalanche of mental aerobics.

OMG. Which trip was this? He went to Fiji in 1992 with work. No, that was too long ago. Was it the one when he was with the other company? What year was that? How many work trips to Fiji has he taken?

I scrambled to remember what, where, how, and when I had been deceived by an affair beginning on a Fijian work trip.

*Yes, **that** affair started in Fiji in 2004, not the time frame I am now recounting, phew!*

I'm OK. I'm here, this is now and we're in Perth. Those memories can't harm me, I'm here, keep breathing, I'm safe…

As rapidly as this trigger hit, once my mind considered all possibilities and landed safely, the intense juggling calmed, my heart rate slowed to normal. Somehow, the mouth continued relaying a story I'd embarked on about Fiji, a narrative completely unrelated to infidelity.

My words persisted while my mind circled at breakneck speed in a totally different direction. Who knows what story my face told, but this gorgeous young lady seemed happy to keep company with me for the duration of the weekend.

NONI YATES & DAVID YATES

Fifty per cent of our married life, Dave has been absent with work travel. This is the bit where I reiterate, we don't boast about 'arriving' anywhere or 'making' it, we're still very much on our recovery journey. A lung removal put a halt on work travel for most of 2019, and a global pandemic has taken care of 2020. Travel will likely be our biggest trigger to master once the world resumes some kind of normalcy. We are both different people because of infidelity, and although we wouldn't wish our experience on our worst enemy, we are different in a good way. If we continue on the path we've begun, we're confident our future holds enormous joy and blessing. One day at a time...

In the early stages of recovery, I was monumentally more invested in finding resources and affair recovery material than Dave. He, like many unfaithful, just wanted it to be done and dusted, but healing is a process that takes time and patience. Dave is now actively committed, and dare I say, even enjoying finding out more about himself and his own growth and path to healing.

November 2019, seven months past our last D-Day, Dave attended a large conference in Sydney. I travelled with him to hang out with family. Before going, we discussed the likelihood of him running into any APs, what he would do if he did, and we comfortably sat with our preconceived plans. Arriving back in our room at the end of conference day one, he was quick to share that he saw Ann. There was no interaction and I thanked him for offering up this information. We had a brief loving discussion around this and nothing more was said. As we were preparing to go home after the conference, I asked if he'd only seen her the once. He had actually seen her again across the room but didn't think to mention it to me. Whilst not a trigger, I was disappointed that he didn't offer the information and I had to ask. These are little things that add up to healthy restoration. We both conceded that it would be better if he offers up info rather than me having to wonder or ask.

Recovery is a process. One moment you feel like your marriage is better than ever and you're both unstoppable and bulletproof. The next is spent questioning why on earth you're putting yourself through such hardship. You wonder if it is all worth it. Our short answer to this: It has been for us.

A safeguard Dave decided to put in place was giving me his itinerary before going on work trips.

Despite his high level of work travel, this is not something I've ever asked for. The gesture is appreciated though, he finds the practice beneficial for him too.

In December 2019, I travelled by myself to Bali to write the final chapters of this book. Dave had a Sydney trip booked while I was away, and I had his details. We had been sailing along nicely, connected and united on all fronts. The weekend before I left, I noticed he seemed agitated and a little short, nothing major, just a little out of whack and mildly unpleasant. The night before my flight, I said something about where he would be staying in Sydney.

This is the moment he chose to mention his change of plans.

He had amended his accommodation booking from Ryde to stay in the CBD because he decided to go to a work Christmas party. WTH! Now, these are 'oversights' or omissions of detail that can flick a switch. Challenging him on this, he became defensive. I was ropeable, not because he was going to a Christmas party or he was staying in the city, but because he chose NOT to share the information with me, pretending he couldn't see why it was a deal. Asking him when he made the changes, he told me Friday. It was now Monday. This made sense as to why he was out of sorts all weekend. He slept in the spare room that night. I told him I would rather spend the night at the airport waiting to catch my early flight than sleep in the same bed as him. The crazy thing is, I meant it... Infidelity is *"the keeping of secrets". (Frank Pittman)*

We had made a pact early on in recovery. We were going to do things differently going forward. This behaviour was old Dave, and even though my mind knew he wasn't, it felt like he was trying to hide something.

∽

DAVE

Staying on the path in recovery is much more than not having extramarital relationships, it is choosing the right actions daily. The power of doing small things regularly cannot be underestimated. In my case, the importance of consistency of my actions matching my words has been a lesson learned through repeated poor choices and indecision. One such example was a sunny Saturday. Noni and I planned to spend the morning together at the beach. Noni was preparing breakfast for us while I went for a short jog for ten or fifteen minutes *(more like a shuffle as I struggled to get a semblance of aerobic fitness)*. On the path home, detouring down the short walkway to check the surf, I was entranced by a spectacular swell, as were half a dozen neighbours. Envious I wasn't able to be out there due to my physical condition, I drank in the scene a little longer. Deciding to sit and immerse myself in the moment, chat to guys who'd enjoyed the waves, watch one more ride, talk about the next big set, and on and on. Finally tearing myself away, I ran the 500 metres home knowing full well I had taken at least forty-five minutes longer than the fifteen I'd set out on.

My cooked breakfast was cold, and Noni had long finished hers. I offered excuses as she stormed out the door and removed herself for an extended period. For twelve months we had been rebuilding our relationship and were in a great place early that morning, filled with anticipation for the day ahead. All was undone by a series of seemingly unimportant decisions on my part.

Without uttering a word, the choices made told Noni emphatically:

- When I agree with Noni, I can change my mind if it suits me
- What makes me feel good on a whim is more important than a commitment to my wife
- I matter more than Noni
- My words and actions cannot be trusted

These four behaviours were consistent through all my infidelities. So, a seemingly small slip- up was a huge reminder that the old unfaithful Dave may not be far away. As acutely painful and disturbing as it was for Noni, it was a sobering reminder for me of how unreliable I have been. Veering off the path is dangerous.

~

NONI

Recovery may be one step forward, two steps back, but if we keep walking, we'll get there!

Putting boundaries in place and having realistic expectations of one another is essential for all relationships to thrive. It tells the other person; this is who I am, and this is what you can expect from me. It says I am a person of integrity; you can count on me. Unfortunately, affairs decimate the trust given to our partners and it is by doing the work necessary that we can eventually re-establish trust.

We will be forever changed because of infidelity.

That's ok, we can change for the better if we choose.

Our marriages can be stronger and better than we imagine, we are powerful together.

Progress not Perfection x

EPILOGUE

DAVE

I f you've read this far, you are well aware of what I'm capable of. How the hell did I become a person who betrays people I love deeply as well as my own values and beliefs? Noni is regularly stopped in the street by complete strangers who compliment her skin, hair, and beauty. She accepts all graciously without developing an inflated ego. She is kind, compassionate, and practices humility. A supremely handsome woman, incredibly strong, infinitely gracious.

Noni exemplifies a Proverbs 31 woman.

> "She is clothed with strength and dignity;
>
> She can laugh at the days to come.
>
> She speaks with wisdom,
>
> and faithful instruction is on her tongue.

She watches over the affairs of her household

and does not eat the bread of idleness.

Her children arise and call her blessed;

her husband also, and he praises her:

"Many women do noble things,

but you surpass them all."

Charm is deceptive, and beauty is fleeting;

but a woman who fears the Lord is to be praised.

Honour her for all that her hands have done,

and let her works bring her praise at the city gate."

Why would I betray a woman such as this? This question has taken me fifty-nine years to answer. Layer by layer, I unlocked the deception and stories I told myself. No excuses, no blame, just truth giving freedom and helping me understand I'm not a complete screwup... and I'm not alone!

Lie number one my seven-year-old self-believed; 'love can't be trusted', was closely followed by confusion.

CONFUSION

The thirteen-year-old boy rummaging around in a storage area off the main garage was looking at tools and scraps of wood. Wedged between a box and the brick wall, I spied a brown A4 envelope. It was addressed to a man; the man's name a variation of my father's.

The address care of a Post Office Box in a neighbouring suburb. Curiosity got the better of me, so I opened the envelope to find pornographic magazines. The images were more explicit than I had ever seen. Until that moment, I had only caught glimpses of similar publications discreetly placed out of direct view, behind the counter at newsagents or service stations.

Intrigued, excited, yet revolted, the images left me extremely confused. The discovery was completely at odds with what I experienced and believed about my father. Who was this man with a similar name? My father had gone to the trouble of assuming another identity to indulge this, and it led to questions. What else was hidden? Is this normal to have a separate identity? I never mentioned my discovery to my father, or anyone else while he was alive.

Forty-five years later, my counsellor and Noni were the first to hear of these experiences.

IDENTITY

Shame and regret became my badge of honour – *I can't be such a bad person if I feel this bad.*

Wallowing in shame seems an easy way out. Keeping the focus on me as the victim provided the accountability avoidance ticket I needed. Shame is an act of selfishness permitting those who relish in it to repeat destructive cycles.

Noni frequently reached out, assuring me of the depth and sincerity of her feelings.

Despite being unable to view the full extent of my struggle, Noni voiced genuine concern for the raging conflict she knew I was tormented by. She saw 'me' and seemed to love the person I was regardless of how I felt about myself.

Confronted and overwhelmed by my desire to be in a relationship with Noni confused me.

Although Noni's heart is genuine and authentic, the scoresheet I referenced told me love couldn't be trusted. Didn't I love and want Noni?

Yes, always. I've never stopped loving Noni. At times, I felt she was much more than I deserved.

Blind to my insecurity and the fear driving the destructive and selfish behaviours, I literally couldn't see the extent of distortion. According to me, this was just the way things were or should be. A reflex honed over many years, disguised as protection that kept me safe and eliminated the risk involved in giving myself to others. For many years before meeting Noni, I carried an underlying sense of inadequacy, not quite fitting in. No one else knew how much I secretly hated myself and this is why I could never commit my whole self to her. I didn't trust unconditional love.

CONTROL

Frustration at not being able to make everything right both within and around me often preceded a loss of control. Feelings and frustrations were so intense at times that I needed to find a way of exerting myself or dulling my discomfort. Gaining acceptance and admiration from others was a good way to prove myself significant in this world – people-pleasing. In contrast, arrogance, sarcasm, and becoming hypercritical of others proved I wasn't inferior and could control my surrounds. Oversensitive to perceived criticism, particularly from those closest to me, my reaction was to withdraw and sulk. I would deflect attention by minimising my actions or attack my 'accuser' by digging up vaguely comparable errors on their part. Any apology for lousy behaviour deflected responsibility off of myself. In my mind, the behaviours were the product of someone else's actions, not mine. I would do anything to avoid taking ownership; a tendency that persisted long into our marriage.

DUALITY

I always experienced a sense of importance or superiority whenever I held the attention of women. This attention wasn't necessarily a prelude to physical intimacy or sexual activity; sexual gratification was never the goal. Recognition and validation were the hooks for me.

Flattery and acceptance, buoying up the fragile inner child.

Emotional distance existed between the two worlds I lived in. My infidelity was separate, or so I thought. Unfaithful behaviour happened over there and wasn't very visible.

'Philandering Dave' was separate to 'husband Dave', father, soccer coach, friend, brother, etc. 'Cheating Dave' dwelt in a separate neighbourhood, far away and hidden from everything else in my life.

That Dave didn't exist when I was with my family. I didn't think of him, and to a large extent, 'family Dave identity' was suspended when with my affair partners. I was living a fragmented existence. If those fragments dare draw near to each other, the internal conflict spiralled dangerously out of control. Medications merely softened the edges of a war raging inside.

PORNOGRAPHY

The mindset that pornography is technically not classified as an extramarital affair is another enormous trap of infidelity. Far from the harmless entertainment or blokey diversion modern society would have us believe, porn consumption is highly addictive, triggering a release of dopamine, the reward transmitter in the brain. Long-term pornographic viewing has been linked to sexual dysfunction, depression and marital quality. Pornography rewires the brain to a more juvenile state, diverting precious attention and energy from where it belongs.

(Barr, R., 2019. Watching Pornography Rewires the Brain to A More Juvenile State. the conversation.com.)

Instead of investing in my relationship, pornography was a quick fix to physical want that required zero emotional effort. My indulgence in porn unwittingly led to a disassociation of sexual fulfilment and emotional bonding. Aside from dehumanizing women, essentially, I was also commoditizing sex. Each time I sought a sexual sensation from online pornography, I undermined my emotional connection with Noni. As with most of my lightbulb moments, the detrimental effects of pornography on my life have been a recent revelation, even though its presence has manifested for years.

> "Most men don't experience the consequences immediately, so they don't believe there will be any. They continue day after day, year after year, not realizing that their lives are being consumed. They are losing thousands of hours; allowing their spiritual, emotional and moral souls to be stunted."
>
> — CLEAN: A PROVEN PLAN FOR MEN COMMITTED
> TO SEXUAL INTEGRITY - DOUG WEISS

ABUSE

More than anything else I have faced in learning about myself, this one aspect has been *the* most difficult to accept. Am I an abusive man? The short answer is yes. If you had asked me this question two years ago, my answer would have been categorically 'NO'. How thankful I am the scales have fallen from my eyes and more layers have been shed. When I first read *Why Does He Do That?* by Lundy Bancroft, my sight and mind recognised several similarities, but I certainly wouldn't identify with or call myself emotionally abusive. This has been the most uncomfortable truth to come to terms with, and not one that I accepted quickly. Over a year or more of learning more about covert abuse and the way I used this method of control for decades, the more I understand I am indeed guilty 100%.

This is definitely nothing to boast about, but unless we can be completely honest with ourselves, we are powerless to change. I've lived too many years hiding from me. Now that I know and accept exactly who I am, I can become the person I am called to be.

CLOSING

Akin to my other discoveries, my experiences are not unique. The more I speak with men who have betrayed their partners, the more I realise we walk to the beat of a familiar drum.

We share driving forces and although our stories differ, our roots appear to be established in the same soil. For years, I foolishly kidded myself thinking that the rules didn't apply to me.

Comparing and judging someone else's 'sin' to alleviate my own.

"I'm not as bad as them."

"At least I don't do XYZ."

Sin is sin, missing the mark, falling short, and yes, it applies to us all.

"Pride comes before a fall."

— PROVERBS 16:8

We can live with regret or we can let it propel us into a brighter future. Nothing excuses the horrendous pain I inflicted upon people I love.

Nothing.

By understanding *why* I acted out in the ways I did, I can prevent the cycle from continuing.

Dave

LESSONS FROM BEYOND

IT'S IMPOSSIBLE TO LIVE WITHOUT REGRET WHEN DECADES OF YOUR LIFE HAVE BEEN TARNISHED BY LIES AND SECRETS. WE CAN'T ERASE OR CHANGE THE PAST, BUT WE CAN CREATE A BRIGHTER FUTURE.

ALTHOUGH THERE ARE REGRETS, WE DON'T DWELL IN THEM, TO DO SO WOULD KEEP THE SHAME CYCLE SPINNING.

NONI IS AMAZING ABOUT MOVING FORWARD AND ALTHOUGH SHE REMEMBERS THE PAST, SHE REFUSES TO LET IT CONTROL OUR FUTURE.

IF ONLY, IF ONLY...

I HAD TAKEN STEPS DECADES EARLIER TO EXPLORE AND ADDRESS REASONS FOR MY SELF-LOATHING, INSECURITY, AND INFIDELITY.

I CAN ONLY IMAGINE HOW DIFFERENT MY LIFE AND THAT OF MY FAMILY WOULD HAVE BEEN HAD I CORRECTED THE DAMAGING STORIES BURIED DEEP WITHIN MY PSYCHE THE BIBLE – A BOOK MORE VERBIAGE OF SELF-WORTH, RELATION-SHIPS, TRUST, PERFORMANCE, ACCEPTANCE ETC.

THE ENORMOUS AMOUNT OF ENERGY WASTED PROTECTING MY 'IMAGE OF SELF' WOULD HAVE BEEN AVAILABLE TO NONI, OUR FAMILIES, AND RELATIONSHIPS.

LESSONS FROM BEYOND continued

TIME AND ENERGY WERE STOLEN FROM MY WIFE AND CHIL-
DREN AND GIVEN TO SOOTHE THE DISCOMFORT OF HIDDEN
SECRETS INSTEAD. TIME, A PART OF OUR LIFE WE WILL NEVER
GET BACK.

REGRET I WILL HAVE TO LIVE WITH.

NOTES, LETTERS, THOUGHTS

As promised, we offer ourselves, unvarnished. The following writings are from our many notes, some stored on devices and some dug up from the archives.

Emotionally scribing feelings and thoughts, sometimes concise, often scrambled. My form of journaling is more ad hoc than disciplined. Whenever a burst of words surface, no matter where I find myself, I write. If I'm driving, I'll pull over, whether I'm in the middle of cooking or ironing or if it is two in the morning, I write. Some are not pretty; you will be forgiven if you think them the ramblings of a madwoman. I can absolutely testify that the trauma of infidelity betrayal will cause even the sanest person to imagine they might be losing their minds. Infidelity can cause a craziness like nothing else. Crimes of passion, legitimate terminology.

I love that Ann Bercht, author of *My Husband's Affair Became the Best Thing That Ever Happened to Me*, and director of BAN, implores us betrayed to find a way to channel our anger without landing us in jail!

I recall reading that swear words may well be invented for use by the betrayed! All I can say to that is forgive the potty mouth of this betrayed bride! Journaling is likely my outlet that prevents me from acting in a way I may later regret. Dave also wrote what he needed to.

Find the healthy outlet that best works for you.

∾

A note from early days post-separation when Dave was being a real jerk:

> *My eyes are raw from the stinging of hot tears,*
> *but I can't stop them from coming.*
> *I love you and though the tightness around my*
> *chest is painful, it's still preferable over*
> *constantly walking on eggshells.*
> *The fatigue from jostling emotion is unbearable*
> *but I want to fight on because what we're*
> *doing is right.*
> *I'm frightened like never before, I want the*
> *comfort of God's arms around me, the*
> *safety and security of His promises, but I'm*
> *walking through a valley, a very deep*
> *valley and I'm scared and I don't feel His*
> *assurance or His presence. I just have to*
> *know and that must be enough.*
> *The practical steps we need to take which offer*

no guarantee of our desired outcome,
terrify me, but we cannot go back to how it
was. I won't go back, so however scary this
may be, I'm going to move forward hour by
hour. Maybe minute by minute, this is
new, x

~

The doozie I wrote to the floozie, purely for my own vent, never sent.

Karen,
Dave came clean about his multiple affairs,
    infidelities and betrayal over our twenty-
    eight years together, betrayal of trust to me,
    our marriage and our family. Betrayal of
    his own core values.
Although there's a few, I must say that you're
    the one female who disappoints me the
    most.
I extended the hand of grace to you twenty-five
    years ago and only said to Dave the week
    before he told me everything, I at least
    respected you for having the guts to face
    me, yep right at that moment he was
    probably crapping himself as those words
    left my lips!
When you turned up in tears on our doorstep
    back then and I counselled you woman to
    woman, you confided if not you that Dave

*had an affair with it would be someone else,
I said to you then, "Yes I agree." I thought
that was the end of the betrayal. What a
fool I was... Did you know that Beth T
from **** was also another in between
hook-up while you and Dave started
screwing again????? He chose to disclose
all the details recently. Then after that
another married f*** from ****. Industry
bonuses eh! Can you even begin to imagine
the pain? Our youngest son Ezekiel born
in Sept 1997, you and Dave reignited your
whatever sometime the year after his birth.
I can tell you that the day before Christmas
Eve 1997 (Ezekiel was only three months
old) I popped an upper chest cavity rib
while I was making love to Dave. Our sex
life has never been dull, but unfortunately
always hindered by lies and deception from
a man frightened of the truth and
demonised by self-loathing.*

*The reason I remember this vividly is that I
suffered excruciating pain for the next six
months while I nursed an infant and cared
for two children and accommodated a needy
husband. I continue to experience pain
associated with this injury. Clearly, I still
failed to fill the void.*

So, here's the equation;

*While Dave was cheating on me with you, he
was cheating on you with Beth, who was*

*cheating on her husband with Dave; then
you were cheating on your husband with
Dave and then cheating on Dave with
Peter P who was cheating on his wife with
you! And then you hooked up with another
from the same company! This is one
hysterical f***** up mess where the only
people who had a choice were the ****
employees, nice culture...and yes, I'm
aware of many others in the company who
were having affairs. I wonder how many
are still married and aware of their
partner's infidelity?*

~

The one I wrote when I didn't give me the name of the unknown affair partner:

*"Your words and intentions are cheap Dave,
nothing more than lip service.
If words were enough, then our marriage vows
would be the guarantee against infidelity
and betrayal. TWENTY-EIGHT F******
YEARS OF YOUR B******* LIES AND
DECEIT!!!!!
Your actions are the ONLY currency we have if
there is to be ANY hope for reconciliation.
I can forgive you, but not trust you.
Even today when I asked you to give me the
name, this was your reply,*

*'I will give you a written history after work. I
would rather be present when you read, so I
can fathom your pain. I guess you read my
correspondence to the recovery website.'
You STILL wouldn't give me the answer to the
straight-forward question. I asked for a
name, not an excuse for not answering! I'm
sorry... did it make you angry that I read
your correspondence?
You've had EVERY OPPORTUNITY Dave
and then some!
Much more than you deserve."*

~

Something to convey how the smallest aberration can
propel us into an emotional freefall and derail
rebuilding trust, this was written one month after
disclosure:

*There's nothing quite like the pain of being
deceived and lied to repeatedly by someone
you've loved for twenty-eight years.
The person you committed your own life to, the
person you trusted your own life with, the
one you gave your heart to, forsaking all
others, the one who is meant to love honour
and protect you. The one person who is
supposed to keep you safe.
The person you thought you knew... this is
excruciating pain that you can't even come*

*close to understanding! You can't even
keep the simplest of promises that you gave
to try to help me feel safe again.*

*From your own mouth, "I'm going to call you
every day I'm away. I see other men step
out of meetings to check in with their
wives." "I only have one or two wines with
dinner when I'm away." "I'll call you this
afternoon when I get back to the room."*

*I interpret all of the above by your actions
Dave, and this is what you are actually
saying; that you will ONLY do any of the
above things if it suits you and fits into
how you 'feel' at any given time. Yep, it's
all about you; I must be one major
inconvenience to you! Do you just expect
me to keep believing your empty promises?*

*This is turning me into someone I don't want
to be. I'm not sure I even know who I am
any more. I'm scared, I'm sad, I no longer
trust, I feel like I'm constantly doubting
myself. I feel like I've lost touch with
what's real. I can't focus, I'm not present
with anyone. I feel like I'm losing my sense
of self and do you know what? I feel like
you really don't care! The words that come
out of your mouth say that you do, but
your actions certainly don't!*

*I SAY IT AGAIN LOUD AND CLEAR.
DAVE, YOU ARE NOT A SAFE
PERSON FOR ME, OUR MARRIAGE*

*OR OUR FAMILY. YOUR ACTIONS
SPEAK WAY LOUDER THAN YOUR
WORDS.*

∽

SOME QUESTIONS ASKED OF ME

Noni

Q; How can you be sure?

A: I can't, I can only learn and grow. Ultimately, I am responsible for myself and how I respond to a situation. Wisdom from Oswald Chambers, My Utmost for His Highest; "Faith never knows where it is being led, but it loves and knows the One Who is leading."

Q: What if it happens again?

A; What if it doesn't? If it does, it's on him, I can't control another person.

If I couldn't prevent Dave from straying when I was a young, slim, confident, attractive, and a successful woman, why would I think this older, larger version of me can? I refuse to live in fear. Dave is in charge of what Dave does and his emotional toolbox is now full of new tools. If he chooses to revert to old ways, then he will be doing it knowingly.

Q: How can you trust him after all this?

A: Dave has had to earn my trust back. It's taken time and hasn't been without glitches. He has worked hard though, painstakingly and patiently standing firm, facing every ounce of my doubt and shredded trust. One of the worst parts of being lied to over and over again is not believing even when he is telling the truth. Dave has had to accept this as reality and a consequence of his choices. Consistently, I am able to see the transformation in his countenance. No longer an angry reactive man, he responds dramatically differently to all manner of situations. The broken eggshells we once walked on have been replaced by velvet. I feel safe to speak and share my deepest thoughts and cares. It has taken time, but what a pleasure to live this freely.

"A soft word turns away wrath, but a harsh word stirs up anger."

— Proverbs 15:1

Q: Where was God for you through all of this?

A: He was with me, beside me, cradling me. He never, ever let me go through this on my own. Through the most heinous gut-wrenching agony, He was there. The nights I spent groaning on my bathroom floor after Dave deflected ownership, God was with me, He cushioned me against the cold tiles. He caught me each time I was thrown from that plane and made certain I wasn't broken beyond repair. He made a way when I thought there was none. God was present and when there was only one set of footprints in the sand, there was never any doubt in my mind who they belonged to.

Q: (from Dave) Knowing what you do now, do you feel like I made a fool out of you when you gave your testimony at the women's meeting years ago?

A: Dave, my testimony had nothing to do with you and everything to do with God and yet another revelation into how amazing He is. It has always been about how much He loves us.

Nothing to do with you, Dave!

AND THE QUESTIONS I ASKED OF MYSELF, ON MORE THAN ONE OCCASION!

How much do I have to suck up?

How much do I have to get over?

Is it possible????

Can I do this?

Am I crazy for even wanting to?

Am I such a faulty human being that I am hanging onto someone who is using me?

Am I hanging onto someone who doesn't want me or want the pure relationship I hope for?

Is my self- worth in the gutter?

Do I not deserve the marriage I desire?

Am I kidding myself?

Am I expecting the impossible?

Should I let it go?

Should I walk away?

Am I keeping Dave from being where he wants to be and doing what he wants to do?

Am I an idiot?

THE ONLY AUTHENTIC ANSWER:

How can one explain what the heart feels?

How can one determine what action they would take unless they have walked in the same shoes?

How can I describe how much I love you?

I have no need to justify, I will die to my flesh.

I only know

Who I am?

Because of us

Because of you

This is who I am

and

Who He has called me to be

This is all I know

28/06/2019

Dear Noni

This year we have been throwing ourselves into rebuilding our marriage, and though it has been difficult, painful and exhausting at times, it has been fantastic as we have brought our relationship so far and look forward to continuing to do so, for rest of our lives.

This Cancer stuff we are going through is throwing another degree of difficulty and challenges to both of us, none of it welcome. But I am thankful it did not occur when we were in the place we were late last year. I doubt I would have had the will to face it.

Given the active rebuilding of "us" has slowed somewhat, I want to take the time to put in <u>writing</u> an apology

~~I am so very sorry~~

Noni you did not deserve the betrayal and the hurt I caused, and especially you did not deserve it from me

I am sorry for the breaking of the vows before God, for dishonouring you, tormenting you with erratic behaviour, and then looking you in the eye and lying over and over again. Please know my lies did not come easy and without my own pain, they did not come from a place of protecting others or preserving affairs, they were reflexes to hide the deep shame I did not want to face.

I was a person I despised, making a mockery of the values I believed but (at the time) not able or willing to face the real "why"

I am sorry for making you doubt your own sanity at times, for the rollercoaster and at times the house of horrors

I am sorry for the secrecy and deceit I lived in and the emotional energies that I robbed our marriage of. You have always been enough for me, but I believed other lies about myself

I am sorry for repeating the same behaviours, for leaving doors open, for not respecting myself, my family or my marriage

I am sorry for the anger that burst out of me regularly and unpredictably and landed on you and the kids.

I am sorry for the lost opportunity of 27 years that should have been so very much better, we have had just a taste of what is possible. I cannot change the past, but I am learning from it and will not stop learning from it.

All my Love Dave
xox

The following is an exercise Dave completed in the Affair Recovery Hope 4 Healing course.

Powerful.

H.U.R.T.

Hurt

Before I married you Noni, I was already lying about my relationship with Karen. I had deceived you in the lead up to our wedding and during our courtship, I was never totally honest. I chose to betray my vow to you soon after we were married. I deceived you and deflected all of your rightful questions and suspicions. I undermined your instincts and belittled your love for our marriage.

During discovery and our reconciliation, I still tried to minimise and control information, your reaction and my image. I continued to manipulate the circumstances and take advantage of your love. I abused your commitment to me and our vows before God.

For the next twenty-six years, I repeatedly choose to indulge myself selfishly with relationships, physical and emotional, outside the one relationship I had sworn to keep sacred. I shared my body and emotions with others when I swore an oath that they were to be reserved for you. In doing so, I undermined our marriage and short-changed you emotionally throughout our marriage. I continued deceiving you, betraying my entire family and even my very own values.

Those closest to me, Ezekiel, Ruby, Corey and you are the ones I was meant to honour and protect. Instead, you bore the brunt of my inner conflict, insecurities and self-loathing - my sarcasm, inconsistency, arrogance, petulance and self-indulgent behaviour created an unstable and at times abusive home atmosphere. I shattered the trust I was given time and time again. I have not been a safe husband or father, and have disrespected, belittled and even ridiculed you out of my own weakness. I abused all of your trust and love that was freely given to me.

Understanding

Noni, I will never be able to properly understand how excruciatingly painful and demoralising this has been for you, the uncertainty and doubts I created over such a long period must have been like torture. Knowing that the person you chose to give your life to gave no regard or value to your precious gift. You are right to be furious with me forever and to be sickened by the very sight of me or the sound of my name. The ongoing betrayal and abuse must have devasted and humiliated you, and I made you feel foolish for trusting me again and again.

It is a miracle that you remained physically, spiritually and emotionally intact at all and that you can still be the loving person you are today.

Remorse

Noni, no words can describe the disgust I have for myself after squandering your pure gift of love. I mourn the years of lost opportunity, as I made choices that undermined all the worthwhile relationships (Ours, our children and my relationship with God).

I have been a fool and a selfish pathetic example of a man. Often, I have been so empty I'm not worthy of the air I breathe, let alone the family we have been blessed with. I have been so ashamed of my actions for so many years that I had believed I would die with them, rather than admitting to my betrayal.

I will always live with the knowledge that I have been responsible for inflicting pain and damage on those who innocently trusted and loved me. I have betrayed my own core and hate what I have done.

Time

It will probably take a lifetime to restore trust in so many broken areas of our lives, but I am committed to doing whatever it takes, for as long as it takes, as often as it takes. I desperately want a future for our family and our marriage, a future that is better than the past ever was.

I realise that the scars and bruises I have inflicted will probably surface for a long time and will need attention, but I will be patient with your journey of healing, I will be present, I will be supportive, I will not run away from what I have created.

I will pursue my own healing and that means to seek a complete understanding of my own vulnerability and history. I will put in place the boundaries to keep us safe. I will seek help and guidance to identify and replace the wrong thinking and destructive habits of the past. This will take practice and time and more practice.

I don't deserve to ask for this time or this chance. Regardless, I will do all I can to build a better US and a safe and strong marriage.

I stumbled across this on the internet in 2019, unfortunately I have been unable to find out who wrote it, but I think it is an incredibly strong and powerful letter.

Letter to my Partner

Addiction, I really hate you. You lying, deceitful parasite.

You knock on the doors of young boys, preying on their ignorance and curiosity, and you promise them excitement and pleasure. And they let you in while their parents look the other way. But what you really deliver is pain and disappointment and an unquenchable thirst for more. You teach boys that women are only objects and that their worth is the sum of their physical parts, so easily measured and found wanting. But the damage of your lies doesn't stop there.

You tell them that no one will love them if they know that you are there, that they are hosting a horrible self-destructive parasite.

You tell them that they are unlovable, unworthy of real joy, real love, etc...

You tell them that they are incapable of being anything more than you, that you and they are one, incapable of change, incapable of being worth more than the soul-staining garbage you consume together.

But I have news for you, addiction, though you may be inseparable, you are not my husband. He is better than you.

You are selfish. He is capable of generosity. You are abusive. He is capable of kindness and patience. You promote contention, disgust, and hatred. But he chooses to love. I cannot control him anymore than I can control you, but I am grateful that for now he is choosing love. He is choosing me.

As for me, I refuse to be your victim any longer. I refuse to believe that I am not enough, not beautiful enough, not sexy enough, not worthy to be loved and respected, not good enough for any man to stay by my side. I refuse to believe that my value is determined by how I measure up or by the number on my scale. I refuse to believe all the crazy making that the anger and violence, the threats of abandonment are my fault and that I deserve to be treated that way. I refuse to apologize to you or to anyone who looks for a fight with me and tells me that I am not good enough simply to justify cheating on me. I only regret that it has taken me so long to recognize your hand in the cycles of contention and pain in my life.

You have made me feel blind and stupid, incapable of even trusting myself. I only wish I had found my own power sooner. But I am claiming it now.

I am rebuilding my trust in myself and in God, even in my husband. I am learning that I am truly enough even just as I am, a very imperfect human being. I deserve to be treated with love, to be told I am beautiful, and to be made love to by a man who is not wishing he was with someone else. You lied to my husband and told him I would leave him so many times he believed it. But I am here to stay. I have news for you, addiction: I am only growing stronger from my encounter with you. And I am also here to stay.

— AUTHOR UNKNOWN

REFLECTIONS; MAY 2019

Noni

At the time of writing, there are so many emotional challenges. Betrayal trauma is a very real and painful form of PTSD. The trauma of infidelity is bestowed upon us by people we love deeply. People closest to us our most intimate attachments, our trusted companions, ones we've trusted our hearts and lives to. They're supposed to protect us, not betray us. The pain inflicted is excruciating at the deepest level. We didn't sign up for this!

Triggers come from all directions. They always smack me right out of the blue. They're as unpredictable as they are intense. Most times, I reign my thoughts and emotions in, other times, the conductor may as well blow his whistle and I jump right on board the train to Crazy Town.

The process is awful, I'm getting better at recognising cues and talking myself through steps of reason. I'm not going to lie though, sometimes I just want a good goddamn tantrum because none of this has been fair. This uninvited and most unwelcome experience took me to places I never wanted to go and, at times turned me into someone I really don't want to be.

There have been times during the unravelling of our ungodly mess when I desperately wanted Dave to feel the pain that I had. I wanted him to experience this hurt as much as I did.

Although this is what my shattered self wanted at times, short of me having a revenge affair and inflicting this grievous assault on him; he could never come close to experiencing the violation I did.

Grief comes in all manner of appearances. Sometimes nothing but numbness, other times it manifests as absolute rage. Many a four-letter word said and not all of them were love.

There are days without appetite and others of overindulgence. At times, I've drunk too much wine to dull out feeling and then there were days of nurturing myself in far healthier ways.

One thing for sure though, through every emotion, every challenge, every heartache, every failure, and every win, God has been with me.

> Be strong and courageous. Do not be afraid or terrified because of them, for the Lord your God goes with you; He will never leave you nor forsake you.
>
> — DEUTERONOMY 31:6

He has never left me. He has never changed, never ever forsaken me, and even when the same mouth and heart that worships and praises him can be so vile, He doesn't even reject me. His spirit is there, willing me on, soothing my pain, lifting me up, loving me unconditionally and drawing near to me.

The Lord is close to the broken-hearted and saves those who are crushed in spirit.

— PSALM 34:18

Another unquestionable and undeniable point of gratitude; I am forever appreciative that Dave is walking this path right alongside me. He encourages me and is generally supportive and sensitive to my needs, even when it is difficult for him.

The truth is, I'm not the only one in recovery. It might be easy to think an unfaithful partner gets off lightly when, in actual fact, the majority of unfaithful husbands and wives wage their own battle. Internal warfare. No one escapes unscathed. Yes, they made their choices. Yes, they reap the consequences of those choices. The bigger question must be 'why' they made those choices. Being honest enough to get to the root cause and dealing with that takes enormous courage, determination, and perseverance. I love and respect my darling husband for taking this leap of faith. For being brave enough to take off his mask and finally let me close to the real him. The true and authentic man that I always believed him to be.

I would rather be with Dave in all his brokenness, with a repentant contrite heart than any persona or superficial perfectionist illusion that he previously thought necessary to be loved completely.

He is my hero and I will champion and support him "until death do us part".

Lying, Losing, Loving, and Living… this is our circle of life…

ONLINE RESOURCES

- Affair Recovery affairrecovery.com
- Beyond Affairs beyondaffairs.com
- Beyond Affairs Network
  beyondaffairsnetwork.com
- Brené Brown, TED talks
- Bible App
- The Heart of Man Movie
- Dr Doug Weiss drdougweiss.com
- Family Drug Support fds.org.au
- Bloom for Women bloomforwomen.com
- The Gottman Institute gottman.com

ESSENTIAL READING

- How to Help Your Spouse Heal From Your Affair author Linda Macdonald
- Not Just Friends, author Shirley Glass
- The Monogamy Myth, author Peggy Vaughan
- Anatomy of an Affair author David Carder
- My Husbands Affair Became the Best Thing that Ever Happened to Me author Anne and Brian Bercht
- The Bible
- Why Does He Do That? Inside the Minds of Angry and Controlling Men, author Lundy Bancroft

ABOUT THE AUTHORS

NONI YATES

A hairdressing career spanning almost four decades, Noni has heard stories most wouldn't believe.

Very little catches her by surprise, however, her own story did just that.

Resilient, introverted, and candidly honest; a description fitting of both Noni's character and the memoir.

BEYOND BETRAYAL is raw, real, without pretence and may just change the way you look at infidelity.

Noni is a proud and adoring mum to three adult children as well as an avid traveller. She lives on Australia's northern New South Wales coast with husband Dave and their array of critters.

DAVID YATES

Dave likes to fix things.

He's a bloke, isn't that what blokes do?

He's learned that fixing isn't always the answer though.

Listening for and hearing the emotions behind the words is a valuable skill for all men to have in their relational toolkit.

Dave learned his biggest lessons later in life and he's thankful for every one of them.

If you're going down a similar path to Dave or you've been there, it's not too late to change if you really want to. Be like Dave, learn your lessons and grow up.

You can contact them at
www.beyondbetrayalrecoverybook.com

David and Noni have completed Levels 1 and 2 Training in Gottman Method Couples Therapy, the Gottman Method for Treating Affairs and Trauma plus Couples and Addiction Recovery.

Noni is currently pursuing her Diploma in Counselling with The Australian Institute of Family Counselling.

facebook.com / nonianddavey
instagram.com / beyondbetrayalrecovery

www.ingramcontent.com/pod-product-compliance
Lightning Source LLC
Chambersburg PA
CBHW060018030426
42334CB00019B/2094